EXETER MEDIEVAL E[...]
General Editors: Mario[...]

rudan rædum ꝛbltom hpilum hit þæt mð þætan be frumeð. beþylc
mið fratiꝼ ꝛange. hꝛilum mð finef ꝛe ꝛyppet. ꝛ ꝛpædpe icꝼaꝛ
beꝛnde lanꝛe hpile. beheolo hꝛæþ etaꝛiꝛ. haꝼtnoiꝛ tꝛiꝛeꝛ.
oðlæ iceꝛhyide þæt hit hlæoꝛiede onꝛan þæt pouð ꝛpꝛtcan
rudu ꝛelꝛta þæt þæt ꝛtapia m. iceþæt ꝛtꝛa ꝛe man. þæt icþæt
ahaꝛin holtiꝼ onꝛide aꝼtypeð oꝛ feꝼene mnil. ꝛenaman
meoæꝛ ꝛepanꝛe ꝛronoaꝛ ꝛe ꝛopꝛtcon. ꝛum þæt to þæꝛꝼꝼꝛꝼ
hꝛcon me hꝛpa pꝛꝛaꝛ hebbun. beꝼon meoiꝛ bꝛopꝛꝛ
onuꝛlum. oðlæ hic me onbꝛopiꝛ aꝛceton ꝛeꝼæꝛt neoon me
þaꝼ ꝛronoaꝛ ꝛenoꝛe. ꝛe ꝛeah ic þa ꝼꝛꝼuꝛ man cynneꝼ ꝛeꝼꝛam
elne mycele. þæt he me polde onꝛe ꝛpaꝛan. þaꝼ icha neoopiꝼ
oꝼꝼꝼ oꝛyhtneꝼ pouð buꝛan oðlæ bꝛꝼꝼtan. þa icbꝛpian ꝛeꝛꝼꝼ
uꝛpioan ꝛeꝛuiꝛa þulle ic mihte ꝛronoaꝛ ꝛepyllan hꝛæopiꝼ
icꝼæꝛte ꝛtrod. Onꝛyptede hine þa ꝛtonꝛ hælto þæt þæꝛ ꝛoð
æolmihtiꝛ ꝛepanꝛ yꝼtio moð. ꝛe ꝛrah he onꝛtulꝛan heanne
meoiꝛ onmaniꝛpa ꝛe ꝛyliꝼe. þa he polde mancyn lyꝼan
lꝛpoꝼe icþa me ꝛe bꝛopn ꝛmb elꝛpte. neoopꝼte ic hꝛæopꝼe
buꝛan to uꝛpioan þullan uoploan ꝛerutu. ile ic ꝛeerloꝛ þæꝼt
ꝼrandan. Roð þæꝼ ic aꝛiꝛaþeð. ahoꝛ ic puene cyninꝛ heoꝛona
hlaꝼopið. hyloan me neoopiꝼe. þuꝼh oꝛiꝼpan hine mð
oꝛpican nælu. onme ꝛyndon þa dolꝛ ꝛe ꝛuhe opine inꝼið
hliꝼmaꝼ. ne oopꝼce ic hꝛ]a namꝛi ꝛreooan byꝛmꝼꝼaoin bm
une buru æꝛæoꝼpꝼ þull ic þæꝼ mð bloðe beꝛuimeð. beꝛocin oꝼ
þæꝼ ꝛuman ꝛioan. ꝛioan he hæꝼde hiꝼ ꝛaꝼe onꝛioeð. þaula
ic onþam beꝛꝼꝛe ꝛebioth hæbbe þꝛaoꝼpa ꝛypoa ꝛe ꝛeah ic þꝼꝼ
ꝛoð þꝼꝼple ꝼunan hꝛꝛpio hæꝛoon be ꝼꝛiꝛin mð polenum
ꝛuloꝛbioꝛ hꝛaꝼ. ꝛeꝛuine ꝛerman ꝼaoaou pouð ioe. þann
unoꝼ polenum prop þulꝛe ꝛeꝛaꝼt cꝛiooon cyninꝛꝛ ꝼyll
cꝛiꝼt þæꝼ onꝛioeð hꝛæopꝼuꝼ þaꝼ ꝼuꝛꝼ ꝼꝛoꝼꝼan cꝛoman to
þam æolinꝛe icþæt þull be hiꝛoð. Saꝼe ic þæꝼ mð ꝛeoþiꝼ
hnaꝛ ic hꝛæopꝼe þam ꝛeeꝛii uo hanoa uao moð elne mycele
ꝛe namon hit þaꝼ ælmihtiꝛne ꝛoð ahoꝛon hine oꝼ oam

The Dream of the Rood

Edited by
MICHAEL SWANTON

UNIVERSITY
of
EXETER
PRESS

First published by Manchester University Press in 1970

Revised edition published in 1987 by
University of Exeter Press
Reed Hall, Streatham Drive
Exeter EX4 4QR
UK
www.exeterpress.co.uk

Reprinted 1992
New edition 1996
Reprinted 2000, 2010

ISBN 978 0 85989 503 3

Printed in Great Britain by
Short Run Press Ltd, Exeter

PREFACE TO THE FIRST EDITION

The Dream of the Rood has entranced generations of scholars.
It is, in the words of the late Professor Wrenn, ' the greatest of
all Anglo-Saxon religious poems ' and ' one of the greatest
religious poems in English literature ', the work ' of a nameless
poet of superb genius '. Immediately attractive, its poetic
content is readily accessible to the modern reader, and while
neither private nor esoteric, being in the main-stream of
Western religious thought, increasing familiarity simply reveals
the poet's further literary sophistication.

Representative of the golden age of Anglo-Saxon culture,
drawing on both visual and doctrinal motifs, it provides a
ready introduction to its own intellectual and artistic milieu.
This is underlined by its intimate links with the Ruthwell
Cross, the documentary context of the earlier version and itself
often justly regarded as one of the finest monuments of
Anglo-Saxon times. The underlying premiss of both is the
same: a statement of the relationship of God to his creation,
out of which the artist constructs a formal meditation on the
nature and power of Christ.

The existence of the poem in two distinct versions, chrono-
logically and dialectally disparate, serves as a useful warning
on problems involved in the development and transmission of
Old English literature. The text is one that has been considerably emended by earlier editors, although no manuscript
form is actually unintelligible. It has been thought best to
present a conservative text with variant readings described in
the notes. Exigencies of space prevent full treatment of every
aspect of the work, but I have attempted to provide sufficient
introductory material for the reader to appreciate the poem
adequately. In particular I have thought it advisable to give
a full account of the Ruthwell Cross, sources for which are
scattered and not normally familiar to students of Old English.

It is obvious how far any new edition of this poem must
lean on the earlier work of Professors Cook, Dickins and Ross

and Dr. Hans Bütow, and on a now growing volume of critical studies. Of friends and colleagues who have so generously made available to me their special knowledge, I am particularly indebted to Miss R. J. Cramp, Professor J. E. Cross, Mr. D. G. Scragg, and to the general editor of this series, Professor G. L. Brook. My thanks are also due to Mgr. Giuseppe Ferraris of the Chapter of Vercelli Cathedral and to the Rev. A. H. Bone, minister of Ruthwell parish church, who gave free access to the antiquities in their care.

Manchester, 1969

                                                                    M. S.

PREFACE TO THE PRESENT EDITION

This book has been reprinted a number of times in the last quarter century. The high cost of resetting unfortunately precludes the accommodation of valuable points made to me in person and in the continually growing body of critical literature. However, a further call for reprinting has enabled me to make minor corrections and to supplement the bibliography.

Exeter, 1996

                                                                    M. S.

CONTENTS

ILLUSTRATIONS

ABBREVIATIONS

AB	*Anglia Beiblatt*
Ælfric, *Homs*	*The Homilies of the Anglo-Saxon Church*, ed. B. Thorpe. Two volumes. London, 1844–6.
Archiv	*Archiv für das Studium der neueren Sprachen und Literaturen*
ASC	*Two of the Saxon Chronicles Parallel*, ed. J. Earle and C. Plummer. Two volumes. Oxford, 1892–9.
BM	*The Burlington Magazine*
Brunner	K. Brunner, *Altenglische Grammatik nach der angelsächsischen Grammatik von Eduard Sievers neubearbeitet*. Second edition. Halle, 1951.
Campbell	A. Campbell, *Old English Grammar*. Oxford, 1959.
EETS	Early English Text Society
ES	*Englische Studien*
Gesetze	*Die Gesetze der Angelsachsen*, ed. F. Liebermann. Three volumes. Halle, 1903–16.
JEGP	*Journal of English and Germanic Philology*
Keiser	A. Keiser, *The Influence of Christianity on the Vocabulary of Old English Poetry*. Urbana, 1919.
MLN	*Modern Language Notes*
MLR	*Modern Language Review*
MP	*Modern Philology*
Napier	A. S. Napier, *Old English Glosses, chiefly unpublished*. Oxford, 1900.
NM	*Neuphilologische Mitteilungen*
N & Q	*Notes and Queries*
PBB	*Beiträge zur Geschichte der deutschen Sprache und Literatur*, ed. H. Paul and W. Braune.

PG	*Patrologiae cursus completus; series graeca*, ed. J. P. Migne. Paris, 1857–1912.
PL	*Patrologiae cursus completus; series latina*, ed. J. P. Migne. Paris, 1844–64.
PMLA	*Publications of the Modern Language Association of America*
Pope	J. C. Pope, *The Rhythm of Beowulf*. New Haven, 1942.
Prosa	*Bibliothek der angelsächsischen Prosa*, ed. C. W. Grein, R. P. Wülcker and H. Hecht. Cassel, Leipzig and Hamburg, 1872–1932.
RC	Ruthwell Cross
RES	*Review of English Studies*
Ross	A. S. C. Ross, ' The linguistic evidence for the date of the Ruthwell Cross ', *MLR*, xxviii (1933), 145–55.
SS	Surtees Society
Studies	K. Sisam, *Studies in the History of Old English Literature*. Oxford, 1953.
VB	Vercelli Book
Wright	T. Wright, *Anglo-Saxon and Old English Vocabularies*, Second edition, ed. R. P. Wülcker. Two volumes. London, 1884.
Wülfing	J. E. Wülfing, *Die Syntax in den Werken Alfreds des Grossen*. Two volumes. Bonn, 1894–1901.

INTRODUCTION

THE VERCELLI BOOK

The full text of the *Dream of the Rood* is found together with other legendary and homiletic matter in Codex CXVII of the cathedral library at Vercelli in northern Italy. This is a well preserved manuscript volume containing 136 uniform parchment folios, each measuring about 31 by 20 cm., and made up into gatherings numbered I–XIX at the head of each first folio and lettered A–T at the foot of each final folio. It is a plain manuscript with no decorative pages nor space left for them, and with only occasionally decorated initials. Each folio has been ruled for between 23 and 33 lines of writing, the number of lines to the page being similar within each gathering.

The handwriting of the entire codex is uniform[1] and quite legible: a square Anglo-Saxon minuscule characteristic of later tenth-century West Saxon scriptoria. Wülcker[2] ascribed the script to the beginning of the eleventh century, while Keller[3] suggested that it might be dated to between 960 and 980. More cautiously, however, Förster[4] assigned the manuscript simply to the second half of the tenth century, drawing attention to the fact that Latin words were written in an insular hand rather than the Frankish cursive which became usual towards the end of the tenth century. Förster's dating is now generally accepted but not so his suggestion of provenance.

Förster favoured a connection with the Worcester scriptorium on account of similarities he recognised between the

[1] Cf. p. 5. Since Förster (*Il Codice Vercellese* (Rome, 1913), p. 15), most scholars have considered the codex to be the work of a single scribe, save that the signatures on the gatherings, a few corrections and minor additions seem to have been added by later hands.

[2] *Codex Vercellensis* (Leipzig, 1894), p. vii.

[3] W. Keller, *Angelsächsische Palaeographie* (Berlin, 1906), i, p. 33; and cf. J. Hoops, *Reallexikon der germanischen Altertumskunde* (Strassburg, 1911–19), i, p. 102.

[4] Förster, *op. cit.* pp. 11–14.

1

language of the Vercelli Book and that of Wulfgeat's copy of Wulfstan's homilies,[1] but this cannot be proved. The language of the Vercelli Book offers little evidence for its history. Few features are common to the whole codex; both Anglian and Kentish forms occur within the classical West Saxon matrix, but too sporadically to be critically used. Several manuscripts containing parallel texts of Vercelli Book homilies were certainly written at Canterbury or Rochester.[2] And a Kentish connection would be supported by the scribe's use of the abbreviation *xƀ*, a sign most common in later tenth-century Canterbury manuscripts.[3] But zoomorphic and knot-work initials on ff. 49, 106ᵛ and 112 might be shown to derive from types found in earlier tenth-century Winchester manuscripts.[4]

There has naturally been some speculation as to how such a manuscript came to be at Vercelli. The fine products of Anglo-Saxon scriptoria were highly prized throughout the continent during early medieval times. But this volume is in no sense decorative, and its contents are hardly likely to have been much sought after in Italy at this time. The only other documents containing Old English which are known to have been south of the Alps in medieval times take the form of fragments which might well have come there as bindings. Certainly none can be shown to have come there so soon after its composition.

The hand which added the words *writ þus* at the foot of f. 63ᵛ and *sclean* on f. 99 suggests that the book was still in England at the beginning of the eleventh century and had not therefore been especially written to be sent abroad.[5] But the manuscript was almost certainly at Vercelli by the end of the

[1] *Ibid.* pp. 20–1; and cf. R. Brotanek, *A B*, xxvi (1915), 229.

[2] D. G. Scragg, ' The compilation of the Vercelli Book ', *Anglo-Saxon England*, ii (1973), 207.

[3] *Studies*, pp. 109–10.

[4] F. Wormald, ' Decorated initials in English MSS from A.D. 900 to 1100 ', *Archaeologia*, xci (1945), 120, 134.

[5] *Studies*, p. 113; and cf. K. Sisam, ' Epenthesis in the consonant groups *sl, sn* ', *Archiv*, cxxxi (1913), 305–10.

eleventh century. In a blank space left at the bottom of f. 24[v] a later hand has recorded a variation in the music of the Italian church service—an extract from *Psalm XXVI* written in the form of a neumed response. Förster[1] assigned this to the thirteenth century, but the small Caroline minuscule and form of notation used are now considered to have been made by a north Italian hand about, or before, 1100.[2]

With this internal evidence as to chronology we can now reject two strongly argued theories as to the manuscript's history, simply because they rely on dates too late in time: i.e. either that the manuscript came to Vercelli at the hands of Cardinal Guala, papal legate in England in the time of king John and the minority of Henry III,[3] or that it took the form of a chance addition to the cathedral library at a much later date, perhaps as a result of Renaissance antiquarianism. If any individual carrier is to be identified, then Ulf, the notorious Anglo-Norman bishop of Dorchester who visited Vercelli in 1050 to be examined before a papal synod, is an attractive candidate.[4] But it is hardly necessary to look for any specific occasion for the manuscript's arrival. Vercelli formed a staging post for the not inconsiderable traffic between England and Rome at this time, and the existence of an ' hospitalis Scottorum ' there probably dates from before the beginning of the twelfth century.[5] The manuscript may have come from the baggage of any one of the more important travellers taking this route during the eleventh century. Alternatively

---

[1] Förster, *op. cit.* pp. 16, 52.

[2] *Studies*, pp. 113–15.

[3] This suggestion was first made by Sir Francis Palgrave in an article in the *Quarterly Review*, lxxv (1845), 398–9, unsigned but identified by M. F. Brightfield, *PMLA*, lix (1944), 507. The case was taken up and strongly argued by A. S. Cook, *Cardinal Guala and the Vercelli Book* (Sacramento, 1888).

[4] S. J. Herben, ' The Vercelli Book: a new Hypothesis ', *Speculum*, x (1935), 91–4.

[5] F. Borgognone, *Il Problema del Vercelli Book* (Alessandria, 1951), pp. 7–10.

the manuscript may have come indirectly to Vercelli by way of some monastery like Fulda or Fleury which had close connections with England. In any case we might have expected such a manuscript to have come to Vercelli at some time during the eleventh-century *floruit* of that city after which time it declined drastically in importance.

What may well be a reference to this manuscript occurs in a cathedral book catalogue of 1426.[1] It was certainly at Vercelli by 1748 when Giuseppe Bianchini of Verona transcribed a short extract from one of the prose homilies.[2] The text did not become widely known however until it was rediscovered by Friedrich Bluhme in 1822, pronouncing that it contained 'Legenden oder Homilien in angelsäxischer Sprache '.[3] The further enquiries of both English and German scholars led the Record Commission in 1833 to engage Dr. C. Maier of Tübingen to make a complete transcript of the contents. It was this transcript, now preserved at Lincoln's Inn, that was used as the basis of Thorpe's edition of the Vercelli poems printed by order of the Record Commission in 1836. Because of the Commission's dissolution in the following year, this edition was not made fully public until 1869, but a few copies were distributed and were apparently used as the basis of both Kemble's and Grein's editions. Not until 1894 was a complete collation of the full text of the Vercelli poems made by Wülcker for his revision of Grein's edition. In the same year he published a half-size facsimile of the Vercelli poems. Förster's facsimile of the entire manuscript, two-thirds full size, followed in 1913.

The Vercelli Book is an eclectic collection. It includes twenty-three anonymous Old English prose homilies, beginning with sermons on Christ's Passion and the Last Judge-

---

[1] M. Halsall, ' Vercelli and the Vercelli Book ', *PMLA*, lxxxiv (1969), 1549.

[2] Ed. G. de Grégory, *Istoria della Vercellese Letteratura ed Arti* (Turin, 1819–24), iv, pp. 556–8; and cf. M. Förster, *op. cit.* p. 41.

[3] *Iter Italicum* (Halle, 1824–36), i, pp. 87, 99.

ment (ff. 1–12) and including others on conventional monitory themes like the evils of intemperance. The twenty-third and last homily takes the form of a version of the prose Life of St Guthlac (ff. 133ᵛ–135ᵛ). The manuscript arrangement seems haphazard, but perhaps—as dialectal differences and groupings suggest—the scribe was copying seriatim from sheaves of different provenances without bothering to impose any other order upon his material.[1] Intercalated with these prose works are found six poems of varying length: *Andreas* and the *Fates of the Apostles* (ff. 29ᵛ–54), the two incomplete pieces called, in Krapp's edition, *Soul and Body I* and *Homiletic Fragment I* together with the *Dream of the Rood* (ff. 101ᵛ–106), and finally and particularly pertinent to the substance of this last poem, *Elene* (ff. 121–133ᵛ), a versified account of St. Helena's successful search for the remains of the True Cross, undertaken at the instigation of her son, Constantine the Great, in the middle of the fourth century.

The text of the *Dream* begins at the sixth line of f. 104ᵛ and finishes at the bottom of f. 106. Gathering XIV, ruled with twenty-four lines to the page, ends with f. 104, and gathering XV, beginning with pages ruled for thirty-two lines of writing, opens with f. 105. Wülcker[2] and Bütow[3] thought they recognised a second hand beginning with *wendan* (22) at the top of f. 105, but they seem to have been misled by the smaller and more closely written characters that were consequent merely upon the change to closer ruling that begins with gathering XV. The hand is regular and quite uniform with what has gone before. Coincidentally, however, the pattern of punctuation also changes with the opening of gathering XV, and this may mark a separate unit of work. The poem opens with two majuscules: a large H enclosing a Ƿ, but

[1] P. W. Peterson, 'Dialect grouping in the unpublished Vercelli homilies', *Studies in Philology*, l (1953), 559–65.

[2] R. P. Wülcker, *Grundriss zur Geschichte der angelsächsischen Litteratur* (Leipzig, 1885,) p. 239.

[3] H. Bütow, *Das altenglische 'Traumgesicht vom Kreuz'* (Heidelberg, 1935), p. 40.

thereafter, as commonly in manuscripts, majuscules occur only sporadically. These are not necessarily arbitrary, however. As throughout the poems of the Vercelli Book, majuscules seem to have been used pragmatically as a reader's guide to rhythm and emphasis rather than syntax, frequently marking the beginnings of clauses or sentences containing significant contrasts in the structure, most commonly signified by *Ac* or *Hwæðre*. But their use is neither consistent nor regular. They have all been retained in the printed text.[1]

Through the text of the *Dream* in general, as in the whole of the Vercelli Book verse, punctuation is irregular and apparently syntactical rather than metrical in intention, simply marking ends of sentences or pauses within sentences.[2] With the beginning of a new gathering, however, it is as if the scribe had temporarily taken up a new scheme of punctuation. At the top of f. 105 from the end of line 22 to the end of line 25 the text is regularly pointed after each half-line (save after *licgende*, 24a), which fact seems to indicate a metrical intention. But this punctuation lapses almost as soon as taken up, and thereafter it is again rare, and apparently syntactical. The sign ꝫ found after *gesceaft* (12) and *treow* (17), like its variant :∼ , which ends the poem, is normally used to mark the ends of sections in the verse of the manuscript, although where they do occasionally occur within a section they do not apparently differ from a simple point.[3]

A small number of acute accents occur sporadically over vowels that are etymologically long: *áheawen* (29), *áhof-on* (44, 61), *fáh* (13), *ród* (136). With the exception of Ꝥ for *ond*,

---

[1] *Ac* (11, 43, 115, 119, 132), *Aledon* (63), *Forht* (21), *Genaman* (30), *Hwæðre* (18, 24), *Hwilum* (23), *Nah* (131), *Ne* (117), *Nu* (78, 95), *Ongunnon* (65), *Ongyrede* (39), *Rod* (44), *Sare* (59), *Syllic* (13).

G. P. Krapp (*The Vercelli Book* (London, 1932), p. xlvii) also takes initial long *i* for a majuscule in *ic* (13, 28, 47) and *inwid-hlemmas* (47). But this was apparently used without discrimination in late OE manuscripts.

[2] For a general account see G. P. Krapp, *op. cit.* pp. xxviii–xxxi.

[3] Cf. *wolde* ꝫ (*Soul & Body I* 83) or *fornam* :∼ (*Elene* 131).

abbreviations are not used consistently in the manuscript. Macrons occasionally mark the omission of a nasal, as in the particles: *poñ* for *ponne* (142) or *pā* for *pam* (146, 149, 150), or, more frequently, mark dative plural endings, as in *manegū synnū* for *manegum synnum* (99). More noticeable is *gebrinḡ*, presumably for *gebringe* (139). All abbreviations have been expanded without comment in the printed text.

As in the rest of the codex, the linguistic forms of this text are predominantly those of classical late West Saxon. Sporadic non-West Saxon forms might have been thought to supply some linguistic evidence as to the historical transmission of the text, but it is now generally believed that such forms might provide proof for a mixed ' poetic ' rather than a dialectal vocabulary.[1]

Within the late West Saxon matrix are found one or two earlier West Saxon forms: *meahte* beside the later *mihte* (18, 37),[2] *gesīene* (36) with *īe* by front-mutation from early OE *īo*, rather than the later WS *ȳ*,[3] and *hiht* beside the regular *hyht* (148, 126). Spelling forms with final *g*, *hnag* (59) *āstāg* (103) survive by the side of more regular forms with final *h*, *fāh* (13) *gestāh* (40).[4]

The distinct Anglian feature of smoothing appears in *wergas* (31) (WS *weargas*), as in the Vespasian Psalter, which regularly displays *e* before *r* followed by a back consonant *c* or *g*.[5] The metre of half-line 22a would suggest the existence of an originally uncontracted Anglian form of the dative plural **blīwum*, smoothed as a result either of a final inorganic *h* or an internal *g*.[6]

In *bestēmed* (22, 48) front-mutation has produced a non-West Saxon form (WS *bestīeman*, *bestȳman*). While this is the form used in the precisely located Ruthwell Cross inscription, it also occurs in the late West Saxon inscription on the Brussels cross-reliquary.[7] And as the same form commonly recurs in the same

---

[1] *Studies*, pp. 119–39.   [2] Brunner, § 425.
[3] Brunner, § 107.   [4] Campbell, § 446; Brunner, § 214.
[5] Campbell, §§ 222–3.   [6] Campbell, § 579(5).   [7] See p. 49.

or similar formulaic phrases elsewhere in Old English verse, it might well be regarded as part of the poetic vocabulary.[1]

Non-West Saxon fronting gives *blēdum* (149) (WS *blǣd*) and *sceððan* (47) (pure WS *scyððan* < **scieððan*) where the stem-vowel of the latter has remained undiphthongised by the initial palatal group.[2] The form *blēd* is found also in *Christ* (1256, 1346) and *Guthlac* (1348), and may well, like *mēce*, represent a ' poetic ' word. The form *sceððan* too is common in verse (e.g. *Andreas* 917, 1147) and has even become the regular form of West Saxon prose.

The past participle suffix *-ad* rather than *-od* in the weak class II verb *geniwian* (148) might be either Anglian or Kentish.[3] Some have considered the suffix *-ed* (*forwunded*, 14) to be characteristically Anglian,[4] but in fact all dialects contain examples of this.[5] It has been suggested that un-contracted forms of the third person present indicative, as in *frīneð* (112), are also indicative of Anglian origin, but this too is questionable.[6]

The usefulness of vocabulary in determining the dialectal origin of Old English verse is similarly open to doubt.[7] The various forms that have been considered specifically or predominantly Anglian in use include: *bearn* (83), (*ge*)*frīnan* (76, 112), *hlēoðrian* (26), *sigor*(*fæst*) (67, 120), *sceððan* (47), and *on* in the sense ' upon ' (56, etc.).[8] In the formation of place-names the second element of *feorgbold* (73) certainly is charac-teristic of Anglian regions, *boðl* being chiefly Northumbrian and the form *bold*, with metathesis, chiefly Mercian.[9] In

---

[1] See note to *bestēmed*, 22.   [2] Campbell, §§ 188–9.   [3] See p. 36.
[4] E.g. Bütow or Mossé, and cf. Brunner, § 414.   [5] Campbell, § 757.
[6] Cf. E. Sievers, ' Zur Rhythmik des germanischen Alliterations-verses ', *PBB*, x (1885), 464–5; J. Hedberg, *The Syncope of the Old English Present Endings* (Lund, 1945); but cf. *Studies*, pp. 123–5.
[7] Cf. *Studies*, pp. 126–31.
[8] Cf. R. Jordan, *Eigentümlichkeiten des anglischen Wortschatzes* (Heidelberg, 1906), pp. 43–4, 94–7, 107, *et passim*.
[9] E. Ekwall, ' Ae. *botl, bold, boðl* in englischen ortsnamen ', *AB*, xxviii (1917), 82–91; A. H. Smith, *English Place-Name Elements* (Cambridge, 1956), i, p. 44, ii, map 8.

general, however, it may be concluded that the linguistic character of the Vercelli Book version of the *Dream* simply conforms with the standard literary language in which the majority of Old English poetical manuscripts were written, that is, predominantly late West Saxon with a strong Anglian element.

THE RUTHWELL CROSS

The lesser text of the *Dream of the Rood* is found inscribed in runes on the sides of a sculptured monumental stone cross of the late seventh or early eighth century at Ruthwell in Dumfriesshire.[1] Until the middle of the seventeenth century it stood close to the altar in the parish church of Ruthwell. Just one account survives of the monument at this time. Between 1599 and 1601 Reginald Bainbrigg of Appleby toured the north to collect material for a new edition of Camden's *Britannia*. It was probably during the course of this tour that he found occasion to describe the monument and transcribe a small part of the inscription. His note was never used by Camden, although the manuscript survives.[2]

In 1642, however, in accordance with an 'Act annent Idolatrous monuments in Ruthwall' passed by the General Assembly of the Church of Scotland meeting at Aberdeen,[3] the

---

[1] Casts of the monument may be seen in Durham Cathedral Library and in museum collections at Copenhagen, Edinburgh, Glasgow, London (Victoria and Albert) and Manchester.

[2] B.M. MS. Cotton Julius F VI, f. 352. Although noticed by Haverfield ('Cotton Iulius F. VI', *Trans. Cumberland and Westmorland Antiquary Society*, N.S. xi (1911), 373–4), it seems to have remained unknown to Anglo-Saxon scholarship until brought to general attention by R. I. Page ('An early drawing of the Ruthwell Cross', *Medieval Archaeology*, iii (1959), 285–8).

[3] In *Acts of the General Assemblies of the Church of Scotland, 1638–1649*; appendix: Index of St. Andrews Acts, 27th July 1642. Only the title of this Act survives and it is not known how many monuments are referred to. Frequently, however, as at nearby Hoddom, several such stone monuments are found in one place. From Ruthwell churchyard comes a fragment of interlace panel which almost certainly indicates a second cross-shaft (W. G. Collingwood, *Northumbrian Crosses of the*

cross was broken down and partially defaced. The piece immediately below the transom was removed to the churchyard and buried, while the remaining pieces were allowed to remain inside the church, where they seem to have been used as paving set into the earthen floor of the nave. It remained in this state for some 130 years, during which it was remarked upon by various local antiquaries. Early transcripts, although taken from the broken and increasingly crumbling pieces, are clearly important for our reading of the inscription.[1] They are often the only authority for letters which were later to be lost. And as those who drew the monument were commonly unfamiliar with the nature of runes, it might reasonably be assumed that their transcripts more or less objectively reproduced what was then visible. In 1697 William Nicolson, canon and later bishop of Carlisle, examined the pieces still inside the church.[2] He gives a full text for the upper fragment of the lower stone, although already local deterioration had rendered part illegible.[3] Other early engravings were

---

Pre-Norman Age (London, 1927), p. 119, fig. 101), and a complete but simpler monument of the cross-pecked fifth or sixth-century Whithorn type (*Trans. Dumfries and Galloway Antiquarian Society*, S3, xxviii (1949–50), 158–60).

[1] Earlier readings may be conveniently compared in G. B. Brown, *The Arts in Early England*, v (London, 1921), 206–11; G. B. Brown and A. B. Webster, *Royal Commission on Ancient and Historical Monuments . . . of Scotland*, vii (Edinburgh, 1920), pp. 270–1; W. Vietor, *Die Northumbrischen Runensteine* (Marburg, 1895), pp. 6–12.

[2] W. Nicolson, *Letters on Various Subjects*, ed. J. Nichols (London, 1809), i, pp. 62–3, 158–9.

[3] Nicolson's work was the basis of the engraving in G. Hickes' *Linguarum Veterum Septentrionalium Thesaurus* (Oxford, 1703–5), ii, p. 5, tab. iv. Nicolson revisited Ruthwell in 1704 to collate his original transcript, but the additions he then made are not found in Hickes (' Bishop Nicolson's Diaries ', ed. H. Ware, *Trans. Cumberland and Westmorland Antiquarian Society*, N.S. ii (1902), 195–6). *Inter alia* Nicolson describes a local tradition as to the origins of the cross which he found remarkable, being so firmly held in a presbyterian parish. The cross was said to have been found lettered and entire in a nearby quarry; in a dream a local labourer is directed to erect the cross with

those of Gordon (1726) and de Cardonnell (1789),[1] and an account claiming at least equal antiquity was later published by Haigh.[2] Important nineteenth-century drawings were made by Duncan (1832) and Gibb (1859).[3]

Towards the end of the eighteenth century, structural alterations to the church building resulted in the remaining fragments being put in the churchyard, where the broken ends of the fine sandstone began to decay rapidly. In 1802 the then minister, Dr. Henry Duncan, probably motivated by the rediscovery of the once buried upper section, reconstructed the monument in the garden of the manse. The missing transom was replaced with a spurious piece at Duncan's direction in 1823.[4] The uppermost arm of the cross head was put on back to front at this time. In 1887 the cross was moved back into the church, where it now stands in the well of a specially constructed apse.[5]

The artistic scheme

The Ruthwell Cross now stands 5·28 m. high, rectangular in section and tapering towards the top (71 × 46 cm. at ground

---

the aid of a team of oxen, and a church is raised over it, ' whereat it miraculous grew like a tree till it touched the roof of the church '.

[1] A. Gordon, *Itinerarium Septentrionale* (London, 1726), pp. 160–1, pls. 57–8; A. de Cardonnell and R. Gough, *Vetusta Monumenta* (London, 1789), ii, pls. liv–lv.

[2] D. H. Haigh, ' The Saxon cross at Bewcastle ', *Archaeologia Aeliana*, N.S. i (1857), 170; *The Conquest of Britain by the Saxons* (London, 1861), pp. 38–9, pl. ii.

[3] H. Duncan, ' An account of a remarkable monument . . .', *Archaeologia Scotica*, iv (1833), 313–26, pls. 13–15; Gibb's plate is published as J. Stuart, *Sculptured Stones of Scotland* (Aberdeen, 1856–67), ii, pls. xix–xx.

[4] H. Duncan, *op. cit.* pp. 318–19. A small fragment of the same material preserved with the cross at Ruthwell probably represents all that remains of the transom. It bears on one side the figure of one of the remaining evangelists. See p. 19.

[5] G. Seton, ' Statement relative to the Ruthwell Cross '; *Proc. Society of Antiquaries of Scotland*, xxi (1887), 194–7.

level to 33×24 cm. below the crosshead). It was originally
made in two sections of local New Red Sandstone joined above
the major figure of Christ in Judgement. The broad principal
faces of the shaft are carved with figural subjects surrounded
by identifying Latin inscriptions. Such explanatory marginal
inscriptions are paralleled only in the elaborate round shaft
from Dewsbury.[1] That parallels to the figural programme are
all ultimately Byzantine is hardly surprising in the church of
Theodore of Tarsus (primate from 668 to 690). The fullest
correspondence is with the sixth-century ivory Ravenna throne,
which has panels illustrating various Old and New Testament
scenes.[2] Similar scenes recur on a group of sixth or seventh-
century gold medallions from Adana, near Tarsus,[3] and a
programme of Christ's life is found in the sixth-century upper
mosaic frieze of St. Apollinare Nuovo, Ravenna,[4] although
this contains neither Nativity nor Crucifixion. Rather later
in the ninth or tenth century a Latin Gospels from St. Gall
contains inscriptions for unexecuted illustrations of various of
these scenes, including both Nativity and Crucifixion.[5] But
no other survives from Merovingian or Carolingian Europe and
none from Anglo-Saxon England, although fragments from a
later Anglian cross at Rothbury might originally have come
from a complete coherent monument of this kind. In this,
as in other respects, the Ruthwell Cross remains a unique
work of art.

The narrower sides of the shaft are more purely decorative,
carved with the so-called ' inhabited vine-scroll '. This is a

[1] W. G. Collingwood, *op. cit.* figs. 13, 91.

[2] Traditionally associated with the name of Maximianus, bishop of
Ravenna (*ob.* 556), but probably of Alexandrian workmanship (C.
Cecchelli, *La Cathedra di Massimiano ed altri avorii romano-orientali*
Rome, 1936–44).

[3] H. Peirce and R. Tyler, *L'Art Byzantin* (Paris, 1932–4), ii, pl. 73b.

[4] P. R. Garrucci, *Storia della arte Cristiana nei primi otto secoli della
Chiesa* (Prato, 1873–81), iv, *tav.* 248–51.

[5] S. Beissel, *Geschichte der Evangelienbücher in der ersten Hälfte des
Mittelalters* (Freiburg i B., 1906), pp. 238–40.

Middle Eastern motif deriving from models like the Ravenna throne, where it fills the narrower panels of the framework. As it appears on the Ruthwell Cross it is made up of a continuous heavy stem with alternately placed side-volutes, each of which encloses a bird or some more fantastic animal which pecks at stylised leaves, flowers and bunches of grapes. The use of this ' Tree of Life ' motif is as rare in Celtic sculpture as it is common in Northumbrian. Referring to the words *Ego sum vitis vera* . . . (*John* xv. 1–7), and conflated by the Psalmist's account of the ' trees of the Lord ' being the refuge of birds and beasts (*Psalm CIV*), it is generally recognised as a symbol of Christ in union with his church and the harmonious coexistence of transformed nature in the living God. Appropriately it is the margins of these panels that bear the text of the *Dream of the Rood*.

It is no mere chance that we should find the *Dream* associated with a carefully planned theological programme. The artist of the cross clearly understood the poem to be an integral part of his conception, underpinning and augmenting his meaning in the sculpture. It is important therefore to assess adequately the character of the monument which forms the intellectual and artistic as well as the ' documentary ' context of the early version of the *Dream*.

It is clearly a preaching cross. Its message is evangelical, stating the role of Christ in the world of men both historically and eternally. In particular, it links the symbol of Christ's death with the Christ of Judgement, and Nature's recognition of his majesty.

The principal face of the cross, now looking north,[1] contains scenes of desert asceticism. The largest panel, as on the Bewcastle Cross,[2] portrays Christ in Judgement, the right hand

[1] Originally, no doubt, as at Bewcastle, where the cross still stands erect, the principal face looked west so as to be seen by worshippers conventionally approaching from that direction.

[2] Both scenes are compared by G. B. Brown, *The Arts in Early England*, V (London, 1921), pp. 128–31, pl. xvii.

raised in benediction, a scroll in the left, and trampling the heads of fawning beasts below. Unidentified quadrupeds replace the conventional asp, dragon, lion or basilisk. The surrounding inscription is disjointed but is clearly intended to read: + IHS XPS IUDEX · AEQUITATIS · BESTIAE · ET · DRACONES · COGNOVERUNT · IN · DES · ERTO · SALVATOREM · MUNDI ·, ' + Jesus Christ, Judge of Righteousness. Beasts and dragons recognised in the desert the Saviour of the World.' This paraphrases Vulgate *Psalm XC.* 13, which contemporary exegesis thought prophetic of Christ's rejection of temptation in the wilderness.[1] Conventional iconography, as in the narthex mosaic of the archiepiscopal chapel at Ravenna or on the eighth-century Genoels-Elderen ivory,[2] represents Christ as a victorious warrior, often transfixing the hostile beasts, using the cross as a spear. Here, however, as indicated in the accompanying inscription, there is to be recognised in the incident an element of adoration, the beasts of the desert acknowledging the divinity in Christ.[3] Perhaps this accounts for the crossed paws of the beasts found in both Ruthwell and Bewcastle representations of the scene.[4] This representation of Christ in Judgement, illustrating both Christ's power over evil and his relationship to creation, dominates the artistic scheme of the cross.

As on the Bewcastle Cross, the panel above this principal figure portrays John the Baptist holding up the paschal Lamb of God, iconography identical with that of the centre-piece of the Ravenna throne. What remains of the inscription reads, in the left-hand margin: . . . ADORAMUS . . ., ' We adore ', and in the bottom margin the runes *tndn . . . u*, which remain un-

[1] Cf. Bede, *PL*, xcii. 369.

[2] C. Ihm, *Die Programme der christlichen Apsismalerei vom vierten Jahrhundert bis zur mitte des achten Jahrhunderts* (Wiesbaden, 1960), pp. 32–3, *taf.* x.

[3] Eusebius, *PG*, xxii. 673 f.; xxiii. 1153–6.

[4] Cf. F. Saxl, ' The Ruthwell Cross ', *Journal of the Warburg and Courtauld Institutes*, vi (1943), 2; M. Schapiro, ' The religious meaning of the Ruthwell Cross ', *Art Bulletin*, xxvi (1944), 235.

explained. The subject of this panel is plainly in agreement with the ' desert ' theme of this face, however. John, the prototype of Christian asceticism, the voice which cried in the wilderness, heralds the approach of the Lord, the Lamb who is to take away the sins of the world.[1]

Beneath the Judgement panel is placed a scene representing Paul and Anthony, considered with John to be the founders of monasticism.[2] The inscription reads: + SCS · PAULUS · ET · A[NTONIUS EREMITAE] FREGER[UN]T · PANEM IN DESERTO ·, ' Saints Paul and Anthony, the hermits, broke bread in the desert '. In Jerome's account of this event the loaf is understood to be heaven-sent through the medium of a raven, while its breaking denotes for the early church the ' confractio ' of the mass.[3] This scene is paralleled only in the Celtic north and west of Britain,[4] which fact is perhaps significant in view of the greater importance placed on the ' vita contemplativa ' there. Paul and Anthony found a special place in Celtic liturgy,[5] which regularly associates with the ' confractio ' rite the two concepts of Judgement and Salvation,[6] here represented in adjacent panels.

Below this desert scene is appropriately placed one of the Flight into Egypt. This is a particularly rare subject in early Christian art, although it occasionally occurs in Alexandrian contexts as in a (now missing) panel of the Ravenna throne or the contemporary Adana medallions. The occasion of the Flight is insignificant in the canonical gospels, and was not

[1] Cf. Bede, *PL*, xciv. 121.

[2] Cf. Aldhelm, *PL*, lxxxix. 120, 126; *The Dialogue of Salomon and Saturnus*, ed. J. M. Kemble (London, 1848), pp. 190, 213.

[3] Jerome, *PL*, xxiii. 25; and cf. *Acta Sanctorum*, 10 January, and *An Old English Martyrology*, EETS, cxvi, p. 16 (a mid-ninth century work but probably deriving from an eighth-century Northumbrian Latin version).

[4] For example at Nigg, Rosshire.

[5] Cf. *Stowe Missal*, ed. G. F. Warner (London, 1906–15), ii, p. 15, and *Irish Litanies*, ed. C. Plummer (London, 1925), p. 32.

[6] *Stowe Missal*, ii, 18, and cf. *The Antiphonary of Bangor*, ed. F. E. Warren (London, 1893–5), ii, p. 10 f.

celebrated by the early church. But greater emphasis was placed on it in apocryphal gospels like the pseudo-Matthew, where it is made the occasion of worship by beasts in the desert,[1] thus linking with the Judgement scene. The top margin contains the remaining fragment of an inscription: + MARIA · ET IO[SEPHUS], but the lettering has been largely defaced, together with the figures of the panel.

The large bottom panel has been all but totally obliterated. Almost certainly, however, this represented a Nativity scene similar to that on the Ravenna throne, the Adana medallions or in the contemporary Rabula Gospel.[2] Such a scene would represent not simply a narrative link between Annunciation and Flight, but correspond with the Crucifixion on the alternate face, bringing together the beginning and end of Christ's incarnation, which were commonly linked in contemporary theology.[3]

The southern face of the shaft bears significant Gospel scenes, all of which seem to have been identified by appropriate sentences from the Vulgate ' textus receptus '. The principal panel of this face, corresponding with the Christ of Judgement on the other, is one of Salvation, representing a forgiving Christ. An impressively monumental Mary Magdalene draws a swathe of hair across the feet of a nimbed Christ standing in a similar posture to that of the Judgement scene, a book in the left hand and the right raised in benediction. The marginal inscription reads: + ATTUL[IT ALABA]STRUM UNGUENTI & STANS RETRO SECUS PEDES · EIUS LACRIMIS · COEPIT RIGARE · PEDES EIUS · & CAPILLIS · CAPITIS SUI TERGEBAT, ' She brought an alabaster box of ointment and standing behind his feet she began to wash his feet with her tears and dried them with the hairs of her head '

---

[1] C. Tischendorf, *Evangelia Apocrypha* (Leipzig, 1876), pp. 85–7. Bede connects the flight with the persecution of *Matthew* x. 23 (*PL*, xcii. 369).

[2] P. R. Garrucci, *op. cit.* iii, *tav.* 130.

[3] Cf. Bede's Christmas sermon, *PL*, xciv. 44, and the Christmas mass of the Gelasian Sacramentary, *PL*, lxxiv. 1056–7.

(*Luke* vii. 37–8). For contemporary exegetes, Mary here represents the individual believer, the church or the converted heathen, bowed at the feet of Christ.[1] The scene is unique in Anglo-Saxon sculpture,[2] but has iconographical affinities with a scene on the fourth- or fifth-century Brescia casket.[3]

Below this is carved the scene of Christ healing the man born blind, familiar from early Christian sarcophagi and ivories and found again on a fragment from Rothbury.[4] The inscription is a paraphrase of the Vulgate *John* ix. 1: + ET PRAETERIENS · VIDI[T HOMINEM CAECUM] A NATIBITATE ET SA[NAVIT EUM A]B INFIRMITATE, 'And passing he saw a man blind from birth, and he cured him of his infirmity'. This is appropriately placed in juxtaposition with the Magdalene scene, being considered by exegetes like Bede to represent the divine power to illuminate a believing soul, mankind having been blinded through the sin of Eve.[5] Traces on the stone suggest that Christ touches the man's eyes, not with the fingers as at Rothbury, but with a wand held in the right hand in the iconographical tradition of the fifth-century Bologna ivory pyxis.[6]

Below this again is an Annunciation scene composed simply of a winged angel confronting a female figure, both nimbed and standing. The inscription might be completed from the Vulgate thus: [ET] INGRESSUS ANGEL[US AD EAM DIXIT AVE

[1] Cf. Bede, *PL*, xcii. 424 f. A link with the desert theme of the opposite face might be recognised in the fact that the *Old English Martyrology* (EETS, cxvi, p. 126) represents Mary Magdalene having become a desert recluse after her conversion.

[2] Although similar iconography is found on a probably ninth-century shaft at Halton, where a crouched figure is shown at the feet of what appears to be an angel (W. G. Collingwood, *op. cit.* fig. 92).

[3] P. R. Garrucci, *op. cit.* vi, *tav.* 441. Where the scene recurs in a ninth- or tenth-century Carolingian ivory, the stance of Mary is similar, but Christ is shown seated (A. Goldschmidt, *Die Elfenbeinskulpturen ... VIII–XI Jahrhundert* (Berlin, 1914–26), i, pl. xlix).

[4] W. G. Collingwood, *op. cit.* fig. 94.

[5] For example *PL*, xcii. 757 f.

[6] G. Bovini, *Avori dell' alto medio evo* (Ravenna, 1956), p. 45, fig. 41.

GRATIA PLENA DOMINUS] TECUM · BE[NEDIC TA TU IN MULIERI-
BUS], ' And the angel having entered, said to her " Hail, full of
grace, the Lord is with thee; blessed art thou among women " '
(*Luke* i. 28). The Hovingham slab[1] (*c.* 800 A.D.) includes an
Annunciation scene, but with Mary shown seated in the Hellenistic manner of the Ravenna throne or Adana medallions.   The
Ruthwell iconography derives from an early Syrian type found
on one of the Monza ampullae.[2]   The Annunciation, for Bede
the 'exordium nostrae redemptionis ',[3] appropriately opens any
selection of scenes from the life of Christ.

As on the Monza ampulla or the eighth-century Genoels-
Elderen ivory, the Annunciation is balanced by the two confronting female figures of a Visitation panel at the top of the
shaft.   The remains of a runic inscription in the right-hand
margin read: ... *dominnæ* ..., ' ladies ', and in the left and
upper margins what might be interpreted: *m[a]rpa ma[riam].*[4]
Martha would be a curious error for Elizabeth here, but the
sequence of such inscriptions is often disjointed and, in the
absence of the greater part, no firm conclusion can be drawn.
However, the iconography of the scene, although not so common in early Christian art as the Annunciation, corresponds
with those of the Adana medallions and a (now missing)
panel from the Ravenna throne, as well as the eighth-century
Langobardic altar of Ratchis at Cividale.[5]

At the foot of the cross, filling the large bottom panel of this
face, are the remains of a once impressive Crucifixion, the
figure almost three feet high.   This has been the subject of
systematic obliteration but it is possible to decipher its main
lines.   In agreement with the majority of early Crucifixion
scenes, and in conformity with contemporary theological

[1] W. G. Collingwood, *op. cit.* fig. 54.

[2] P. R. Garrucci, *op. cit.* vi, *tav.* 433.

[3] *PL*, xciv. 9.

[4] Cf. G. F. Black, *Academy*, xxxii (1887), 225, who curiously reads not
dominnæ but *ma. . .isnæ* (or *a*).

[5] P. R. Garrucci, *op. cit.* vi, *tav.* 424.

thought, an upright and vigorous Christ, bearded but naked save for a loin-cloth, extends over the entire area, reaching to the four sides of the panel. Symbols of sun and moon are seen above and there is some evidence for two figures by the cross below.[1] No part of any inscription remains.

Only the upper and lower arms of the original crosshead survive. Disjointed ornament along the sides shows the uppermost piece to have been reconstructed the wrong way round, and should therefore be understood reversed in the original artistic scheme. Originally the upper arm of the principal face bore the half-length figure of St. John with his eagle attribute, and in the margin the remains of what are probably the opening words of his Gospel: IN [PRINCIPIO ERAT VERB]UM. The lower arm contains what must be the figure of St. Matthew with his angel attribute, but the whole composition is blurred and no inscription is legible. Almost certainly the missing transom bore on this face the corresponding figures of SS. Mark and Luke with their respective attributes of lion and bull.[2] Such evangelist motifs might have surrounded a centre-piece containing an Agnus Dei as at Durham.[3]

The possible significance of the ornament on the southern face of the cross-head has been the subject of considerable speculation. A bird stands in foliage on the upper arm while the lower contains the crouched form of an archer aiming obliquely upwards. The archer is a frequent motif on Northumbrian sculpture,[4] but in a monument like the Ruthwell Cross so packed with religious significance this sort of juxtaposition of motifs is unlikely to be fortuitous. On the Halton cross, as on a contemporary Ravennate capital at

[1] See especially A. S. Cook, ' The date of the Ruthwell and Bewcastle Crosses ', *Trans. Connecticut Academy*, xvii (1912), fig. 8. For early types of Crucifixion iconography see pp. 52–4.

[2] See p. 11, n. 4.

[3] W. G. Collingwood, *op. cit.* p. 81, fig. 98.

[4] Cf. sculptures at Bakewell, Durham, Halton, Hexham, Jarrow, Sheffield or St. Andrew Aukland; and found in MSS. like the Corbie Psalter, about 800 (Amiens, Bibl. Municip. MS. 18, f. 95r).

Brescia,[1] the archer is plainly shooting *at* the bird.   A variety
of allusive interpretations are possible.[2]   But if the archer is in
fact aiming at the bird, one very straightforward interpretation
presents itself.   In early Christian art a bird, like those of the
inhabited vine, conventionally represents the Christian soul,
and an archer the Devil. Similarly in Anglo-Saxon literature an
archer shooting arrows generally signifies the promptings of sin.[3]
However, in the absence of the transom it is not possible to
assess the character of the entire composition with any con-
fidence, and it is always possible that the archer and bird have
no significance other than a realistic and secular one.[4]   No
assistance is to be derived from the remains of a runic inscription traceable on this side of the cross-head, all interpretations
of which are highly disputable.[5]   All that can now be deciphered
reads: *mæfauœþo*.

[1] Brescia, Museo Civico Medioevale, no. VI.

[2] E. H. Kantorowicz ('The archer in the Ruthwell Cross', *Art
Bulletin*, xlii (1960), 57–9) supposes that it might represent the story of
Ishmael, the archetypal archer of *Genesis* xxi, in which case it would
continue the desert theme of the other face.   According to Saxl (*op. cit.*
pp. 6–7), referring to liturgical comment on *Psalm CII.* 5, *renovabitur ut
aquilae iuventus tua*, the bird might represent the Ascension of Christ.
And if it could be assumed that the centre piece contained an Agnus Dei,
then lamb, archer and bird together might represent a complex of such
Christ symbols; cf. B. C. Raw, 'The archer, the eagle and the lamb ',
Journal of the Warburg and Courtauld Institutes, xxx (1967), 391–4.

[3] For the arrows of sin and related images see E. G. Stanley, 'Old
English poetic diction ', *Anglia*, lxxiii (1955), 418 f. Occasionally
arrows represent the words of God (cf. comments on *Psalm CXIX.* 4 by
Augustine, *PL*, xxxvii. 1600, or Alcuin, *PL*, c. 620). But where
depicted thus the Divinity is easily recognisable (e.g. B.M. MS. Harley
603, ff. 11, 11v, 22, 73v, etc.).

[4] Cf. M. Schapiro, 'The bowman and the bird on the Ruthwell Cross
and other works ', *Art Bulletin*, xlv (1963), 351–5.

[5] Of the more fantastic, F. Magnussen (*Annaler for Nordisk Oldkyn-
dighed* (1837), 266) claimed to read a memorial to Offa: *Ofa vodo
khonmeð*, i.e. ' Offa Wodanis genere procreatis ', pointing out that the
' eagle ' was a royal bird. In the left-hand margin of the bird panel
F. E. C. Dietrich (*Disputatio de Cruce Ruthwellensi* (Marburg, 1865),
p. 4) read *æfæ uœtho*, and in the right-hand, *uæ. efth*, which he compared

The style and composition of the Ruthwell Cross are normally considered together with that at Bewcastle,[1] less than
thirty miles away in Cumberland. The two works clearly
belong to the same school, if not to the same hand, characterised by fine, bold, monumental carving in the Roman tradition.
While Roman monuments were preserved and still appreciated
in the seventh century,[2] there cannot be shown any direct and
unbroken line of insular Roman sculpture, although this is
certainly in the main tradition. No doubt it was reintroduced
from the eastern Mediterranean through the medium of the
church. The technical competence displayed by the artist is
unparalleled at this time in Europe and is not found again in
England until the twelfth century. Striking proof of the
sculptor's plastic skill is found in the St. John panel of the
cross-head, where originally fine cutting is betrayed by the
leg of the eagle free-standing above the claw so as to allow a
finger to pass behind. While there may be two hands at work
in the Ruthwell carvings,[3] they have more in common than

with Lindisfarne Gospels gloss, *voed(ð)o:* ' vestimenta ' (*John* xiii. 4).
In the following year G. Stephens, *The Old-Northern Runic Monuments
of Scandinavia and England* (London, 1866–84) i, thinking that he read
the name Cadmon on the cross also, interpreted the whole as ' Cadmon
me fawed (made) ', taking *fauœþo* as 3 sg. pret. of *fegan.* (Of course,
even if this reading is accepted, *me* would refer to the monument rather
than the inscription merely.) S. Bugge (*Studien über die Entstehung der
nordischen Gö:ter- und Heldensagen* (Munich, 1889), pp. 494–6), followed
by Cook (*MLN,* v (1890), 153–5), maintained Stephens' reading, but
rejected his interpretation; taking the bird in foliage to represent a dove
and olive branch, he suggested instead: [*ic ne*] *god mon mæ fah œþo,* ' I
God no longer destroy men in anger ', referring to *Genesis* viii. 21.

However, in fresh readings made shortly afterwards G. F. Black
(*Academy,* xxxii (1887), 225) declared the name Cadmon illegible.
Traces of an inscription thought by Vietor to have been runes still exist
in the margins of the archer panel, but no part is now decipherable.

[1] The relationship between the two monuments is described by G. B.
Brown, *op. cit.* p. 102 f.

[2] For instance at nearby Carlisle (cf. *Two Lives of Saint Cuthbert,* ed.
B. Colgrave (Cambridge, 1940), p. 122).   [3] F. Saxl, *op. cit.* p. 19.

separates them. The Magdalene panel is typical: a deeply cut and confident composition with a fine sense of the plastic. The sculptor uses the entire available area for his figure in a broad and heavy monumental manner, the background cut well away to give the impression of free-standing sculpture, and left entirely empty to add even further weight to the figures. The interplay of curved and straight lines is stylised rather than anatomical. The form and stance of Christ here, as in the Judgement scene, are virtually identical with that incised on the wooden coffin of St. Cuthbert, made at Lindisfarne in 698[1], while in the mannered drapery both have much in common with figure work in the Lindisfarne Gospels, themselves made about the year 700, or in the *Codex Amiatinus*, copied from an Italian model at Wearmouth–Jarrow at about the same time.[2]

Other chronological considerations have centred on the nature of the inhabited vine-scroll which formed such an important feature of earlier Northumbrian art. In its classical state, as on the Ravenna throne, this takes the form of a naturalistic vine rising from an urn and fed upon by a wide variety of realistic animals: lions, bears, deer, peacocks. In the north there probably exists just one monument—fragments of a slab from Hexham[3]—which exhibits vine-scroll ornament directly inspired by a classical model of this kind (probably an ivory introduced during the seventh century), and perhaps from the hand of a foreign sculptor. While still discernibly associated with the Ravennate, the Northumbrian version was a considerably devolved form, the tendrils forming a merely schematic scroll in which the leaves and flowers are now scarcely identifiable, and bunches of grapes rarely hang down. And apart from the occasional bird, the animals which inhabit this vine are rarely realistic—fantastic bipeds and quadrupeds

---

[1] C. F. Battiscombe, ed., *The Relics of Saint Cuthbert* (Oxford, 1956), pp. 241–4, pls. v (1–2), vii.

[2] *Codex Lindisfarnensis*, ed. T. D. Kendrick *et al.* (Lausanne, 1956–60), ii, p. 142 ff., pls. 21–4.   [3] W. G. Collingwood, *op. cit.* fig. 28.

Plate I
Ruthwell Cross, east face
*by courtesy of the Warburg
Institute*

Plate II
The Ruthwell Cross, Magdalene panel
by courtesy of the Warburg Institute

whose hind quarters often grow from the foliage stem. Nevertheless the Ruthwell form of this vine-scroll is still in a relatively pristine state.

Collingwood had attempted to construct a pedigree for Northumbrian sculpture based on a cross at Hexham commonly ascribed (but on doubtful grounds) to the grave of bishop Acca (*ob.* 740), and placing the Ruthwell and Bewcastle Crosses some time in the second half of the eighth century.[1] However, the so-called Acca Cross has no figural subjects, while its vine-scroll ornament is very much developed upon that at Ruthwell. Collingwood's method was in any case questionable. He ignored the possibility of any stylistic relationship between one art medium and another, totally divorcing his consideration of sculpture from contemporary manuscript illumination or metalwork. And his chronology would place the whole inception, *floruit* and decline of this remarkable Northumbrian school in a period of political decadence, and then crowd the entire series of pre-Viking Anglian crosses into a mere 130 years. On purely stylistic grounds, relating the plant and animal ornament to other art forms, art historians now generally agree that in the ' acclimatised classicism ' of the Ruthwell and Bewcastle Crosses there is nothing incompatible with a date in the late seventh or early eighth centuries.[2]

The subject matter of the Ruthwell Cross could probably only have been brought together in the Hiberno-Saxon

[1] W. G. Collingwood, *op. cit.* pp. 112–19, and ' A pedigree of Anglian crosses ', *Antiquity*, vi (1932), 35–54. E. Mercer (' The Ruthwell and Bewcastle Crosses ', *Antiquity*, xxxviii (1964), 268–76) has recently revived Collingwood's use of the ' Acca Cross ' as a fixed chronological point.

[2] Cf. N. Åberg, *The Occident and the Orient in the Art of the Seventh Century* (Stockholm, 1943–7), i, pp. 50–1; J. Brøndsted, *Early English Ornament* (London, 1924), pp. 78–9; T. D. Kendrick, *Anglo-Saxon Art to A.D. 900* (London, 1938), p. 128 ff.; E. Kitzinger, ' Anglo-Saxon vine-scroll ornament ', *Antiquity*, x (1936), 61–71; L. Stone, *Sculpture in Britain: the Middle Ages* (Harmondsworth, 1955), p. 13.

church, its iconographical scheme fitting best the artistic ethos of the Northumbrian Golden Age. But there was no monumental tradition in Anglo-Saxon England, nor any in the Celtic hinterland, from which the conception and technique of the high stone cross might immediately derive. The origin of the free-standing stone cross—a form of monument unique to the British Isles—is still obscure. It is unlikely that the simply incised memorial slabs of the Celtic Whithorn type had any direct influence on these elaborate monumental carvings, and the parallel development in Ireland seems not to have been related to that of Northumbria. These distinct schools probably arose simultaneously, inspired by that same impulse from the Byzantine east which carried the cult of cross veneration to seventh-century Northumbria.[1] And in all probability the technique of high-relief stone carving developed in England together with the first stone church buildings.

The iconography of the Ruthwell Cross, like so much contemporary insular art, certainly did derive from the eastern church. With a wholesale exodus of eastern clerics due to both militant schism and Mohammedan insurgence, the whole of western Christendom was strongly influenced by east Mediterranean culture at this time. In any case, there had survived from Roman times a not inconsiderable traffic in both works of art and craftsmen from the east Mediterranean to Gaul and the Rhineland.[2] There is no question that the best of the Ruthwell sculpture has a grace and elasticity that find their closest affinities with the latest good work of the Hellenistic east. And although there is no direct model for the total artistic scheme, such parallels as can be adduced derive ultimately from the same area.

---

[1] See pp. 45–7. J. Strzygowski (*Origin of Christian Church Art* (Oxford, 1923), p. 230 f.) drew attention to Coptic *stelae* and Armenian shafts with panels enclosing the standing figures of saints and evangelists.

[2] Cf. L. Bréhier, ' Les colonies d'orientaux en occident au commencement du moyen-âge ', *Byzantinische Zeitschrift*, xii (1903), 1–39.

With an overall artistic scheme at once ascetic and mission-
ary, the Ruthwell Cross is a monument highly appropriate to
the extending Celtic frontier of the Northumbrian church.
Since the opening years of the seventh century the upper waters
of the Tweed and south-western Scotland had been dominated
by Northumbria; Edwin had extended his power to the
Forth, and his successors beyond. After the defeat of
Ecgfrith at Nechtansmere (685) the Picts, together with the
Dalriadan Scots and certain of the Strathclyde Britons,
recovered their liberty, but at the time of Bede the Solway
littoral at least remained firmly in Northumbrian hands. In
705 a synod was held near to Ruthwell on the River Nith, and
by 731 Anglian settlement was such as to require the establish-
ment of a Northumbrian bishopric farther to the west at the
originally Celtic centre of Whithorn.[1]

A singularly appropriate milieu for so grandiose a monumental conception as the Ruthwell Cross might well be found
in the court of Aldfrith (685–704), described by Bede as *vir
undecumque doctissimus*,[2] who we know patronised the eastern
traditions[3] and who so nobly restored the estate of Northumbria
albeit in more limited bounds, after the setback at Nechtansmere.

The inscriptions

The form of the Roman lettering round the figural panels
corresponds with that in general use in Northumbria during
the later seventh and earlier eighth centuries, and found for
instance on the Hartlepools name-stones (675–725), the coffin
of St. Cuthbert (698) and manuscripts of the Hiberno-Saxon
school. Elements common to the Lindisfarne Gospels and the
Ruthwell Cross include the use of both square and round O and
both majuscule and minuscule T, but minuscule forms alone of
h, m and *q*. They also share the early form of the ligature ET,
Ꝋ, while the writing of TERGEB$_t^A$ in the bottom margin of the

[1] Bede, *PL*, xcv, 268, 285.
[2] *PL*, xcv, 251; and cf. Alcuin, *PL*, ci. 830.   [3] Cf. p. 45.

Magdalene panel, with majuscule *A* surmounting a minuscule *t* in order to fit the available space, is exactly paralleled in the form ER^A_t on Lindisfarne Gospels f. 211. The Ruthwell epigraphy has certain elements in common with the *Codex Amiatinus*, written at Wearmouth–Jarrow at least in part by a scribe signing himself in the Greek manner—*ΣΕΡΒΑΝΔΟΣ*, and perhaps therefore utilising Byzantine conventions: minuscule for majuscule H in the IhS formula, the curled form of P made like an R in the XPS formula, and the use of B for V in NATIBITATE.[1] In general, therefore, the evidence of the Latin epigraphy tends to confirm the conclusions drawn from the artistic scheme of the Ruthwell Cross.

The use of runic lettering for Latin words round the Visitation scene is paralleled on the coffin of St. Cuthbert (698) and on the more or less contemporary Northumbrian Franks Casket. It must be assumed that these runic words were cut at the same time as the Latin, being part of the same scheme. And there is no reason to suppose separate hands to have been responsible for the runes on this broad face, and those on the narrower sides. It is not only the overlap of runes expressing Latin words which relates the runic and Roman lettering of the monument. Both are executed in much the same manner, finished with a kind of dot not made with a drill, but a pick; and the depth and sharpness of both is the same. The same workman may very well have cut both. There are some differences between the size of lettering cut on either face, but this applies equally to both Roman and runic inscriptions. The disposition of the sequences from the *Dream* is different from that identifying the figural scenes, but this might simply be due to the different requirements of a lengthier narrative with no direct pictorial guide. If the fragment *dægisgæf* on the upper stone is to be identified as part of the poem, there exists a further connection in the disposition of the runes.

There is no reason to doubt that the runes were an original

[1] Cf. G. B. Brown and W. R. Lethaby, ' The Bewcastle and Ruthwell Crosses ', *BM*, xxiii (1913), 48.

part of the monument, but, in the absence of an adequately dated series of comparable inscriptions, it is difficult to assess the relative date of the futhorc used. Save for one or two details, the Ruthwell futhorc corresponds with that used on the Hartlepools name-stones, the coffin of St. Cuthbert and the Franks Casket.

It represents an extension of the normal Anglo-Saxon twenty-eight letter futhorc, and seems to correspond with the more extensive Northumbrian series as represented in B.M. MS. Cotton Otho B X.[1] Six of the final Northumbrian maximum of thirty-three do not occur. There was no occasion to use some, but it is interesting that neither the *ior*-rune ⋇ *io* nor the *stan*-rune ⋈ *st* were used. Probably these were not yet in common use.[2]

Like the Bewcastle Cross, although more consistently, the Ruthwell Cross employs distinct symbols to distinguish between the several phonetic values of OE *c* and *g*. Whereas the Franks Casket, for instance, uses the *giefu*-rune ᚷ indiscriminately to represent both palatal and velar qualities of *g*, the Ruthwell Cross rune-master used a formal variant ᚸ for the latter, represented in the text as *ḡ*. Thus while the normal sign ᚷ is used for [g] in [*ond*]*geredæ* and *alegdun*, ᚸ is found for the velar [ɣ] in *ḡod* and *ḡalḡu*. Runic inscriptions regularly distinguish between the palatal and velar qualities of *c*, representing them by the *cen*-rune ᚻ and *calc*-rune ᚼ respectively, although these are not systematically distinguished in the Latin alphabet of OE manuscript orthography.[3] In

---

[1] See R. Derolez, *Runica Manuscripta* (Brugge, 1954), p. 16 f., pl ii, or H. Arntz, *Handbuch der Runenkunde* (second edition, Halle, 1944), pp. 122 f., 173 f., *taf.* ix.

[2] The Franks Casket similarly does not use the *stan*-rune. And there seems to have been some confusion as to the value of the ⋇ symbol; on the Brunswick Casket and the Dover and Thornhill stones, for instance, it is sometimes used as the equivalent of the *giefu*-rune (G. Stephens, *op. cit.*, i, pp. 381, 465, ii, p. 415).

[3] Campbell, § 427; K. Bülbring, ' Was lässt sich aus dem gebrauch der buchstaben *k* und *c* im Matthäus-Evangelium des Rushworth-Manuscripts folgern? ', *AB*, ix (1899), 289–300.

addition, however, the Ruthwell Cross rune-master identifies two uses of [k]. While the normal sign ᚴ is used for [k] where it precedes consonants and back vowels, as in *Krist* and *kwomu*, before front vowels the form ᛤ is used (shown as *k̄*), in *uŋket* and *kyniŋc*. The sign is similar to, and probably derived from, that used for velar *g*.

The *eoh*-rune ᛇ occurs only once, as the fifth character of *almehttig* (39). This rare form occurs with varying values,[1] but here, as in the Urswick Cross form *toroᛇtredae*, it appears to represent the fricative [x]. Commonly in runic inscriptions the combination [xt] is represented by *ht*, although on the Franks Casket it is found as *gt* in the form *fegtaþ*. In early manuscript texts it is represented *ct*, but *ht* is the normal form of later orthography.[2]

The *ing*-rune ᚷ ŋ occurs twice: *kyniŋc, uŋket*. Its original value was probably that of *n + g*; here it clearly represents guttural [ŋ]. In manuscript orthography this sound is not distinguished from the ordinary dental nasal [n], the runic ᚾ.

The *ear*-rune ᛠ is normally transliterated *ea*, as in *heafunæs*, *fearran*, although in Northumbrian, where the diphthongs *ea* and *eo* were often confused, it might also be taken to represent the latter.[3]

The use of doubled runes on the Ruthwell and Bewcastle Crosses is of interest. It is generally believed that the earliest runic inscriptions did not employ double runes,[4] but whatever might have been the case elsewhere, no such general conclusion seems valid for insular inscriptions. At first sight RC usage seems to represent a systematic reversal of the convention—of

[1] Cf. A. C. Paues, ' The name of the letter ȝ ', *MLR*, vi (1911), esp. 450–1, and R. I. Page, 'The Old English rune *Eoh, Ih*, " Yew-tree " ', *Medium Aevum*, xxxvii (1968), 125–36, esp. 129.

[2] Campbell, § 57(3); Brunner, § 221.1, *Anm.* 1.

[3] Campbell, § 278(b), n. 2. This might reflect an actual phonemic coalescence (J. W. Watson, ' Northumbrian Old English *ēo* and *ēa* ', *Language,* xxii (1946), 19–26). If Haigh's transcript be credited, the Ruthwell rune-master rendered the diphthong in *biheold* (58) by two separate runes, ᛗᚠ.   [4] Cf. H. Arntz, *op. cit.* pp. 78–9.

single consonants for double.[1] Single runes are found in contexts where on grounds of etymology and general manuscript usage double might have been expected, in *almehttig* and *men*, and rather more instances in which double runes are found where, by the same token, single letters might have been expected, in: *almehttig*, *æppilæ*, *gistoddun* or Latin *dominnæ*. This feature is by no means unparalleled in other Northumbrian runic inscriptions, but the assumption of a regular epigraphic convention is too facile.[2]

Instances of single for double and double for single characters are easily enough paralleled in Northumbrian manuscripts, occurring in both OE and Latin, and this becomes almost characteristic of later Northumbrian texts like the Lindisfarne Gospels gloss.[3] The only form which seems to have no exact parallel, *æppilæ*, if not a straightforward dittograph error, might simply have gone unrecorded. The double vowel in *riicnæ*, for which early manuscripts especially provide adequate parallels, probably represents vowel length.[4] The Ruthwell Cross inscription is a singularly sophisticated phonetic document but, in this respect, that consistency which might indicate a distinct epigraphic spelling convention is lacking. Many factors other than phonetic or orthographic exigency will have affected the work of the rune-master. His medium is equally communicative and ornamental, and a fitting occupation of the space available will have been an important consideration.

It is the lower stone which bears the runic inscription of part of the *Dream*. It is cut in horizontal rows of two to four characters in the narrow margins of the ornamental panels down the sides of the shaft. The text is arranged in four sections, in sequence: across the top, then down first the right

---

[1] As assumed by e.g. Ross, pp. 151–2, 154, etc., and R. W. Elliott, *Runes* (second edition, Manchester, 1963), pp. 88, 95.

[2] As shown in the important study by R. I. Page, ' The use of double runes in Old English inscriptions ', *JEGP*, lxi (1962), 897–907.

[3] Cf. Campbell, §§ 65–6, 457–8, 489.   [4] Campbell, § 26.

and then the left margin of each panel, first on the east and then the west face. The sequences correspond respectively to Vercelli text lines 39-42, 44-5-48-9, 56-9 and 62-4. As usual in runic inscriptions, there is no attempt at systematic word division, although one or two points were recognised in early transcripts. Bainbrigg's reading opened the inscription with a +, as on the Urswick, Falstone and Thornhill stones, and on most of the Latin panels of the Ruthwell Cross. Early drawings show the third section also to have begun thus, + *Krist* (56), but this probably disappeared towards the end of the eighteenth century.[1] Several early transcripts show points, a small dot, after *almehttig*[2] and *kyniηc*,[3] at the ends of lines 39 and 44 respectively. Bainbrigg shows another beginning the second sequence: ·*icr* / *iicnæ* (44).

When the stone was broken down in 1642 the critical lower stone broke in two, and where the exposed ends crumbled a row or two of runes have been lost from each of the four sequences where they cross the break. The edges of the shaft also seem to have been damaged either at this time, when used as paving, or during subsequent exposure in the church-yard; and many of the runes along the outermost edges are either entirely obliterated or only partly legible. This has affected especially the lowest part of the stone.

The printed text represents what may easily be read at present; italicised forms indicate partially obliterated but probable readings. Restorations from early transcripts are printed within square brackets. The italicised letters within brackets represent speculative restoration, and the number of dots an estimated number of characters now totally lost. The runes now missing or indecipherable almost certainly account for the substance, if not the actual form, of the greater part of the intermediate matter of the Vercelli text. This main

---

[1] Plain in Gordon, less clear in de Cardonnell and absent in independent later engravings.

[2] Those of Bainbrigg, Gordon, Duncan and Gibb.

[3] De Cardonnell, Duncan and Gibb.

inscription was first correctly[1] deciphered by Kemble in 1840, four years before he learnt of the existence of the Vercelli text.[2]

The runes in the margin of the upper stone are no longer legible save for a single line in the lower right margin of the east face which reads ... *dægisgæf*. ... The suggestion that this fragment might be reconstructed [*wœp*]*dæ gisgæf*[*t*], thus corresponding with VB *Weop eal gesceaft* (55),[3] is attractive. There is no reason to believe that the upper stone did not bear further extracts from the poem; Bainbrigg described the monument as ' ab apice descendo ad basim peregrinis literis, sed fugientibus, incisam '. These letters are set differently from the other runes, running in a single vertical row down the margin, but the distinction might be considered appropriate to such a broad, universal statement: an important theme in the poem suited to a dominant position on the cross. At the same time its position on the shaft would be correct for a sequence immediately preceding that below, beginning: + *Krist wæs on rodi* (56). On the other hand, the upper stone might well have contained some sort of memorial inscription, which is the implication of Dickins–Ross, who suggest that, instead, *dægisgæf* might represent an otherwise unrecorded personal name.[4] However, the fragment of inscription remaining is so small as to make speculation unfruitful.

[1] Two early Scandinavian scholars resorted to the invention of a ' Pictish ' language to offer interpretations. T. G. Repp (' Letter regarding the runic inscription on the monument at Ruthwell ', *Archaeologia Scotica*, iv (1835), 327–36), considered it the record of a grant of fort, cattle and lands at a place called Ashlafardhal at the instance of the monks of Therfuse. F. Magnussen (*op. cit.* 243–337) interpreted it as the record of a marriage settlement given to one Ashlaf by Offa.

[2] ' On Anglo-Saxon runes ', *Archaeologia*, xxviii (1840), 352–9; when Thorpe's publication was brought to his attention, he found it necessary to emend his interpretation only to the extent of three letters, *ibid.* xxx (1844), 31–9.

[3] J. L. N. O'Loughlin, *Times Literary Supplement*, xxx (1931), 648; and cf. B. Dickins and A.S.C. Ross, *The Dream of the Rood* (London, 1954), p. 4, n. 4. [4] *Loc. cit.*

Language

As might be expected from its geographical location, the
language of the Ruthwell inscription broadly corresponds with
that of major Northumbrian texts like the tenth-century
glosses to the Durham Ritual or Lindisfarne Gospels. Evidence as to date, however, is much less certain. It is possible
neither to confirm nor refute the commonsense assumption that
the language should be contemporary with the erection of the
cross on which it is carved. We simply have no independent
knowledge of the dialect of western Northumbria. The few
surviving early texts are associated with the eastern part of
the kingdom. While we might expect to find many points of
linguistic contact with these, it would not be surprising if the
language of the distant trans-Pennine frontier were more or
less advanced than that of the cultural heartlands of Northumbria. While the earliest texts are as short as that of the
Ruthwell inscription itself, so that no meaningful statistical
evidence is to be adduced, all significant Ruthwell forms can
be shown to exist in these earliest texts.

From the earlier eighth century come manuscripts of Bede's
Historia Ecclesiastica and Cædmon's Hymn; Bede's Death
Song and the Leiden Riddle are probably to be ascribed to the
same date. The rather longer text of the Durham *Liber
Vitae* belongs to the earlier ninth century. From the eighth
or early ninth century comes an important series of probably
Mercian glossaries: the Leiden, Epinal, Erfurt and Corpus
Glossaries, of which the last is probably the latest.

A number of significant features are found in the sounds of
stressed syllables.

In *pēr* (57, 64) and *strēlum* (62), CGmc. $\bar{æ}$ (possibly > West
Gmc. $\bar{a}$)[1] has been raised to $\bar{e}$. This is a common non-WS
feature, the equivalent VB forms being *pǣr* and *strǣlum*. It
is regular in earlier Anglian texts, although less so in later ones.
Where single examples of $\bar{æ}$ occur in the Leiden Riddle, Franks

[1] Campbell, § 129, n. 1.

Casket inscription and Corpus Gloss, they are probably due to lack of differentiation between symbols which were equivalent in Latin.[1]

Several instances illustrate a characteristically non-WS lack of breaking. In *almehttig* and *[ond]geredæ* (39), where OE *æ*, from the fronting of CGmc. *a*, should have been broken before [x] and *r*-groups respectively, no diphthong is found.[2] (The VB forms *ælmihtig*, *ongyrede* represent developments from broken vowels.) This feature is common to early non-WS dialects, however, occurring in the earliest Kentish charters as well as in the English names of early Bede manuscripts and in the Epinal and Corpus Glossaries.[3]

Similar lack of breaking is observable in the stem-vowels of *ǧalǧu* (40), *al* (58) and *walde* (40). The first two represent CGmc. *a* fronted to early OE *æ* and retracted instead of broken before an *l* or *l*-group (cf. VB *gealga*, *eall*). The last derives from CGmc. *o*, which was sometimes unrounded to *a* in Anglian texts; *a* of this origin was never subject to fronting and breaking before *l* or *r*-groups.[4]

Breaking, however, has apparently affected CGmc. *e* to produce the diphthong in *fearran* (57). This regularly occurs before an *r*-group in all dialects, but normally produces *eo*, as in the corresponding VB form *feorran*.[5] While *ea* would be the appropriate equivalent for the rune ᚣ according to the usual method of transliteration, it cannot be proved that the value of ᚣ was in fact *ea* rather than *eo* in this inscription.[6] However,

[1] Campbell, §§ 128–9.

[2] Campbell, § 139 ff. K. Luick (*Historische Grammatik der englischen Sprache* (Leipzig, 1914–29), § 194.2) suggested that this *æ* had in fact been broken to *æo* (*eo*) and then smoothed to appear written as *e*.

[3] Campbell, § 140.

[4] The same form *walde* is thus found in the Vespasian Psalter. It does, however, occasionally occur in purely WS texts by the usual *wolde* (Campbell, §§ 143, 156; Brunner, § 428 *Anm.* 4).

[5] Campbell, § 146.

[6] Campbell, § 278(b); cf. M. L. Samuels, ' The study of Old English phonology ', *Trans. Philological Society*, 1952, 37, n. 2.

in the Lindisfarne Gospels gloss and in the Durham Ritual, *eo* is regularly represented by *ea*, save where *w* follows or *o* or *u* stands in the next syllable.   A similar digraph *ea*, deriving from CGmc. *eu*, occurs in *[bi]hea[l]du[n]* (64).   This diphthong, spelt *eu* or *iu*, is occasionally retained in some earliest texts such as the early Bede manuscripts, the Durham *Liber Vitae* and early glossaries.   But already forms in *eo/io* predominate in these texts.[1]   The digraph *ea* recurs again in *heafunæs* (45) by back-mutation from CGmc. *e*.

Several forms occur resulting from front-mutation of a characteristically Anglian kind.   In *hælda* (45) CGmc. *a* fronted to *æ* and retracted before an *l*-group has once again been fronted by this mutation.   This entire process is regular in Anglian texts such as the Vespasian Psalter, where the identical form *-hældan* occurs.[2]

In the nom. acc. pl. *men* (41, 48) CGmc. *a* rounded before a nasal has been mutated to *æ* and then raised to *e*.   While this becomes universal only later, from the time of the earliest texts words in *e* exist beside those with the original umlaut *æ* (cf. the forms *Hængist*, *Hengist* in early Bede manuscripts).[3]

œ, runic ᚧ, in the second syllable of *gidrǣ[fi]d* (59) and *limwǣrignæ* (63), represents the front-mutation of CGmc. *ō*.[4] While this remains as an occasional fossil in earliest West Saxon, it is most characteristic of Anglian texts.   Represented by the digraph *oi*, this mutation occurs commonly in names like Coifi in early Bede manuscripts.[5]

In *[b]istēmi[d]* (48) the front-mutation of the CGmc. diph-thong *au* is represented by *ē*.   This is regular in non-WS dialects.   The WS mutation would regularly have given *īe* (cf. *Beowulf* 486, *bestȳmed* < *bestīemed*), although Anglian forms with this sound-change frequently intrude into WS texts.

---

[1] See p. 28, n. 3.   [2] Campbell, §§ 143, 193(a).

[3] Campbell, §§ 193(d), 291; Ross, 146–7.

[4] Cf. Campbell, § 67; R. I. Page, ' A note on the transliteration of Old English runic inscriptions ', *English Studies*, xliii (1962), 484–5.

[5] Campbell, § 198.

In the corresponding line of the Vercelli text this Anglian form is found, and indeed seems almost entirely to have replaced the WS form in poetic texts.[1]

Back-mutation has produced a distinctive form in *heafunæs* (45), the diphthong deriving from CGmc. *e*. In Cædmon's Hymn and in some early Bede manuscripts *e* is regularly found, but occasional forms with diphthongs occur in other early Bede manuscripts, the Leiden Riddle and the Epinal and Corpus Glossaries.[2]

The vowels of unstressed syllables present a relatively pristine picture. While the *æ*, *e* and *i* of unaccented syllables later fell together in a sound usually written *e*, here, as in other early Northumbrian texts, these sounds remain largely undisturbed.[3] Early OE nasalised *a* or *o* is spelt *a* in such forms as *gistīga*, *hælda*, *fearran* or *giwundad*; *æ* is found commonly in *heafunæs*, *līcæs*, *riicnæ*, *limwǣrignæ*, *æppilæ*, etc.; *i* appears in [*b*]*istēmi*[*d*], *æppilæ*, *ni* and the *bi*-, *gi*- forms;[4] *u* remains in e.g. *ālegdun*, *bismærædu*, *ḡalḡu*, *gistōddun*, *kwōmu* or, resisting syncope,[5] *heafunæs*. While the vast majority of these early forms remain, three are already represented by *e*: *æ* in *walde*, and *i* in *uŋket* and [*ond*]*geredæ*.

In the earliest Bede manuscripts, Bede's Death Song, Cædmon's Hymn and the Epinal Glossary, early OE *æ* is generally retained in unaccented syllables, although occasional examples written *e* are beginning to appear.[6] (The fact that *æ* is found conversely for *e* in the second syllable of *bismærædu*

---

[1] See pp. 7–8; Campbell, § 200(5).

[2] Campbell, § 210(2); F. Dieter, *Ueber Sprache und Mundart der ältesten englischen Denkmäler* (Göttingen, 1885), p. 20

[3] Campbell, § 369.

[4] The suffix in *almehttig* and *modig* (39, 41) may belong with these, or alternatively may derive from CGmc. -*aʒ*.

[5] Contrasting with later Northumbrian texts in which syncope is regular in this word (Ross, 151; and cf. U. Lindelöf, *Die Sprache des Rituals von Durham* (Helsinki, 1890), p. 56).

[6] Cf. E. Sievers, 'Der angelsächsische Instrumental', *PBB*, viii (1882), 324–33.

as in the Franks Casket form *gibrōpær*, may indicate a stage at which confusion between these two sounds was possible.) Similarly in these texts early OE *i* is generally retained,[1] although replaced by *e* sporadically in the Leiden Riddle and more commonly in the Durham *Liber Vitae*.[2] This trend seems to have begun equally early in the south, being found in an original East Saxon charter of 692–3.[3] Unaccented *u* is preserved in all instances in the early Northumbrian short texts, as here.

Breaking seems not to take place in Old English in unaccented syllables. Instead we find the retraction of *æ* from CGmc. *a*, to *a* before *l* or *r*-groups, later tending to become *o*. Thus we find *a* retained in the second element of *hlāfard* (45), which is the normal form of the Vespasian Psalter and Durham Ritual for the regular WS *hlāford*, later occasionally *hlāfurd*.[4]

The past participle suffix *-ad* for regular WS *-od* in weak class II verbs, like *giwundad* (62) beside VB *forwundod*, is characteristic of all non-WS dialects.

One or two features of the consonant system of the Ruthwell text are of interest. The most remarkable feature is the relatively frequent loss of final *-n*. It is missing in *bismærædu*, *ḡalḡu*, *gistīḡa*, *hælda* and *kwōmu*, whereas it has been preserved in *ālegdun*, *fearran* and *gistōddun*. This loss of final *-n* is normally regarded as one of the chief characteristics of the Northumbrian dialect. It is already lost in weak nouns in the earliest Bede manuscripts, Cædmon's Hymn, the Leiden Riddle and Franks Casket inscription, and is extended, although by no means universally, later.[5]

In medial positions the bi-labial voiced fricative [ƀ], regularly represented by *f* in RC *gidræ[fi]d*, *heafdum*, *heafunæs* and

---

[1] K. Luick, *op. cit.* § 325; E. Sievers, *loc. cit.*

[2] R. Müller, *Untersuchungen über die Namen des nordhumbrischen Liber Vitae* (Berlin, 1901), p. 21.

[3] *The Oldest English Texts* (ed. H. Sweet, EETS, lxxxiii), p. 426; and cf. M. D. Forbes and B. Dickins, ' The Ruthwell and Bewcastle Crosses ', *MLR*, x (1915), 29.   [4] Campbell, § 338.

[5] Campbell, §§ 472, 735(e); and cf. Ross, 152–3.

hláfard, is occasionally represented by *b* in the earliest Northumbrian texts, but *f* already predominates.[1]

The group *-ŋc* in *kyniŋc* (44) (and cf. *uŋket*, 48) is not unfamiliar in early texts, the spelling *-ngc* being found in an original East Saxon charter of 692–3, while the use of *c* for *g* plosive is well attested in eighth-century Mercian charters.[2]

Few features of RC accidence can be said to have any dialectal or chronological significance, assuming that these are not plain errors or due to false etymology. The likelihood of runic error in these cases is slight.

After *miþ* the dative form *blódæ* must clearly be interpreted as an instrumental. Perhaps, as in OS and OHG, the dative case came to be used for the instrumental even before the two cases fell together for phonological reasons.[3] These forms remain distinct in the Epinal Glossary, but it may well be that syncretism took place at different times in different dialects.[4]

The form of the instrumental suffix in *ródi* (56), when we might have expected *-æ*, is curious. Parallels occur in the strong *ó*-stem noun forms: Franks Casket *cæstri*, Epinal Glossary *gitiungi*, *mégsibbi*, and possibly Leiden Glossary *tyndri*. It may be that this represents the analogical introduction into the paradigm of *ó*-stem nouns, the locative-instrumental ending of the *a*-stem nouns.[5] Perhaps at a time when both unaccented *æ* and *i* were falling together into

---

[1] Campbell, §§ 57(1), 444; and cf. E. Sievers, ' Altangelsächsisch F und B ', *PBB*, xi (1886), 542–5; ' Zu Cynewulf ', *Anglia*, xiii (1891), 15–16.

[2] M. D. Forbes and B. Dickins, *op. cit.* 33.

[3] Ross, 149; and cf. B. Delbrueck, *Synkretismus* (Strassburg, 1907), p. 163 f.

[4] B. Dickins and A.S.C. Ross, *op. cit.* p. 11, n. 3; E. Sievers, ' Der angelsächsische Instrumental ', *PBB*, viii (1882), 324–33.

[5] Campbell, §§ 369, 572, 587, 591; Brunner, § 252, *Anm.* 1; Ross, 150; E. Sievers, *op. cit.* 330. But cf. G. K. Anderson, ' Some irregular uses of the instrumental case in Old English ', *PMLA*, l (1935), 951 f., and C. E. Bazell, ' Case-forms in -i in the oldest English texts ', *MLN*, lv (1940), 136–7.

a sound written *e*, *rōdi*, like *blōdæ*, simply represents a confused transitional stage. This might also account for the
variant locatives: Franks Casket *on hærmbergæ* beside
Thornhill Cross *on bergi*.

The weak noun form *ḡalḡu* ending in -*u* reflects (although
with loss of final -*n*) the West Gmc. thematic element -*un*-.
Similar forms are confined to the Northumbrian dialect, found
early in Cædmon's Hymn and the Leiden Riddle, but also in
later texts.[1]

A wide variety of dates have been suggested for the language
of the Ruthwell Cross inscription, complicated by the suggestion
that deliberate archaism may possibly have been involved,[2]
but the question of an absolute date is not to be resolved. It
is reasonable only to conclude that it occupies a relative position
contemporary with, or shortly after, the earliest Northumbrian
manuscript texts.

RELATIONSHIP BETWEEN THE TEXTS

The three-hundred-years history that links two such texts,
geographically disparate and distinct in style and form, must
surely have been, as Sisam remarked,[3] one of movement and
change that stretches the imagination. The Ruthwell Cross,
probably erected in the last years of the seventh or the first of
the eighth century, and the Vercelli Book, written in the
later tenth century, provide two more or less fixed chronological points, but the process of historical transmission is

[1] Campbell, § 617; W. v. Helten, ' Grammatisches ', *PBB*, xv
(1891), 461.

[2] Attempting to reconcile art-historical and philological evidence,
Cook ascribed both monument and inscription variously to the tenth
and twelfth centuries, arguing that the early linguistic forms were
archaisms (*Academy*, xxxvii (1890), 153–4; *PMLA*, xvii (1902), 375–90;
Scottish Historical Review, xii (1915), 213–15). More recently Wrenn,
accepting Collingwood's late eighth-century date for the cross, similarly
supposed the early forms to represent deliberate archaising (' The value
of spelling as evidence ', *Trans. Philological Society*, 1943, 19 f.)

[3] *Studies*, p. 122.

unlikely to have been simple. The Northumbrian Renaissance would provide a singularly appropriate milieu for the composition of the *Dream*, but there are no historical reasons why a poem composed in the south should not have passed to the north or midlands, assumed an Anglian colouring there, and returned subsequently to the south.

If the sprinkling of Anglian dialectal forms[1] throughout the Vercelli text, and not simply in those lines that correspond with the Ruthwell version, are not to be dismissed as merely part of the poetic vocabulary, they suggest the previous existence of a full northern text. Indications of style and metre as well as the intellectual substance of the poem might place this early in the eighth century, with the flowering of the cross cult in Northumbria.[2] The small number of early West Saxon forms might indicate at least one intermediate version, perhaps stimulated by Alfred's acquisition of important cross relics in 885.[3]

The essential literary identity of the two texts cannot be questioned; the verbal parallel is too close to be accounted for simply by the use of common material. *A priori* three possible relationships might be said to exist between the two texts. It may be that an original inscription on the cross, partly poetic in form, inspired the composition of a much fuller poem. Or the sculptor may have chosen and modified appropriate extracts from an already extant poetic text. This in turn may either have been in a form approximating to the Vercelli text as we have it, or an earlier version of it.

It is difficult to assess the relative merits of each of these possibilities in view of the only partial survival of the Ruthwell inscription. There are sometimes lengthy breaks in the text, the restoration of which is largely conjectural and usually based on the Vercelli version. And there may well have been further material, perhaps of an explanatory nature, on the upper stone.[4] However, given that the Ruthwell lines are

---

[1] See pp. 7–8. [2] See p. 45.
[3] See p. 48. [4] See p. 31.

obviously incomplete in sense and metrically imperfect, the significant verbal discrepancies seem to be as follows:

In line 39 the subject of RC [*Ond*]*geredæ* is *ḡod almehttig*, and in VB *geong hæleð*, with *þæt wæs God ælmihtig* as an additional explanation in the second half-line. This could be considered an unnecessary expansion of the RC line, which might therefore be thought a more pristine form.[1] But this is just the sort of variation which, while essential to the poetic mode, adds nothing to the requirements of the monument and can therefore reasonably be dispensed with. In the full context of the *Dream*, however, it might well be insisted that the line as it stands usefully underlines the dichotomy central to the poem's organisation—the existence of two persons in the figure of Christ.[2]

In line 58 RC *æppilæ til anum* compares with VB *to þam æðelinge* with a displacement of the attribute. It is just possible that the form *æðelinge* might be due to the construing of an earlier *æppilæ* as a Northumbrian dat. sg. instead of a nom. pl. masculine case,[3] whereas it is difficult to arrive at any convincing formula to link the two forms in the reverse direction.

In line 41 RC *f*[*ore allæ*] *men* compares with VB *on manigra gesyhðe*. Cook assumed the Ruthwell Cross phrase to have been transposed from VB 93, which would presuppose the existence of a fuller text available to the sculptor. But of

[1] Cf. B. Dickins and A. S. C. Ross, *op. cit.* p. 17. In hypermetric verse it is normally the second chief stress that bears the alliteration, and Pope (p. 135, n. 22, p. 226, n. 15) points out that by omitting VB 39b together with 40a it is possible to produce a sound hypermetric line: *Ongyrede hine þa geong hæleð; gestah he on gealgan heanne*, with proper alliteration on the noun *gealga* rather than on the finite verb *gestah*.

[2] Cf. J. A. Burrow, ' An approach to *The Dream of the Rood* ', *Neophilologus*, xliii (1959), 129.

[3] Cf. B. Dickins and A. S. C. Ross, *op. cit.* p. 17; H. C. Carpenter, *Die Deklination in der nordhumbrischen Evangelienübersetzung der Lindisfarner Handschrift* (Bonn, 1910), p. 230.

course, although without strict verbal correspondence, this line quite adequately and appropriately paraphrases its Vercelli Book equivalent.

Other points of comparison—as in line 45, where for VB *hyldan me ne dorste* RC omits the object which *hyldan* usually takes and repeats the subject: *hælda ic ni dorstæ*; or 48, where RC has no form corresponding with VB *eall*; or 63, in which VB *ðær* is replaced by RC *hinæ*—might all be marks merely of sensible paraphrasing on the part of the Ruthwell sculptor. This is not to assume, however, that the sculptor necessarily knew the poem in the form we have it in the Vercelli Book.

Attention might also be drawn to the metrical arrangement, or lack of it, in the Ruthwell lines. Some, like lines 39, 45 or 48, are clearly intended to represent conventional Old English alliterative verse, while others, like 40, 56 or 62, although adequate in syntax and sense, are metrically incomplete without alliterative continuation. Had the verse been composed especially for the monument it is inconceivable that it should have contained such defective lines. And while a beginning and end may well be missing, what remains of the inscription hardly represents the substance of a poem in itself. Rather it has all the appearance of reference to or quotation from some familiar text. *A priori* this seems the most reasonable connection between the two versions. The Ruthwell artist was an habitual quoter, not only in the allusive nature of the material he portrays, but also in his use of the Vulgate to illustrate the theological content of his work. Just as he had used familiar verses from the Bible, some quoted direct, others appropriately modified or paraphrased, to identify the figural panels of his artistic scheme, so no doubt he chose appropriate parts from a singularly pertinent and masterly poem to fill the margins of the more universal motifs along the sides of the shaft—the central words of a poem that celebrates the relationship between Christ and the cross. The same source of quotation seems to have occurred as naturally to the artist of the Brussels cross-reliquary some three centuries later in the first years of the eleventh century.[1]

DOCTRINE AND ICONOGRAPHY

In both the content and structure of his work the poet of the *Dream* betrays a fine appreciation of the more important theological issues of his day. For a proper understanding of his achievement, therefore, we need to know something of this background—of the remarkable cult of the cross which spread across Europe to reach its zenith in later seventh- and eighth-century England, and the developments in contemporary Christology with which this cult was intimately linked.

The cult of the cross

The emperor Constantine's conversion to Christianity on the eve of his victory over Maxentius in 312 had been directly related to his dream or vision[2] of the 'heavenly sign' of a cross, which he believed to be the divine pledge of his triumph. Thereafter, concomitant with the adoption of Christianity as the State religion, Constantine promoted as symbols of the new faith both the *chi–rho* monogram of the name of Christ and the long-abhorred cross itself. They were exhibited separately and in combination upon his weapons and armour, his statues and in the decoration of his palaces. In particular the standard of the imperial troops was remodelled, the so-called *labarum* taking the form of a cross surmounted by the *chi–rho* monogram.[3] Ultimately the church itself was to adopt the imperial *labarum* as an ecclesiastical banner. But imperial patronage seems to have resulted in the immediate popularity of these symbols, which from the middle of the fourth century are found extensively in lay as well as ecclesiastical contexts. And

[1] See pp. 48–9.

[2] Eusebius represents this as an actual apparition seen in the sky (*PG*, xx, 944–5, 948), and Lactantius as a dream vision (*PL*, vii. 260–2). It was the second of these traditions that the Anglo-Saxons adopted.

[3] Cf. Eusebius, cited in note to *wædum* (15).

as an abstract devotional sign, use of the cross among the faithful became ubiquitous, accompanying almost every action and found on almost every object of daily use.[1]

An additional stimulus to this vogue came with the erection at Constantine's initiative of a basilica and rotunda at Jerusalem over the supposed sites of the crucifixion and resurrection respectively.[2] The discovery of a cross, however, is first mentioned by Cyril of Jerusalem about 350, remarking on the dissemination of pieces of the wood of the cross and on such cross cult portents as the apparition of a great cross of light in the sky above Golgotha.[3] But by the end of the fourth century an ' Invention ' tradition, which ascribed the discovery of the true cross to Constantine's mother Helena on a visit to the holy land in 326, was well known.[4]

According to this legend three crosses had been found deep in the ground, together with the superscription placed over Christ's head and the iron nails with which he was crucified. A miraculous cure identified the true cross. Helena sent two of the nails to her son, one in a diadem, the other in a bridle, while the other two are variously said to have been made into a sword or spear for the emperor.[5] Pieces of the wood were dispersed to different centres, part together with the superscription being preserved at the basilica of St. Croce, built in Helena's own Sessorian palace at Rome. The western church seems to have embraced entirely this tradition in one form or another. It was certainly well known to Anglo-Saxon England, where it received detailed vernacular treatment in Cynewulf's poem *Elene* and in later prose homilies.[6]

[1] Cf. Tertullian, *PL*, ii. 99; Cyril of Jerusalem, *PG*, xxxiii. 816; John Chrysostom, *PG*, xlviii. 826.

[2] Eusebius, *PG*, xx. 1085 f.   [3] *PG*, xxxiii. 468–9, 776–7, 1168–9.

[4] Cf. Ambrose, *PL*, xvi. 1463, or Rufinus, *PL*, xxi. 475–7.

[5] A variety of such ' holy weapons ' survive in different Western regalia. See p. 48, n. 5; and cf. P. E. Schramm, *Herrschaftszeichen und Staatssymbolik*, vol. ii (Stuttgart, 1955), *passim*.

[6] Ælfric, *Homs*, ii, pp. 302–6; *Legends of the Holy Rood*, EETS, xlvi, pp. 3–17; M. C. Bodden, ed., *The Old English Finding of the True Cross*, Cambridge, 1987.

In the court between basilica and rotunda at Jerusalem was erected a large commemorative metal cross which the emperor Theodosius later in 417 had encased with gold and jewels.[1] This Jerusalem cross seems to have inspired many representations of both jewelled and burgeoning, flowering crosses, perhaps best represented in that of the eighth-century Pontianus cemetery fresco at Rome—its arms jewelled, the stem putting forth flowers.[2] The fifth-century Syrian Nilus, however, had urged that a single cross placed in a conspicuous position in the apse should be enough to decorate ecclesiastical buildings.[3] And indeed probably deriving from the east, such great apsidal crosses are a characteristic feature of fifth- and sixth-century church buildings surviving at Ravenna and elsewhere in western Europe.[4] The earlier form, as represented in the cupola mosaic of the mausoleum of Galla Placidia, sets a small cross or monogram in the centre of a starry sky.[5] By the sixth century, however, as in the basilica of St. Apollinare-in-Classe, this seems to have been replaced by an impressive jewelled cross stretching right across and quartering the cosmic round.[6] The example cited contains a small medallion portrait of Christ at the centre, already anticipating an artistic link between the corporeal person of Christ and the abstract symbol.

Two cross festivals commemorate these traditions. The more ancient, and a major feast of the eastern churches, is the Exaltation of the Holy Cross, celebrated on 14th September, which goes back to the dedication of the Holy Sepulchre in 335. This is referred to in all early western martyrologies like those of Jerome, Bede and Hrabanus Maurus, and was taken into the Gelasian and Gregorian sacramentaries. It was probably fully established in the early seventh century, when it became

[1] A representation of this cross together with the surrounding buildings as they appeared in the late fourth century was reproduced in an apsidal mosaic at St. Pudenziana, Rome (C. Ihm, *op. cit.* pp. 130–2, *taf.* iii). [2] P. R. Garrucci, *op. cit.* ii, *tav.* 86.

[3] *PG*, lxxix. 577. [4] C. Ihm, *op. cit.* p. 76 f.

[5] M. v. Berchem and E. Clouzot, *Mosaïques Chrétiennes du IVme au Xme siècle* (Geneva, 1924), fig. 104. [6] *Ibid.* fig. 202.

doubly famous by Heraclius' recovery of the cross relics seized by the Persians when they had captured Jerusalem in 614, and now in 628 lifted up for the adoration of the faithful at St. Sophia in Byzantium. Similarly in the seventh century a feast of the Invention of the Holy Cross appears in the calendars of Gallican and Mozarabic service-books for 3rd May,[1] with special offices in the Gelasian and Gregorian sacramentaries probably added some time in the eighth century.[2]

This eastern veneration of the cross spread rapidly across the west during the course of the seventh century, carried like the relics not only by eastern ecclesiastics like Theodore of Tarsus, expelled as a result of doctrinal schism or political disruption, but also by western pilgrims to the holy places. A particular stimulus to the cross cult in Northumbria seems to have derived thus from Arculph's *De Locis Sanctis* describing the cross relics at Byzantium, the silver memorial cross at Jerusalem and another of wood standing in the Jordan where Christ was baptised. Adamman's translation of this account[3] was dedicated to Aldfrith of Northumbria (685–704), who ordered copies of it to be made for use throughout his kingdom. But this only gave impetus to an already living tradition. In 633, at Heavenfield, Oswald of Northumbria had re-enacted the original Constantinian story,[4] erecting a great wooden cross and praying for the assistance of God before engaging battle, the wood of this cross being subsequently believed to work miracles. And what is believed to be the sole surviving coin-type of Aldfrith's predecessor, Ecgfrith, bears a cross surrounded by rays of light and the inscription + LUX.[5] It was this Constantinian vision of the Ravennate cosmic symbol

[1] *PL*, lxxii. 614, 620; lxxxv. 98, 739.

[2] *PL*, lxxiv. 1162; lxxviii. 101, 687.

[3] *PL*, lxxxviii. 779 f.   [4] *PL*, xcv. 117–18.

[5] C. F. Keary, *A Catalogue of English Coins in the British Museum; Anglo-Saxon Series* (ed. R. S. Poole, London, 1887), i, p. 139, pl. xx(1). But cf. C. S. S. Lyon, ' A reappraisal of the Sceatta and Styca coinage of Northumbria ', *British Numismatic Journal*, xxviii (1955–7), 227–42.

aligned with sun, moon and stars which seems to have arrested the Anglo-Saxon mind. Here the image provoked new visions[1] and entered liturgical phraseology.[2]

The legend of the cross as received by the early Anglo-Saxon church was already showing signs of that detailed elaboration that characterised medieval exegesis. And no doubt independent insular particulars were soon added.[3] Certainly various versions were current of the different types of wood which made up the cross. The pseudo-Chrysostom's inference from *Isaiah* lx. 13[4] that it was made up from cypress, cedar, pine and box was adopted by Bede,[5] but the vernacular *Riddle LV* suggests a more homely list: ' maple, oak, the hard yew and pale holly ' (9–10). The composition remained a matter for individual speculation, although its fragrance and miraculous powers, as recorded in Bede's own *De Locis Sanctis*,[6] were generally agreed. Probably already too its Old Testament antecedents were already worked out, types being recognised in both the trees of Paradise, *ligna vitae et scientiae*.[7]

[1] For instance, at the death of Hilda of Whitby (*c.* 679) a nun is reported to have seen a great shining cross carried up into the sky by angels, that *scean swa heofenes tungol* (*An Old English Martyrology*, EETS, cxvi, p. 206); and cf. Ælfric, *Lives of the Saints*, EETS, xciv, p. 150, or *Legends of the Holy Rood*, EETS, xlvi, p. 103.

[2] E.g. York Breviary, *O crux splendidior cunctis astris* (SS, lxxv, 275).

[3] For instance, the concept of the cross itself being soaked in blood, common to the *Dream* and *Christ* but not found in e.g. the Latin source of *Christ*, might well indicate the existence of a distinct vernacular cross tradition (cf. C. Schaar, *Critical Studies in the Cynewulf Group* (Lund, 1949), pp. 35, 39). [4] *PG*, lii. 839.

[5] *PL*, xciv. 555. [6] *PL*, xciv. 1190.

[7] There is a hint of the physical descent of the actual tree in the works of Ephraem Syrus (*Corpus Scriptorum Christianorum Orientalium*, ccxviii. 38). The crucifixion scene of an early eleventh-century psalter (Cambridge University Library MS. Ff. I 23, f. 88v) has the words *lignum vite* written along the cross-piece of the gallows. Cf. generally W. Meyer, ' Die Geschichte des Kreuzholzes vor Kristus ', *Abhandlung der königlich bayerischen Akademie der Wissenschaften* (Philos-Philol. Klasse, xvi (2) 1882), 101–65; R. E. Kaske, ' A poem of the cross

With the seventh century the cross became an all-pervasive symbol of ecclesiastical life. It is found lifted up in processional use and adopted as a form of pastoral crosier; jewelled pectoral crosses seem to be first found at this time. And, in Northumbria at least, church buildings are said to be constructed *in modum crucis*.[1] Crosses would certainly have ornamented such buildings. At Jarrow a slab cross has the inscription: *in hoc singulari [sig]no vita redditur mundo*, the opening words of which are clearly reminiscent of Rufinus' account of the inscription on the monument commemorating Constantine's vision of the cross—and which was certainly known to Bede.[2]

The most remarkable feature of this time, however, is the rise of a great series of standing stone crosses, some of them of a memorial nature like that apparently set up by Æthelwald[3] in memory of St. Cuthbert (*ob.* 687), but most no doubt preaching crosses of the kind set up by Cuthbert in his lifetime.[4] These were especially popular in the mission field; by 744 Boniface complains that worship at such crosses was detracting from attendance at regular churches.[5] The carved stone cross was to become a singular and important feature of Anglo-Saxon art. The remains of some one and a half thousand survive—most of them in Northumbria. Many others made of wood have certainly decayed.[6]

---

in the Exeter Book ', *Traditio*, xxiii (1967), 65–6; N. R. Ker, ' An eleventh-century OE legend of the cross before Christ ', *Medium Aevum*, ix (1940), 84–5.

[1] *The Historians of the Church of York*, ed. J. Raine, RS, lxxi (1879–94), i. p. 434; and cf. S. Lewis, ' The Latin iconography of the single-naved cruciform basilica Apostolorum in Milan ', *Art Bulletin*, li (1969), 205–19.

[2] W. Levison, 'The inscription on the Jarrow Cross ', *Archaeologia Aeliana*, S4, xxi (1943), 121–6.

[3] Bishop of Lindisfarne, 721–40; *Symeonis Monarchi Opera*, ed. T. Arnold, RS, lxxv (1882–5), i, p. 39.

[4] Cf. Bede, *PL*, xciv. 777.   [5] *PL*, lxxxix. 752.

[6] The remains of a large wooden cross said to have been recognised buried beneath the tenth-century church of St. Bertelin, Stafford, may

In 701 the Syrian pope Sergius I was led by a vision to the discovery of a jewelled reliquary containing a fragment of the true cross large enough to put the church at Rome on an equal footing with Byzantium in the matter of relic worship. Ceolfrith of Wearmouth–Jarrow was in Rome in the same year and may well have witnessed the celebrations; the event certainly seems to have caused some excitement in the north of England.[1] Such relics were not uncommon in western Europe, however;[2] Alcuin probably got the fragment he asked for in 796.[3] Perhaps the two best known Anglo-Saxon cross relics are those said to have been presented respectively to king Alfred by pope Marinus in 885[4] and, with other Constantinian relics, to Æthelstan by Hugh, duke of the Franks, in 926.[5]

A lively interest in cross relics was maintained well into the end of the Anglo-Saxon period.[6] From the earlier part of the eleventh century comes an important cross-reliquary now at the church of SS. Michael and Gudule, Brussels.[7] Badly

possibly have been the preaching cross of Bertelin himself, c. 700 (A. Oswald, ed., *The Church of St. Bertelin, Stafford, and its Cross* (Birmingham, 1955), pp. 15–18, 26–7).

[1] It is commented upon at length by Bede, *PL*, xc. 569.

[2] See A. Frolow, *La Relique de la Vraie Croix* (Paris, 1961); M. Förster, *Zur Geschichte des Reliquienkultus in Altengland* (Munich, 1943).

[3] *PL*, c, 203.   [4] *ASC*, (A) *sa.* 885, (E) *sa.* 883.

[5] This gift is said to have included a fragment of the crown of thorns, the sword of Constantine with a nail from the cross in its hilt, and the spear of Charlemagne with which the centurion has pierced Christ's side (William of Malmesbury, *PL*, clxxix. 1102–3).

[6] The late tenth-century *Chronicon Æthelweardi* (ed. A. Campbell (London, 1962), p. 46) enthusiastically multiplies the single gift of Marinus; and an eleventh-century hand has inserted a Latin note into a late tenth-century copy of the Anglo-Saxon Chronicle, remarking on Sergius' discovery of 701 (N. R. Ker, *Catalogue of Manuscripts containing Anglo-Saxon* (Oxford, 1957), p. 249).

[7] H. Logeman, *L'Inscription anglo-saxonne du reliquaire de la vraie Croix au trésor de l'église des SS. Michel-et-Gudule à Bruxelles* (Ghent, 1891); and cf. S. T. R. O. d'Ardenne, ' The Old English inscription on the Brussels Cross ', *English Studies*, xxi (1939), 145–64, 271–2.

damaged, its once jewelled front missing, this takes the form of a large piece of cross-shaped wood covered with a silver plate bearing medallions containing evangelist symbols on the arms and an Agnus Dei at the centre. An inscription in a mixture of Latin majuscules and minuscules round the edges reads first: + *Rod is min nama; geo ic ricne Cyning bær byfigynde, blode bestemed,* which bears a close relationship to the *Dream* 44 and 48,[1] and then a common form of dedication: *þas rode het Æþlmær wyrican and Aðelwold hys beroþo Criste to lofe for Ælfrices saule hyra beroþor.* The transom bears the inscription + *Drahmal me worhte.* Although it has not proved possible to identify with any certainty the persons mentioned,[2] the WS language of the inscription, like the art and epigraphy of the reliquary, is clearly ascribable to the late tenth or eleventh century.

The presentation of an important cross relic by the emperor Justin II to princess Radegund, abbess of Poiters (560–87), had been the inspiration for the two most famous cross panegyrics of Venantius Fortunatus, bishop of Poitiers (*ob. c.* 600): ' Vexilla regis prodeunt ' and ' Pange lingua '.[3] These in turn stimulated a long line of hymns and poems in veneration of the cross. Most notable of the imitators of Fortunatus was the Northumbrian Alcuin, frequently composing in the form of a cruciform acrostic, followed in turn by Hrabanus Maurus and Johannes Scotus Erigena.[4] Some such

[1] The metrical character of the Brussels inscription was first recognised by J. Zupitza, *Archiv,* lxxxvii (1891), 462.

[2] A. S. Cook (' The date of the Old English inscription on the Brussels Cross ', *MLR,* x (1915), 157–61) would identify them with three of the six brothers of Eadric Streona mentioned by Florence of Worcester, *c.* 1007. S. T. R. O. d'Ardenne (*op. cit.* 158–9) favours the identification of Æþelmær with the well known patron of Ælfric and founder of Eynsham; Æþelmær was a member of the West Saxon royal house and it is just possible that the Brussels reliquary contains the relic given to Alfred.   [3] *PL,* lxxxviii. 87–96.

[4] Cf. J. Szövérffy, ' Crux Fidelis . . .; prolegomena to a history of the Holy Cross hymns ', *Traditio,* xxii (1966), 1–41.

poems were no doubt occasioned by special events in the church calendar. The seminal hymns of Fortunatus in particular were splendidly suited to liturgical use. Veneration of the cross was especially prominent at Good Friday in Gelasian and Gregorian sacramentaries. More elaborate ritual occurs in the Mozarabic liturgy into which the ' Pange lingua ' was first taken, followed by a prayer, *O sancta crux*, three antiphons *de ligno domini* and an *oratio ad crucem*.[1] Such adoration elements were increasingly extended in western liturgies,[2] and a wide variety of independent prayers and addresses to the cross are found in both Latin and Old English.[3] When Alcuin retells Bede's story of Heavenfield he introduces an element of cross adoration into the story, having the army now prostrate themselves before the cross at Oswald's command.[4]

An address to the cross contains the implication of its possessing some kind of personality. Already in the fifth century Paulinus of Nola considered it accepted doctrine of the Jerusalem cross that *in materia insensata, vim vivam tenens*,[5] and thereafter it is not infrequently seen as having an individual life and persona. However, Christian devotion to the cross still centred in its abstract representation of the Saviour's victory over the powers of evil and death. Behind the simple Ravennate image of a cross stretching out across a starry sky to the four corners of the earth lie the works of early fathers like Jerome or Augustine,[6] for whom, referring to *Ephesians* iii. 18, the cross is a sign of Christ's universal dominion, its

[1] *PL*, lxxxvi. 609 f; and cf. Isidore, *PL*, lxxxv. 429 f.

[2] For a full account of the Western development of ' depositio ' and ' elevatio ' cross rituals, see K. Young, *The Dramatic Associations of the Easter Sepulchre* (Madison, 1920).

[3] J. Zupitza edits a number from eleventh-century manuscripts (' Kreuzandacht, Kreuzzauber ', *Archiv*, lxxxviii (1892), 361–5).

[4] *PL*, ci. 819; cf. Ælfric, *Lives of the Saints*, EETS, cxiv. 126.

[5] *PL*, lxi. 329.

[6] *PL*, xxvi. 522, xxxv. 1949–50; ultimately presumably from Irenaeus, *Patrologia Orientalis*, xii. 685–6.

four projections reaching out to embrace and bring under his subjection ' the length, breadth and height of all creation '. In the pseudo-Cyprian poem *De Pascha*, the cross finds a reasoned place in universal cosmography, conceived as a great tree identical at once with both Christ and the church, and embracing all creation, uniting heaven and earth.[1] Both these essentially cosmic conceptions survive strongly in the seventh and eighth century in the works of, for instance, Alcuin:

> Jacens vero crux quatuor mundi partes appetit, orientem videlicet, et occidentem, aquilonem et meridiem, quia et Christus per passionem suam omnes gentes ad se trahit . . .
> . . . Nam ipsa crux magnum in se mysterium continet, cuius positio talis est, ut superior pars coelos petat, inferior terrae inhaereat fixa, infernorum ima contingat; latitudo autem eius partes mundi appetat.[2]

To the early church, then, this simple sign represented the living Christ, not only in his death but in his triumph. It is often shown as a living, budding stem, sprouting leaves and

---

[1] The poem *De Pascha* was copied with the pseudo-Tertullian until the ninth century (*PL*, ii. 1171–4). For the archetypal form see the scholarly work of E. O. James, *The Tree of Life; an archaeological study* (Leiden, 1966).

[2] *PL*, ci. 1208; and cf. Bede, *PL*, xcii. 913, etc., or Hrabanus Maurus, *PL*, cvii. 157–8, cxii. 423–4.

Systematic theologians like Alanus de Insulis elaborate on the significance of this towering link between heaven and earth in a manner very similar to that of the *Dream* poet: *vere crux Christi scala est a terra in coelum attingens quia per fidem crucis, per imitationem passionis, redit homo de exilio ad patriam, de morte ad vitam, de terra ad coelum, de deserto huius mundi ad paradisum* (*PL*, ccx. 224). Both the angels and knowledge of Christ himself come down to mankind by means of this mystic ladder.

This grandiose mystical conception of the cross was particularly popular with such later writers, and according to E. S. Bugge (*op. cit.* p. 421 f.) this was the source of northern mythology's Yggdrasil, the world-tree whose roots touched hell, the top heaven, and whose branches stretched out across the earth.

wreathed with flowers.[1]   It is as frequently found jewelled,
taken thus to summarise the differing qualities that the cross
might signify, as in the words of a cross dedication first found in
a pontifical associated with the name of Egbert of York (732–
66):

> radiet hic Unigeniti Filii tui splendor divinitatis in auro,
> emicet gloria passionis in ligno, in cruore rutilet nostrae mortis
> redemptio, in splendore cristalli nostrae vitae purificatio.[2]

No human form is mentioned here, but clearly Christ and the
instrument of his death are not separated.   Familiar materials
seem to be endued with some kind of sacramental power and
personality over and above that wrought merely by consecra-
tion.

The portrayal of Christ

Any realistic depiction of Christ on the cross had long been
avoided; the later medieval form of Crucifixion certainly would
have presented too shocking a picture to the imagination of the
early church.   Sometimes the person of Christ is represented
by an Agnus Dei, occasionally bearing the cross or shown with
wounds in its feet and side, but most commonly it is simply
comprehended within the cross itself or the monogram, which
we often find figured within an otherwise realistic tomb.[3]

[1] P. R. Garrucci, *op. cit.* vi, *tav.* 433–5; and cf. the eighth-century
Pontianus fresco (see p. 44) or later Anglo-Saxon sculptured fragments
from Sherburn, Yorks.   (W. G. Collingwood, *op. cit.* fig. 124). In literature the concept is familiar from e.g. *Elene* 1224–6.

[2] SS, xxvii, p. 112.   The Egbert Pontifical seems to represent the
most pristine of a small group of tenth-century English MSS. in which
this form of cross dedication appears (cf. H. A. Wilson, *The Benedictional
of Archbishop Robert* (London, 1903), p. 184).

[3] Cf. P. Thoby, *Le Crucifix des Origines au Concile de Trente* (Nantes,
1959–63), i. pp. 21, 27, pls. iii, vi.   The dramatic Easter deposition ritual,
in which the cross is made to impersonate the body of Christ
in the tomb, is first mentioned in the later tenth-century *Regularis
Concordia* of Æthelwold (*PL*, cxxxvii. 493–4), but may well have occurred
earlier.

Immediately below the broad cosmic symbol of St. Apollinare-in-Classe[1] occur the words ' Salus Mundi ', the whole composition being thus made to denote the sacrificial death of the Saviour. On ten out of the twelve Monza ampullae (c. 600) which represent the Crucifixion, while the two thieves are shown corporeally crucified, only a simple cross in the centre stands for Christ, though sometimes with a portrait medallion above.[2] Similar in its doctrinal implication is an eighth- or ninth-century Celtic iconography in which the body of Christ is superimposed by a large cross, obliterating all but the features of head, hands and feet.[3] By this means the office of Christ is distinguished from his person. And at the same time the symbol can be seen to subsume the entire persona of Christ for any purpose linked with his sacrificial function.

The earliest figural Crucifixion scenes to have survived in the west are those of a probably fifth-century ivory casket now in the British Museum,[4] and a cypress panel from the sixth-century doors of St. Sabina, Rome.[5] More precisely dated from the east is that of the Syriac Rabula Gospel, made in 586.[6] These all depict Christ alive, nimbed, eyes wide open, and standing rigid against the cross with arms stretched out to fill the available space; his God-head is manifest with cosmic symbols of sun and moon on either side. Early insular models are more schematic, preserving more faithfully many of the abstract elements of the Byzantine conception. In the Durham Gospels (c. 700),[7] for instance, the figure forms a conceptual type rather than a realistic representation. The face, like the drapery of the long eastern colobium, is made up of an interplay of lines against an ornamental cross, a dispassionate calligraphic exercise stretching across the page, which seems decisively to reject any personal involvement.

---

[1] See p. 44.   [2] P. R. Garrucci, *loc. cit.*

[3] Cf. H. M. Roe, ' A stone cross at Clogher, Co. Tyrone ', *Journal of the Royal Society of Antiquaries of Ireland*, xc (1960), 191–206.

[4] P. Thoby, *op. cit.* p. 22, pl. iv.   [5] *Ibid.* p. 23, pl. iv.
[6] *Ibid.* p. 24, pl. v.   [7] *Ibid.* ii. pp. 9–10, pl. cxc.

Certainly any portrayal of human suffering seems studiously to have been avoided. Clearly, iconographical traditions were already established in the west by the time the church can first be said to have positively encouraged such representations, when the Quinisext Council of 692 decreed that, the antitype being better than the type or symbol in all representation, the literal presentation of Christ should figure in all emblems of his sacrifice.[1]

This promotion of figural realism in the Crucifixion seems, however, to have paved the way for a further significant development in the west, where the iconodule transition was found especially suited to the newly adopted sacramentary theory of pain. Deriving particularly from Augustine, the western view of the Crucifixion was less concerned than the eastern with abstract cosmic connotations. More devotional, and therefore more subjective, it chose to emphasise in the cross the supreme expression of divine love, finding in the suffering of the Redeemer, remedy for sin and consolation for the tragedy of life. Western portrayals of the Crucifixion therefore show an increasing tendency to depict the pain and agony of the scene as the period progresses. By the middle of the ninth century artists had begun to depict realistically the extreme agony and death of Christ on the cross.[2] In later Crucifixions like that modelled for Gero of Cologne (970-6)[3] the body, no longer stiff and alive, droops in agony, straining the arms, the dead head lolling to one side. Interestingly, the artistic representation of the cross as a hacked and mutilated tree seems to have arisen together with the agonised Christ.[4]

[1] *Die Kanones der wichtigsten altkirchlichen Concilien* (ed. F. Lauchert, Leipzig, 1896), p. 132.

[2] P. Thoby, *op. cit.* i. p. 41, pl. xiii; cf. J. R. Martin, 'The dead Christ on the cross in Byzantine art ', *Late Classical and Mediaeval Studies in honor of Matthias Friend Jr.*, ed. K. Weitzmann (Princeton, 1955), pp. 189-96; L. H. Grondijs, *L'Iconographie byzantine du Crucifié mort sur la croix* (Brussels, 1941); ' La mort du Christ et le rit du Zéon ', *Byzantion*, xxiii (1953), 251-74. [3] P. Thoby, *op. cit.* ii. p. 14, pls. cxcv-cxcvii.

[4] *Ibid.* i, pl. xiii; ii, pl. cxciv.

Any triumphal aspect of the Redemption has to be reserved for the Harrowing of Hell, which we now find for the first time popularly taken up as an artistic subject.

In the meantime, however, the principle involved in the material portrayal of Christ did not go unquestioned. At various times in both east and west, iconoclastic movements arose which opposed the veneration not only of images but occasionally of the cross itself. The early fathers had been at pains to avoid the accusation of adoration of the cross rather than the person of Christ that it represented,[1] and the same careful distinction is maintained into the eighth century by, for instance, Alcuin, for whom *prosternimur corpore ante crucem, mente ante Dominum*.[2] But critics remained. By the end of the seventh century had developed that particularly militant form of Paulician iconoclasm which maintained that the true cross was Christ himself and not the wood on which he hung.[3] In all probability from this time date the two remaining Monza ampullae which show between the two crucified thieves a representation of Christ with hands outstretched but nailed to no cross.[4]

The iconoclastic controversy was to persist with varying degrees of acrimony for some time. As late as 820 Claudius of Turin published a fierce attack on the adoration of crosses, ordering their removal from all churches in his diocese.[5] By the end of the ninth century, however, the dispute seems

[1] Thus Eusebius of Constantine (*PG*, xx. 994, 1167) or Ambrose of Helena (*PL*, xvi. 1464).

[2] *PL*, ci. 1210, and cf. John Damascenus, *PG*, xciv. 1132, or Ælfric, *Homs*, ii. p. 240.

[3] Georgius Hamartolos, *PG*, cx. 889; and cf. Photius, *PG*, cii. 25, or Petrus Siculus, *PG*, civ. 1284. A similar equation occurs in the pseudo-Bede's identification of Christ with the *lignum vitae*, *PL*, xciii. 486.

[4] P. R. Garrucci, *op. cit.* vi, *tav.* 434. There can be no doubt that this is intended as a crucifixion scene, however; the iconography is otherwise complete.

[5] Claudius' *Apologetic* survives only in so far as it was the subject of detailed refutation by Jean of Orleans, *PL*, cvi. 305 ff.

generally to have resolved itself in a compromise over the technical differentiation between images and icons.

Aspects of contemporary Christology[1]

The theological origins of the iconodule dispute were closely related to questions concerning the person of Christ and the nature of his suffering. The significant controversy derived from fifth- and sixth-century disputes as to the corporeal substance of Christ. Monophysite proponents, especially strong in the east, maintained that Christ had only one, albeit composite, nature or *physis*. The extreme monophysite position generally associated with the name of the fifth-century theologian Eutyches held that Christ's body being inseparably united with the *Logos* was therefore incorruptible and without physical agony. At the other extreme the view normally associated in the sixth century with the name of Severus of Antioch laid great stress on the human infirmities of the body, which were believed to extend to the soul of Christ, being entirely man-like. Opposed to both, however, an ' orthodox ' compromise insisted precariously on the existence of two distinct natures, human and divine, balanced in the one person of Christ—the person undivided and the natures unconfused, albeit in some way mystically resolved.

Now while the Eutychan denial of the mortality of Christ inevitably questioned the propriety of representing his humanity in figural form, and therefore insisted on the use of a plain cross, the Severan insistence on his human frailty promoted the literal representation of Christ, together with the implication of his physical agony on the cross. This issue was complicated yet further. Reluctance to portray Christ was confirmed by an unwillingness to believe that the incarnate *Logos* possessed human beauty. Some, like Clement of Alexandria[2]

[1] See further the important study by R. Woolf, ' Doctrinal influences on *The Dream of the Rood* ', *Medium Aevum*, xxvii (1958), 137–53.

[2] *PG*, viii. 557.

referring to the words of Isaiah, *non est species ei, neque decor . . . et non erat aspectus, et desideravimus eum* (liii. 2), could not believe Christ beautiful on the cross. Others, however, and western teachers in particular, preferred to refer to the words of *2 Samuel* xiv. 25, *vir non erat pulcher in omni Israel, et decorus nimis; a vestigio pedis usque ad verticem non erat in eo ulla macula,*[1] from which conception derives the beautiful warrior-Christ typified in Ravennate iconography. By the early eighth century this latter Apollonic tradition was firmly established in both east and west.[2]

With the seventh century, however, the controversy had entered a new phase with an attempt to resolve the theological impasse in which Eutychans denied that Christ was fully man, and Severans that he was fully God. The Persian campaign, ostensibly for the recovery of Jerusalem and the holy relics, had highlighted the need for Byzantine solidarity on all fronts, and Heraclius proposed to resolve the issue with a significant doctrinal revision. This introduced the so-called monothelite doctrine that the divine and human natures of Christ, while quite distinct in one person, were subject to but one activity or will, *thelos*. This was adopted by the Byzantium Council of 626, but immediately aroused such violent controversy that Heraclius' successor, Constans II, was obliged to forbid all discussion of the subject on pain of penal consequences. Silence was maintained in general except for a western protest at the Lateran council of 694. There it was considered that as will is the property of nature and there were two natures in the person of Christ, there must consequently exist two wills, although the human naturally determined itself conformably with the divine. At the accession of Constantine Pogonatus in 688 general controversy revived, and it was resolved to call another great council at Byzantium in 680.

This council was regarded as particularly important in the west. Pope Agatho lost no time in inviting declarations of

[1] Cf. Jerome, *PL*, xxii. 627.
[2] Cf. John Damascenus, *PG*, xcv. 349.

adherence to the Lateran conclusions from each of the western churches. In England a pan-national assembly called at Hatfield in 679,[1] and presided over by the eastern theologian Theodore of Tarsus, subscribed to the Lateran declaration, decisively rejecting, amongst others, both Eutychan and Severan positions. In the event the monothelite position was opposed by the western legates at the Byzantium Council, which reached no agreement. Subsequent councils vacillated, and the theological position remained confused during the greater part of the eighth century.

The intense importance attached to the sophistications of orthodoxy by the earlier medieval church is difficult to understand, unless these were felt to be the bases of social order, without which mankind faced anarchy. These particular controversies were clearly living issues in England for at least the half-century 675–725, when Anglo-Saxon writers found it constantly necessary to refute heretical views concerning them. A literate and religious audience would have been well aware of the exact limits of doctrinal opinion within which poetic speculation was possible. To deal with the theme of the *Dream*, therefore, required of the author a fine sense of theological balance.

STYLE AND STRUCTURE

Style

Past scholars have ascribed the *Dream* variously to both Cædmon and Cynewulf.[2] Because of the early date of the monument, some, like Haigh,[3] supposed the Ruthwell version to represent fragments of a lost poem by Cædmon which a

---

[1] *Councils and Ecclesiastical Documents relating to Great Britain and Ireland*, ed. A. W. Haddan and W. Stubbs (Oxford, 1871), iii. pp. 145–51. The Lateran documents had been brought to Wearmouth by the papal legate, arch-chanter John, and were copied there for distribution (*PL*, xcv. 200).

[2] See generally A. S. Cook, *The Dream of the Rood* (Oxford, 1905), pp. ix–xli; and cf. H. Bütow, *op. cit.* pp. 170–1.

[3] D. H. Haigh, *op. cit.* at p. 11, n. 2; (1857), 173, (1861), pp. 39–41.

tenth-century poet then undertook to modernise and adapt to
the taste of his own times—a supposition encouraged by
Stephens, who claimed to have read 'Cadmon' on the (now
obliterated) upper stone of the cross.[1] But while Bede's list of
Cædmon's work certainly includes verse *de incarnatione domini
ac passione, resurrectione, et ascensione in caelum*,[2] we might
have expected a narrative work rather more diffuse in style and
perhaps more like the Old Saxon *Heliand* treatment of the
crucifixion than the tight, almost lyrical structure of the *Dream*.

Others, like Dietrich,[3] recognised a variety of verbal and
thematic resemblances with the signed Cynewulf poems.
Drawing attention in particular to the supposedly autobio-
graphical envoy to *Elene* in which Cynewulf tells how the
mystery of the cross was first revealed to him, and assuming
the persona of the *Dream* to be as realistic as that of the
Cynewulf signatures, they concluded that the *Dream* might
represent a prologue or epilogue to *Elene*. But such evidence
was at best merely circumstantial. And, in view of the highly
formalised nature of Old English poetic diction, it was clearly
unsafe to link one poem with another simply because certain
expressions are common to both. More recently the studies
of Das[4] and Schaar[5] have shown that while the *Dream* poet
and Cynewulf quite naturally have features in common, there
is no question of metrical or stylistic interdependence.

Chronological tests which, relying on evidence from metre or
syntax, might accord the *Dream* a place later than *Beowulf* and
Exodus but earlier than *Guthlac* and the Cynewulf canon,[6] are

[1] G. Stephens, *op. cit.* pp. 419–20; and cf. pp. 20–1, n. 5.

[2] *PL*, xcv. 214.

[3] F. E. C. Dietrich, *Disputatio de Cruce Ruthwellensi* (Marburg, 1865),
pp. 12–14.

[4] S. K. Das, *Cynewulf and the Cynewulf Canon* (Calcutta, 1942),
pp. 180, 234, *et passim.*   [5] C. Schaar, *op. cit.*, *passim.*

[6] Cf. C. Richter, *Chronologische Studien zur angelsächsischen Literatur*
(Halle, 1910), p. 101; A. J. Barnouw, *Textkritische Untersuchungen nach
dem Gebrauch des bestimmten Artikels und des schwachen Adjektivs in der
altenglischen Poesie* (Leiden, 1902), pp. 210–11.

in principle questionable, but in this instance at least would be supported by the early date that the existence of the Ruthwell text implies. Similarly the doctrinal content of the poem most convincingly fits a date in the Northumbrian Renaissance.

An early date would necessarily suggest some sort of relationship with the poetry of the Cædmonian school, which we might assume to have flourished for perhaps half a century after Cædmon's entering Whitby (658–79). The ascription of the bulk of the so-called Cædmonian paraphrases to a later period makes the association of this poem with Cædmon more credible. But the *Dream* remains stylistically very distinctive. Heroic elements in the poem are largely allusive and a matter of mere vocabulary. The poet is concerned to illuminate aspects of the Redemption rather than to linger on the theme of victor prince. Nevertheless the heroic elements of the vocabulary are used with an apparent freshness, like the word *hilderincas* for Christ's disciples (61, 72). Of the extensive range of epithets for the divinity, only three are shared with Cædmon's Hymn: the common *heofonrices Weard* (91), *Frea* (33) and *Dryhten*. This last recurs some seven times, whereas most of the remaining dozen are used only once, and some, like *Sunu* (150), nowhere else. This poet's vocabulary is in general remarkable. The use of a large number of unusual and some perhaps original words, like *ærgewin* or *bealu-ware* (19, 79), and the employment of others, like *begeotan, gang* or *deorc* (7, 23, 46), in unusual senses, all betray a highly individual mind. The fact that roughly a fifth of the verses are paralleled elsewhere is hardly surprising. Just as this poet's free use of liturgical allusion suggests that he might have drawn freely on authors who had gone before, his own attested inventiveness makes it likely that many subsequent poets would gladly have drawn on the *Dream*.

The work is both syntactically and metrically curious. A fine sense of arrangement of the language to accommodate material of varying complexity, a discriminating play of metre over syntax and a sophisticated appropriateness of style and sense achieve a total effect unlike any other in Old English. The poem is largely made up of rapidly moving short lines composed almost entirely of short inverted clauses, the sense contained within the line. Such variation as exists[1] is of the traditional close Germanic variety, making for brief staccato sequences within the overall structure. There are no instances of mere accumulation, inessential expansion or any of the heaped-up constructions so typical of Cynewulf's Latinate syntax.[2]

Against this are set blocks of hypermetric verse[3] used contrapuntally to accommodate significantly more complex thematic material. This adds dignity but without loss of pace or precision. There is a marked tendency throughout to syndectic combinations which make for smoothness in oppositions—marked especially by an extensive use of *ac*, *hwæðre* and *ond*. This feature was apparently noticed by the Vercelli Book scribe, who picked out many of them with capitals.[4] The use of a large number of verbs following each other with rapidity, many verses opening both first and second half-lines with active forms, serves both to move the narrative at a steady pace and to increase the emotional intensity of the poem. Many are perfective in sense, beginning *a-*, *be-*, *ge-*.

While a lengthy history of transmission is unlikely to have left the poet's work in a totally pristine state, it remains clearly too highly wrought for the hand of other than a distinctly original craftsman. Like the Ruthwell Cross with which the

---

[1] Only 14·1 per cent according to W. Paetzel, *Die Variationen in der altgermanischen Allitterationspoesie* (Berlin, 1913), p. 160.

[2] C. Schaar, *op. cit.* pp. 208–9.

[3] The major blocks of hypermetric verse are: 20–3, 30–4, 39–43, 46–9, 59–69; lines 8–10 may have been corrupted at some stage. See generally J. C. Pope, *Seven Old English Poems* (New York, 1966), p. 189 f., and R. D. Stevick, ' The meter of *The Dream of the Rood* ', *NM*, lxviii (1967), 149–68, and C. B. Hieatt, ' A new theory of triple rhythm in the hypermetric lines of Old English verse', *MP*, lxvii (1969), 1–8.

[4] See p. 6, n. 1.

Dream is so intimately linked, it should probably be considered an early masterpiece. Perhaps tentatively one might regard the poet as a late offshoot of the Cædmonian school and a forerunner, perhaps the stimulator, of the Cynewulfian.[1]

Theme and structure

The highly individual style of the poet merely complements his fresh and original form. It is quite without parallel; no model is to be found among any of the large number of contemporary Latin cross panegyrics. And it has not proved possible to identify a convincing source for any large part of its material. While the poet of the *Dream* shows himself familiar with both contemporary liturgy and current exegetics, this amounts to little more than common phraseology or allusion; it cannot be shown that there lies behind the *Dream* a series of Easter antiphons, like the Advent antiphons which lie behind the probably ninth-century *Christ I*, or that it derives directly from patristic theology like Cynewulf's *Christ II*. The remoteness of apparent analogues to any part merely confirms the originality of the poet. We are obliged to consider the poem entirely in its own terms as an easy and natural development out of the religious concerns of its day.

The question as to whether or not an actual dream occasioned the poet's work, which so exercised those scholars who chose to attribute it to Cynewulf, is irrelevant. The church of Bede was thoroughly acquainted with the dream or vision as vehicle of prophecy or universal truths, often vouchsafed through the medium of a heavenly messenger or guide.[2] Such visions may well have been considered appropriate to the religious poet at this time. The dream which occasioned Cædmon's Hymn affords a convenient parallel.[3] Both require

---

[1] Cf. R. Woolf, *op. cit.* 153.

[2] Cf. *PL*, xcv. 102, 145–8, 186–8, 194–5, 217, 241–2, 248–55, 268. And cf. C. Fritzche, ' Die lateinischen Visionen des Mittelalters bis zur Mitte des 12 Jahrhunderts ', *Romanische Forschungen*, ii (1886), 247–79; iii (1887), 337–69.   [3] *PL*, xcv. 213.

the poet to celebrate a particular theme—Cædmon the Creation and the *Dream* poet the Redemption. The dream convention must in any case have been recognised as particularly appropriate to a cross cult poem. After all, the Constantinian tradition as it was received in England attributed the very origins of the cult to such a dream.

This choicest of dreams takes the form, as in *Daniel*,[1] of the vision of a strange tree, the brightest of wood, towering into the heavens, wound round with light (4–6). This contrives to reflect the Constantinian vision while postponing any explicit identification with the cross of Christ. The use of *treow*, later to become a common figurative equivalent for the cross, may already have carried such a connotation as early as the eighth century, being used like Latin *lignum, arbor*, for special effect. But here the primary denotation of the word is of the greatest structural importance, the concept of the living, natural tree subsequently fulfilling a number of poetic functions.

Instead of an immediate recognition of the vision's significance, a gradual revelation is brought about. A complex series of oblique statements erects a sophisticated structural conception of the meaning of the cross in a way not open to straightforward prose; the theme is one of paradoxical complexity which even theologians found difficult. Possibly already in the context of these opening lines, not only the use of *treow* but phrases like *on lyft lædan, leohte bewunden* may have been recognised as reminiscent either of relevant church liturgy or vernacular cross tradition. The choice of words indicates that the vision is of no simple forest tree merely; it is at the same time a symbol or standard, *beacen* ' vexillum ', appropriately covered with gold and jewels like the *labarum* (6–9). The verb *begeotan*, ' to sprinkle, drench ', normally associated with

---

[1] It is interesting that whereas the ' Cædmonian ' author of *Daniel* passes over or scarcely mentions the various dreams of Nebuchadnezzar, he is particularly engaged by the (biblically unimportant) dream of the great tree, which is recounted in detail together with the prophet's interpretation (495 ff.).

water or blood, is unexpected in the phrase *begoten mid golde*. The application of such an unusual, and perhaps original, word as *eaxlegespann*, ' shoulder-joining ', to the part which bears jewels, similarly requires explanation. The use of the word *sigebeam* is puzzling. And why should it be denied that this was a criminal's gallows? Statements follow one after another, arousing a series of expectations in the mind of the reader which the poet must subsequently satisfy in the body of his work.

The abstract import of the vision is already implicit, however. Like the great Ravennate cross, this jewelled ensign stretches across the entire world, quartering the universe, where it is the subject of adoration by hosts of angels as well as men upon earth and the whole of creation (7–12). Now this abstract Byzantine concept is shown to be in a direct relationship with the individual man the dreamer represents. Lines 13–14 contrast the state of the tree with that of the visionary. Applied to *synnum*, *fah* might mean both ' stained ' and ' hostile ', thus providing implicit contrasts with both the shining visual character of the symbol and its abstract virtue. This is not the only line of the *Dream* in which poetic density is contrived by the use of verbal paronomasia or circumstantial ambiguity.[1]

Now in a unique fusion of symbol and realism, abstract and physical aspects of the tree are brought into direct juxtaposition as the poet introduces personal, spiritual qualities to the material object: *þurh þæt gold ongytan meahte earmra ærgewin, þæt hit ærest ongan swætan on þa swiðran healfe* (18–20). The bleeding tree was not without significance for the early Anglo-Saxon church. Trees were believed to have bled at the crucifixion in recognition of Christ's divinity[2] and a similar sign would

---

[1] See generally M. J. Swanton, ' Ambiguity and anticipation in *The Dream of the Rood* ', *NM*, lxx (1969), 407–25.

[2] Cf. *Christ* 1174–6, *Ða wearð beam monig blodigum tearum birunnen under rindum, reade ond þicce; sæp wearð to swate.* The concept presumably derives from the Apocrypha, 2 *Esdras*, v. 5: *et de ligno sanguis stillabit.*

herald the approach of Judgement Day.[1] The image here therefore tightens the structure of the poem, anticipating not only its climax in the crucifixion but also its final apocalyptic vision. The use of the verb *swætan* to describe the bleeding similarly looks forward to the identification of the tree with the physical person of Christ. And that the tree is specifically said to bleed on the right-hand side clearly anticipates the view not of the dreamer but of the tree and therefore of Christ himself.[2]

The mutability appropriate to the dream convention serves also to define further the mystery of the symbol while still only partially revealing its identity. The poet thus obliquely contrives to introduce the dual role which, deriving from Christ's own, forms the visual representation of the cross. It is at once both the shameful instrument of pain and death and the means of triumphal victory and life eternal. At times, therefore, it seems the simple rough wood of the gallows, squalid, stained with blood; at other times it reverts to a bejewelled treasure. This change of dress and colours recurs in contemporary cross literature and might be underlain by the actual images of church ritual at Passiontide and Easter. In the Egbert Pontifical these elements are simultaneously present.[3] The emblem is in addition said to be *fus* ' eager, hastening, moving, doomed '[4] and therefore also appropriate to the cross at Judgement Day, which contemporary poets similarly visualised lifted on high, shining, but bloody with gore.[5] Only now with so many aspects of the vision explored, is it clearly recognised to be the symbol of the

---

[1] Cf. Bede, *PL*, xciv. 555, or the apocalyptic Vespasian homily: *On þan fiften dæige, ealle wyrte and ealle treowwes ageafeð read swat swa blodes dropen* (EETS, clii, p. 90).

[2] Cf. notes to *swætan* and *þa swiðran healfe* (20).

[3] See p. 52 and notes to *wædum* (15, 22).

[4] For the semantic field of *fus* see note to line 21.

[5] Vulgate *Matthew* xxiv. 30, *tunc parebit signum Filii hominis in caelo*; and cf. *Christ*, 1064 ff., 1080–90, or the Blickling homily for Easter, EETS, lviii–lxxiii, p. 91.

Saviour's universal dominion, *Hælendes treow* (25). Still, how-ever, until the actual moment of crucifixion the poet hesitates to employ the bluntly explicit word *rod* (44).

This position has been rapidly built up in a series of swift economical movements: rapid compound sequences of short half-line syntactic units in a staccato rhythm with no elaborate repetition or loose variation to impede progress. Now a different tone is introduced with the words of the cross, no less flowing, but with a broader more dignified movement brought about by an extraordinary use of hypermetric verse.

That the gallows speaks is in no sense grotesque. We have seen that the early church considered the cross possessed of life and an individual identity and power. Personal addresses and prayers directed to it implied some kind of understanding on the part of the recipient. And certain crosses, like that over the gate of Heraclius' palace at Byzantium or another formerly at Glastonbury, were popularly accorded the power of speech.[1] And as a literary device the speaking cross was not unknown to early religious writings. The apocryphal Gospel of Peter, for instance, tells of a cross towering into the skies that at the Resurrection is given a divine errand to preach to those that sleep—in this case the soldiers at the tomb.[2] But in any case the attribution of personality to inanimate objects was an Anglo-Saxon commonplace. Valued objects such as swords or jewels sometimes bore inscriptions in the form of personalised statements of identity or origin.[3] The eleventh-century Brussels cross-reliquary inscription which begins + *Rod is min nama*,[4] is simply one of the last of a long tradition.

---

[1] William of Malmesbury, *PL*, clxxix. 1698.

[2] A. Harnack, *Bruchstücke des Evangeliums und der Apokalypse des Petrus* (Leipzig, 1893), p. 11; and cf. the dramatic passage in a pseudo-Augustinian sermon, *PL*, xlvii. 1155.

[3] Cf. inscriptions on the Sittingbourne scramaseax: +S GEBEREHT ME AH, +BIORHTELM ME WORTE, a gold ring from Lancashire: +ÆDRED MEC AH, EANRED MEC AGROF (in mixed roman and runic lettering), or perhaps best known of all, the Alfred Jewel: +ÆLFRED MEC HET GEWYRCAN.

[4] See p. 49.

A more literary precedent for the mode probably already existed in the popular type of Anglo-Saxon riddle in which an enigmatic object is made to describe itself in oblique terms, sometimes telling its history—and behind which there may have lain classical forms employing the rhetorical device of *prosopopoeia*.[1] The riddle genre seems to have been particularly popular in the seventh and eighth centuries both in Latin and in the vernacular, and was defended as a religious form by Aldhelm.[2] There are Latin cross riddles by Hwætberht, abbot of Wearmouth–Jarrow from 716,[3] and Tatwine, Mercian archbishop of Canterbury (731–4),[4] and others in the Old English Exeter Book which might be resolved thus.[5] Others from the Exeter Book collection, however (like LIII, ' Battering Ram ', or LXXII, ' Spear '), afford a better structural analogy to the words of the cross here. They tell much the same history— how, living in the forest, they had been cut down and fashioned by men for a particular purpose.

Whether or not the author of the *Dream* consciously imitated such riddle forms in this part of the poem,[6] his

[1] For probable Anglo-Saxon knowledge of this form see M. Schlauch, ' *The Dream of the Rood* as prosopopoeia ', *Essays and Studies in Honor of Carleton Brown* (New York, 1940), pp. 23–34.

[2] *PL*, lxxxix. 170–1.

[3] Per me mors adquiritur et bona vita tenetur;
Me multi fugiunt multique frequenter adorant;
Sumque timenda malis, non sum tamen horrida iustis;
Dampnavique virum, sic multos carcere solvi.
           (*Corpus Christianorum*, Series Latina cxxxiii, 227.)

[4] Versicolor cernor nunc, nunc mihi forma nitescit.
Lege fui quondam cunctis iam larbula servis,
Sed modo me gaudens orbis veneratur et ornat.
Quique meum gustat fructum iam sanus habetur,
Nam mihi concessum est insanis ferre salutem.
Propterea sapiens optat me in fronte tenere.
           (*Corpus Christianorum*, Series Latina cxxxiii, 176.)

[5] For example, XXX, LV, or LXVII, to which the power of speech is specifically attributed as one of several enigmatic features.

[6] As supposed by F. E. C. Dietrich, *op. cit.* p. 11, G. Sarrazin, *Von Kädmon bis Kynewulf* (Berlin, 1913), p. 128 f., and most recently W. F.

employment of an articulate persona for the cross brilliantly contrives to propound the theological subtleties of his theme while simply sidestepping the many difficulties. The attribution of personality, and therefore volition, allows a moral as well as physical parallel to be established between Christ and the cross. Thus it is that the words of the cross can bring us dramatically close to the events of the crucifixion, enabling the reader to share in a unique imaginative reconstruction of Christ's suffering, but at the same time evading the bewildering problem as to the nature of Christ's consciousness, and without the assumptive blasphemy that might have been involved. However, in coalescing the persona of the cross with that of Christ himself the poet draws upon a concept implicit within the traditional liturgical use of the cross and explicitly propounded in the Paulician doctrine that the real cross was not the gallows but the body of Christ himself.[1] This complex theological analogue between Christ and the cross for which we have been prepared since the opening vision of the poem is elaborated in the subsequent narrative. The cross had been chosen from all the trees of the forest simply because it stood convenient at the edge of the wood (29), as arbitrarily singled out as Mary from among all women (90–4);[2] it has a mysteriously mixed nature, at once mundane and precious; abstract qualities like ' victory ' are attributed to its physical substance; it is made a spectacle, mocked, and suffers pain and indignity which it had the power to avoid; it is buried, rediscovered, and achieves a final state of glory in heaven, honoured by men and a power in their lives, and looked to for a second coming. Physical contact between Christ and the cross is provided in the nails which, driven through the hands and feet of the one into the other, link the two. That the

---

Bolton, ' Tatwine's *De Cruce Christi* and *The Dream of the Rood* ', *Archiv*, cc (1964), 344–6.

[1] See p. 55.

[2] Chosen, most famous of trees (cf. *Elene* 1224–6), made holy through him ' although it grew in a wood ' (cf. Ælfric, *Homs*, ii. p. 306).

cross itself thus suffers, allows the agony of the Saviour to be succinctly and dramatically represented without putting unwarranted words into the mouth of Christ himself. The device thus allows the poet to maintain a fine balance between Eutychan and Severan points of view, offending neither those who maintained that the incarnate *Logos* could experience no suffering nor those who insisted upon his real human frailty.

The particular function of the cross in the act of Redemption is explained in terms of its own natural history. Beginning with the forest tree not only draws naturally on contemporary representations in which the cross is seen as the burgeoning stem of the Tree of Life, putting forth leaves, fragrant with flowers, but derives thematic significance from its apparent simplicity. There is no confusion as to the different types of wood of which the cross could have been composed; neither is there any unnecessary reference to the tree's Old Testament antecedents, both of which so engaged contemporary exegetes. The use of the simple, natural tree, while concealing within its metaphor this body of traditional theology, remains a convenient and convincing symbol of the beauty in creation perverted by the evil in men for their own ends. The narrative device begins with what contemporary rhetoricians would have defined as the ' oratio passionalis ', provoking immediate sympathy. The tree recalls its fate with pained outrage: hacked down, torn from its root, seized and turned into an unnatural, shameful spectacle by powerful and wicked men. The evil in men is represented not only by the *wergas* he is ordered to lift up; those who oblige him to do so are also *feondas* (30–3). It is not simply individual men nor even mankind that is involved in the crucifixion, however, but the whole of creation represented in the archetypal world-tree—now the cosmic Ravennate symbol stretching to the four quarters of the universe. With an almost eastern abstract simplicity the poet contrives to embrace within the one concept so much extranea which a later age might have allowed to detract from the philosophic content of the event. There are no explicit bystanders, soldiers or Jews; the *feondas* are forgotten—no weeping women; all are subsumed within the one representative, the sympathetic and yet unwilling instrument of death.   The creator is destroyed by his creation.   This is a poetically dense concept, involving here also the tragic heroic dilemma of the follower not only refused permission to avenge the death of his lord, but himself the *bana* (66) obliged to play a major part in it.   The poet has avoided the obvious temptation to utilise the heroic implications of the disciples' wavering loyalties and ultimate desertion of their Lord.   Instead the conflict between heroic ideal and Christian obedience is utilised powerfully to augment the personal perplexity of the cross, reinforced by a repetition of the words *ne dorste ic* four times within a short space (35–47).   It is in the circumvention of this dilemma that the author has recourse to the rhetorical device of ' purgatio ', accounting for otherwise culpable acts through ' necessitudo '.[1]

The actual crucifixion is presented in simple, starkly dramatic terms.   The poet seems less concerned with specific details of the biblical narrative[2] than to provide an economic representation of what were considered the theological essentials of the event.   The imaginative construction that the poet erects so as to tread so careful a path between doctrinal niceties results in a singularly memorable visual effect.   Natural pathos is absent.   No flogged, suffering, stumbling Christ drags the cross to Calvary; it stands already, a stark symbol set up on a

[1] Described by e.g. Alcuin (*PL*, ci. 927); cf. M. Schlauch, *op. cit.* pp. 32–3.   Later ME dialogues between Mary and the cross similarly employ this form.

[2] The lack of specifically detailed adherence to the biblical narrative disturbed Dietrich, and even recent scholars feel it necessary to identify the allusions.   Dickins–Ross, for instance, point out that the *fuse* (57) are ' presumably Joseph and Nicodemus ';   Mossé recognises the two Marys in *mæte weorode* (69);   Magoun–Walker add a note to line 30, ' presumably Simon of Cyrene '.   But such comments detract from the bare dramatic effect the poet has so carefully contrived from the opening of the poem.   The *Dream* is not a riddle, and clue-hunting is unnecessary.

hill. We have been led to infer that the cross has already been used to execute felons (31, 87–8) so that a gallows image is already established, contrasting implicitly with the innocence of Christ, which need not therefore be mentioned to detract from the heroic status of the warrior-Lord. Christ indeed is not led there by a jeering mob; he is stripped by no mocking soldiers. Instead, as in Ravennate iconography or as seen by Ambrose or Cynewulf, he is a young and confident champion striding from afar,[1] *efstan elne mycle þæt he me wolde on gestigan* (34). Vigorous and single-minded, he strips himself for battle and a kingly victory. The action is entirely his, an eager sacrifice; there is no question at this point of his being nailed to the cross. Instead he climbs to embrace it (40–2).[2] It is pre-eminently an act of dominant free will by a prince confident of victory. With the agony transferred to the cross, Christ can sensibly be seen to rule from the gallows.[3]

It is at this point rather than several hours later that the earth's surface shakes (36–7), thus tightening the structure of the narrative, and allowing for a contrast between trembling earth and steadfast cross, firm at the command of Christ. It is at the climax of the event that darkness covers the earth, shadows serving at once to heighten and subdue the radiance of the Lord's body (52–5), thus utilising a biblical incidental to involve the whole of nature in the recognition of Christ on the cross. If there are no weeping women, as might have been used by later writers to emphasise the pathos of the scene, the whole of creation weeps, laments the fall of the king, the poet returning now to stark, simple half-line syntactic units: *Crist wæs on rode* (55–6). In human terms, misery is absent; the lament of all creation is on far larger a scale.

---

[1] *PL*, xv, 1923–4; *Christ* 744–6, or (presumably referring to the *Song of Solomon*, ii. 8), 715 ff.

[2] Cf. notes to *gestigan* (34, 40), *ymbclyppan* (42).

[3] As in the line of Fortunatus' hymn ' Vexilla regis ', *regnavit a ligno Deus*, apparently taken from the textus receptus of *Psalm XCV*, 10, *dominus regnavit a ligno*.

Nails are driven into the cross, which is mocked together with Christ, but the source of this pain is not specified. Suffering is implied, but nowhere described so as to detract in pathos from the broad doctrinal significance of the action. In later writings this was to become too great a temptation as a visual concept of the suffering Christ arose. The author of *Christ III*, for instance, in dwelling on the brutality of the crucifixion, achieves quite a different effect: the cruel hands of sinful men seize their Saviour, inflicting gaping wounds; the white hands and feet are pierced with nails; he is spat upon and struck and thorns are twisted into his head.[1] There is none of that here. The emotional intensity of Christ's agony is conveyed by a device that evades the awkward issue of his susceptibility to pain. Christ's humanity is transferred to the person of the cross, which insists that the nails were driven into *himself*, on *him* the malicious wounds are to be seen; it is *he* who is stricken with arrows, covered with blood (46-8, 62), the culmination of all the cruel deeds he had endured (50-1). The parallel is maintained; the cross takes on aspects of Christ's dual will and operation. Its whole inclination is to bow before its creator, to shrink from the task set before it, but against the will of God it dare not bend or break; like Christ himself[2] it might so easily have slain all its enemies, but it stands firm at the Lord's command (35-43). This is all very cleverly done, but without straying from orthodox theology. If at the climax we are told of Christ that *his gast onsended* (49), it is certainly not to die in the conventional sense. The paradoxical issue of the death of God is resolved in the Augustinian manner[3] preserved by Bede,[4] which sees this death in terms simply of sleep, the Resurrection therefore implicit in a consequent reawakening. This contrives to suggest both its voluntary and temporary character while avoiding Severan emphasis on the

---

[1] *Christ* 1103 ff.   [2] Cf. Ælfric, *Homs*, i, p. 226.

[3] *PL*, xxxv. 1952; and cf. M. B. Ogle, ' The sleep of death ', *Mems. American Academy at Rome*, x (1932), 81-117.

[4] E.g. *PL*, xcii. 915; and later cf. Ælfric, *Homs*, ii, p. 260.

corruption of his corporeal person which would have been the
logical consequence of his agony. If it is a corpse (*hræw*, 53,
72) we see that grows cold, then it simply sleeps *limwerig*,
resting for a while, exhausted after the great struggle (63–5).[1]

The crucifixion story is completed and the Invention
tradition, found *in extenso* in *Elene*, briefly introduced within a
few allusive lines.[2] The treatment is still swift and compact,
conflating the narrative in simple but concretely dramatic
terms. Men eager to serve their lord, but doomed in his
departure,[3] come to take down their exhausted God and carve
for him a tomb in the sight of his slayer. Even as the corpse
grows cold the cross is cut down and hidden in a deep pit.
But rediscovery by the Lord's *pegnas* leads to its decoration with
the gold and silver of the reliquaries, an echo of the opening
vision of the poem. All this is achieved in rapid, impersonal
terms which allow for no impediment to the dramatic doctrinal
outline. Those who come to take the body down from the
cross are not named. The body is not taken to a distant cave,
but an Anglo-Saxon coffin is carved out at the foot of the
cross. The rediscovery of the cross, we are led to infer, is
made, not centuries later by fresh people,[4] but promptly by
Christ's own disciples. As before, the treatment is carefully
restrained. The poet introduces no unnecessary detail which
might diffuse his material and disperse its impact. Nothing is
allowed to detract from the essential theological relevancies.
There is in the poem an almost Byzantine insistence on the

---

[1] *Limwerig* (RC *limwœrignæ*) occurs only here, although compounds
containing *werig*, (e.g. *adl- deap- fyl- hra-werig*), commonly connote
death.

[2] It is not clear how much, if anything, has been lost after line 76a,
but probably no more than a half-line.

[3] Comparison might be made with the previous use of *fus* (21); see
p. 65 and note to line 21.

[4] In the historical Constantinian account some three centuries inter-
vene between the burial of the cross and its rediscovery. Even then,
however, as in *Elene*, it is convenient to have the anachronistic person of
a still-living Judas, brother of Stephen, to link the two periods.

importance of ideas, to which the shallower matter of narrative
and descriptive detail are totally subordinate.

As throughout, these passages betray a fine artistic accommodation of style to sense. The sequences of expanded verse
which end with the ' death ' of Christ (*his gast onsended*, 49),
are replaced by the rapid movement of normal lines in the
asides of the cross commenting on his fate, the response of nature
and the shadow and weeping which build up to the climax:
Crist wæs on rode (56). The sequence dealing with the deposition, however, reverts to broadly moving hypermetric lines,
suitably underlining at once the grave dignity of the events and
the bewildering theological proposition which underlies it.
Hitherto the extent of Christ's physical condition had been
carefully masked in favour of his victorious rule from the
cross. Now close contact with physical reality is inevitable,
and his essentially corporeal humanity—his nature not only
as God but also as frail man—is expressed through a literary
use of the theological ' communicatio idiomatum '.[1] This
device is found here some ten times within thirty lines, providing all the shock and astonishment of violent paradox in a
deliberate distancing of verb and subject: *Genamon hie þær
ælmihtigne God,* ... *gestodon him æt his lices heafdum* ...
heofenes Dryhten, ... *gesetton hie ðæron sigora Wealdend* (60–7).
In this the Old English habit of variation, using fresh words to
emphasise different attributes of the subject, is employed ironically. The majesty and omnipotence of God are unexpectedly
diminished by the use of such startling verbs, underlining the
orthodox doctrine central to the poem—that of a God who
was fully man. The violence of this paradox is not lessened
here by the use of syndectic combinations which elsewhere
make smooth transitions from one thought to another. The
force of the idea remains. With the end of this doctrinally
dense deposition sequence the block of hypermetric verse comes
to an end, and, beginning with line 70, the Invention narrative

[1] Cf. R. Woolf, *op. cit.* 151–2.

returns to the rapid movement of short lines which continue to the end of the poem.

Once the crucifixion has been acted out and the function of the cross as symbol of the act of redemption made plain, the vision reverts to its opening character (recapitulating over lines 12 and 82). Now it can explain to the dreamer in its evangelical capacity the motivating force behind the cult of the cross—how now in glory it is revered and feared by men upon earth for the healing power it possesses. Its doctrinal significance is underlined by rhetorical balance: although once the instrument of squalid death, it is now become the means of eternal life (87–9). The word used of those to whom salvation is brought is *reordberend*, inevitably recalling the use of the word at the beginning of the poem. The significance of the opening scene in anticipating such an end is now clear. It had contained significant features of the conventional doomsday vision as it is represented in, for example, the beginning of *Christ III*,[1] when the day of the Lord should come in darkness *æt midre niht*, suddenly surprising careless men wrapped in sleep and bringing misery to those unprepared, while the faithful are gathered in from the four corners of the earth. Here, however, there is yet time. Salvation is to be brought to those that sleep, careless of their suffering Lord, ignorant of the word of his messengers. It is to these that the dreamer is given his evangelical mission. Like the cross itself in the Gospel of Peter, he is to preach to them that sleep.[2] As in the artistic scheme of the Ruthwell Cross, the Crucifixion is linked naturally with a view of Judgement Day. A fast compound sequence running over the antithetical balance—*Ne*

[1] Lines 867–89.

[2] See p. 66; and compare the words of a hymn of Ephraem Syrus: ' To thee be glory, watcher [*or* angel] that didst come down after them that slept, and utter the word from the Tree and waken them ' (*Corpus Scriptorum Christianorum Orientalium*, ccxl. 104). In the familiar Easter readings taken from 1 *Corinthians* xv. 20 (cf. *Durham Ritual*, SS, cxl, p. 27), Christ, the second Adam, is described as *primitiae dormientium*.

mæg þær ænig unforht wesan. . . . Ne þearf ðær ænig unforht wesan (110–17)—contrasts the terror then of the unjust with the calm of the righteous, reliant on the simple power of the cross to save. This concludes the words of the cross, which have amounted to some three-fifths of the entire poem.

The view then reverts to that of the original visionary. In the past, scholars have found different parts of these concluding lines unsatisfactory for various reasons, supposing what they considered to be stylistic or thematic breaks to indicate a later redactor's hand.[1] But the conclusion can be seen to have arisen naturally from what has gone before, a congruent part of a coherent and unified whole.[2] To have finished simply with the words of the cross would have been structurally and emotionally inadequate. The whole of Anglo-Saxon religious writing leads one to expect a homiletic coda of some kind at this point, whether following the broad Augustinian model of 'exhortatio' following 'narratio', a sermon to strengthen the reader's response to the story,[3] or the more detailed pattern of contemporary rhetorical analysis: 'exordium, narratio, partitio, confirmatio, reprehensio et conclusio'.[4] The final words here are therefore no more out of place than Cynewulf's signatures, or the homiletic endings to the *Wanderer* or *Seafarer*, which also at one time were considered to have been later additions.

[1] Cf. S. A. Brooke, *The History of Early English Literature* (London, 1892) ii, p. 283. R. Woolf, *op. cit.* 153, n. 34, and recently S. B. Greenfield (*A Critical History of Old English Literature* (London, 1966), p. 136), consider a stylistic break discernible subsequent to the actual crucifixion. Cook (pp. xlii, liv–v) reserved his objections for the last nine lines. Dickins–Ross consider the ending stylistically inferior; Bütow disagrees.

[2] The form recognised by A. Brandl (' Zum ags. Gedichte *Traumgesicht vom Kreuz Christi* ', *Sitzungsberichte*, 1905, 718), as an eighth-century poetical sermon with a practical liturgical end, has recently been re-examined by J. A. Burrow (*op. cit.* 130–3), and J. Fleming, (' *The Dream of the Rood* and Anglo-Saxon monasticism ', *Traditio*, xxii (1966), 54 ff.). [3] Cf. *PL*, xl. 317f.

[4] Cf. sources associated with Alcuin, *PL*, ci. 947–8.

If the style differs at this point, then it is appropriate. The memorable static imagery of the opening vision is replaced by a swifter, simpler style. The conclusion to the poem may be more diffuse than its highly wrought opening, but it is no less organised structurally. The poet's theme is developed consistently and meaningfully. It is perhaps best seen as a formal progression in our view of the cross: from that of the dreamer persona for whom the cross represents a tropological symbol of practical faith—the exhortation to a religious life, through a central allegorical resolution in which the cross is shown as institutionalised doctrine on the person and death of Christ, to its final anagogical development here in an apocalyptic consummation.[1]

Catalysed by his vision, the poet's resolution forms the directly devotional basis of the poem's conclusion. The visionary no longer lies passive and silent. Now an independent personal identity, he declares his veneration for the cross powerfully, but within conventional machinery. As commonly with the religious persona,[2] he is now old and friendless, his soul yearning to follow those who have already sought and won their heavenly home. The confession of world-weariness (*langung-hwila*, 126) is linked with a hope of heaven, the Christian *hyht*, in many cross poems.[3] But although made possible by the sacrificial death of Christ, it is to the deified cross, living symbol of the deed,[4] that he looks to

---

[1] Cogently argued by F. Patten, ' Structure and meaning in *The Dream of the Rood* ', *English Studies*, xlix (1968), 394–401; and cf. L. H. Leiter, ' *The Dream of the Rood*: patterns of transformation ', *Old English Poetry*, ed. R. P. Creed (Providence, 1967), pp. 93–127.

[2] Cf. *Resignation* 91, 102; *Seafarer* 19 ff.; *Wanderer* 37 f., 45, 78 f.; *Wife's Lament* 10; etc.

[3] J. Stevenson, *The Latin Hymns of the Anglo-Saxon Church* (SS, xxiii), p. 156; and cf. line 148.

[4] The cross stands separate from Christ, a symbol of the deed, as on the later cross at Burton-in-Kendal (W. G. Collingwood, *op. cit.* fig. 195), where Mary and John stand by an empty cross while Christ triumphant tramples the serpent below.

fetch him from this transient life to the joys of heaven.[1] The tension contained within the heroic conception of the cross is pursued. ' Securus et gaudens ',[2] the dreamer now ironically finds his patron, *mundbyrd*, in the slayer, *bana*, of his lord (130–1).

However, the cross is more than simply a symbol of individual salvation. As anticipated from the beginning in the bleeding tree image, it will reappear set up in the sky as a sign of sovereignty to herald Christ's second coming and to summon all men into the presence of their creator.[3] We are thus provided with the rationale of an otherwise arbitrary vision. Only a brief and oblique allusion to the harrowing of hell is necessary to complete the doctrinal scheme, for unlike later Crucifixion poems, Christ's victory is already implicit in the battle on the cross. As common to contemporary Ascension poems,[4] there is allowed no delay between the harrowing of hell and the entry into heaven. The two are brought into dramatic juxtaposition to maintain the impetus of the poem. The theological structure is therefore brought to a rapid and triumphal conclusion as Christ together with the visionary and the whole company of saints ascend to their heavenly *eðel* in a final great eschatalogical vision.

[1] The cross traditionally conveys the soul to heaven (cf. W. Bousset, ' Platons Weltseele und das Kreuz Christi '. *Zeitschrift für die neutestamentliche Wissenschaft und die Kunde des Urchristentums*, xiv (1913), 283).   [2] Cf. note to line 127.

[3] See pp. 64–5; and cf. *Christ* 1061–8, *Judgment Day I*, 105.

[4] Cf. *Christ* 558–81; Bede, *PL*, xciv. 624–6; Fortunatus, *PL*, lxxxviii. 132–3.

SELECT BIBLIOGRAPHY

MANUSCRIPT

AVONTO, L. *L'Ospedale di S. Brigida degli Scoti e il 'Vercelli Book'*, Vercelli, 1973.

BORGOGNONE, F. *Problema del Vercelli Book*, Alessandria, 1951.

COOK, A.S. *Cardinal Guala and the Vercelli Book*, Sacramento, 1888.

FELL, C.E. 'Richard Cleasby's notes on the Vercelli Codex', *Leeds Studies in English*, NS, xii (1981), 13–42; xv (1984), 1–19.

FÖRSTER, M. *Il Codice Vercellese con Omelie e Poesie in Lingua Anglosassone*, Rome, 1913.

——'Der Vercelli-Codex CXVII nebst Abdruck einiger altenglischer Homilien der Handschrift', *Festschrift für Lorenz Morsbach*, Halle, 1913, pp. 20–179.

HALSALL, M. 'Vercelli and the Vercelli Book', *PMLA*, lxxxiv (1969), 1545–50.

——'Benjamin Thorpe and the Vercelli Book', *English Language Notes*, vi (1969), 164–69.

——'More about C. Maier's transcript of the Vercelli Book', *English Language Notes*, viii (1970), 3–6.

HERBEN, S.J. 'The Vercelli Book: a new hypothesis', *Speculum*, x (1935), 91–94.

KELLER, W. *Angelsächsische Palaeographie*, Berlin, 1906.

KER, N.R. 'C. Maier's transcript of the Vercelli Book', *Medium Ævum*, xix (1950), 17–25.

——*Catalogue of Manuscripts containing Anglo-Saxon*, Oxford, 1957.

MAIER, C. *Beschreibung des Codex Capitulare Vercellensis, n. CXVII* (1834). Lincoln's Inn MS. Misc. 312.

MARTIN, M. 'A note on marginalia in the Vercelli Book', *N&Q*, ccxxiii (1978), 485–86.

Ó CARRAGÁIN, É. 'How did the Vercelli collector interpret *The Dream of the Rood*?', *Studies in English Language and Early Literature in Honour of Paul Christopherson*, ed. P.M. Tilling, Coleraine, 1981, pp. 63–104.

RICCI, A. 'Il codice Anglossassone di Vercelli nel primo centenario della sua scoperta', *Rivista delle Biblioteche e degli Archivi*, xxxiii (1923), 13–19.

SCRAGG, D.G. 'Accent marks in the Old English Vercelli Book', *NM*, lxxii (1971), 699–710.

——'The compilation of the Vercelli Book', *Anglo-Saxon England*, ii (1973), 189–207.

SISAM, C. *The Vercelli Book*. Early English Manuscripts in Facsimile, xix, Copenhagen, 1976.

SISAM, K. 'Marginalia in the Vercelli Book', *Studies*, pp. 109–18.

SZARMACH, P.E. 'The Scribe of the Vercelli Book', *Studia Neophilologica*, li (1979), 179–88.

TEMPLE, E. *Anglo-Saxon Manuscripts 900–1066*, London, 1976.

WÜLCKER, R.P. *Codex Vercellensis. Die angelsæchsische Handschrift zu Vercelli in getreuer Nachbildung*, Leipzig, 1894.

EDITIONS

ALEXANDER, M.J. *The Earliest English Poems: A Bilingual Edition*, Berkeley, 1970. (VB 1–77)

BOLTON, W.F. *An Old English Anthology*, London, 1963. (VB)

BOUTERWEK, K.W. *Cædmon's des angelsachsen biblische Dichtungen*, Gütersloh, 1854. (VB)

BÜTOW, H. *Das altenglische 'Traumgesicht vom Kreuz'*, Heidelberg, 1935. (VB, RC)

CAMPBELL, J.J. and ROSIER, J.L. *Poems in Old English*, New York, 1962. (VB)

CASIERI, S. *Poemi, Frammenti ed Iscrizioni Anglosassoni*, Milan, 1956. (RC)

COOK, A.S. *The Dream of the Rood*, Oxford, 1905. (VB, RC)

COPPOLA, A. et al. *Il Sogno della Croce*, Messina, 1978. (VB)

CRAIGIE, W.A. *Specimens of Anglo-Saxon Poetry, II*, Edinburgh, 1926. (VB)

DICKINS, B., and ROSS, A.S.C. *The Dream of the Rood*, Fourth edition, London, 1954. (VB, RC)

DIETRICH, F.E.C. *Disputatio de Cruce Ruthwellensi*, Marburg, 1865. (RC with corresponding VB lines)

DOBBIE, E.V.K. *The Anglo-Saxon Minor Poems*, New York, 1942. (RC)

FLOM, G.T. *Introductory Old English Grammar and Reader*, Boston, 1930. (RC)

FOWLER, R. *Old English Prose and Verse*, London, 1966. (VB)

GREIN, C.W. *Bibliothek der angelsächsischen Poesie, II*, Goettingen, 1858. (VB). Second edition, WÜLCKER, R.P. Leipzig, 1894. (VB, RC)

HAMMERICH, P.F.A. *De episk-Kristelige Oldkvad hos de Gotiske Folk*, Copenhagen, 1873. (VB 1–69)

KAISER, R. *Alt- und mittelenglische Anthologie*, Third edition published as *Medieval English*, Berlin, 1958. (VB, RC)

KEMBLE, J.M. *The Poetry of the Codex Vercellensis*, II, London, 1856.

KLUGE, F. *Angelsächsisches Lesebuch*, Fourth edition, Halle, 1915. (VB, RC)

KRAPP, G.P. *The Vercelli Book*, New York, 1932.

LEHNERT, M. *Poetry and Prose of the Anglo-Saxons*, Second edition, Halle, 1960.

MACLEAN, G.E. *An Old and Middle English Reader*, London, 1893. (RC with corresponding VB lines)

MAGOUN, F.P. *The Vercelli Book Poems, done in a normalised orthography*, Harvard, 1960. (VB, RC)

MICHELSEN, A. *Aelteste christliche Epik der Angelsachsen, Deutschen und Nordlander*, Gütersloh, 1874. (VB 1–69)

MOSSÉ, F. *Manuel de l'Anglais du Moyen Âge des origines au XIVe siècle*, Second edition, Paris, 1950. (VB 1–89, RC)

PACIUS, A. *Das heilige Kreuz; angelsächsisches Lied, stabreimend übersetzt und erklärt*, Gera, 1873. (VB)

PEZZINI, D. *Il Sogno della Croce e Liriche del Duecento Inglese sulla Passione*, Parma, 1992.

POPE, J.C. *Seven Old English Poems*, Second edition, New York, 1966. (VB)

QUIRK, R. et al. *Old English Literature: A Practical Introduction*, London, 1975. (VB 1–74)

RICCI, A. *Cynewulf: Il Sogno della Croce*, Florence, 1926. (VB)

STEPHENS, G. *The Old-Northern Runic Monuments of Scandinavia and England*, Four volumes, London, 1866–1901.

——*Handbook of the Old-Northern Runic Monuments. ...* London, 1884.

SWEET, H. *An Anglo-Saxon Reader in Prose and Verse*, Oxford, 1876 (VB 1–89), Ninth edition, ONIONS, C.T. 1922 (VB 1–94, 131–48), Fifteenth edition, WHITELOCK, D. 1967. (VB, RC)

——*The Oldest English Texts*, EETS, lxxxiii, London, 1885. (RC)

——*A Second Anglo-Saxon Reader: Archaic and Dialectal*, Oxford, 1887. (RC)

THORPE, B. *C.P. Cooper's Report on Rymer's Foedera*, Appendix B. Printed, 1836; published, London, 1869. (VB)

VIETOR, W. *Die northumbrischen Runensteine*, Marburg, 1895. (RC with corresponding VB lines)

WYATT, A.J. *An Anglo-Saxon Reader*, Cambridge, 1919. (VB 28–89, RC)

ZUPITZA, J. and SCHIPPER, J. *Alt- und mittelenglisches Übungsbuch*, Seventh edition. Leipzig, 1928. (RC with corresponding VB lines)

TRANSLATIONS

BERGNER, H. *Die englische Literatur in Text und Darstellung*, I, *Mittelalter*, Stuttgart, 1986.

BONE, G. *Anglo-Saxon Poetry*, Oxford, 1943.

BRADLEY, S.A.J. *Anglo-Saxon Poetry*, London, 1982.

BROOKS, H.F. *The Dream of the Rood*, Dublin, 1942.

COOK, A.S., and TINKER, C.B. *Select Translations from Old English Poetry*, Third edition, Harvard, 1935.

CRÉPIN, A. *Poèmes héroïques vieil-anglais*, Paris, 1981.

CROSSLEY-HOLLAND, K., and MITCHELL, B. *The Battle of Maldon and other Old English Poems*, London, 1965.

GARNETT, J.M. *Elene* (and other) *Anglo-Saxon Poems*, Second edition, Boston, 1900.

GORDON, R.K. *Anglo-Saxon Poetry*, Second edition, London, 1954.

GREIN, C.W. *Dichtungen der angelsachsen stabreimend übersetzt*, II, Göttingen, 1859.

HAMER, R. *A Choice of Anglo-Saxon Verse*, London, 1970.

HEWISON, J.K. *The Dream of the Rood: a metrical translation*, Dumfries, 1911.

KANAYAMA, A. '*The Dream of the Rood*: a Japanese translation', *Osaka Gaidai English and American Studies*, xi (1979), 147–54.

KENNEDY, C.W. *The Poems of Cynewulf*, London, 1910.

——*Early English Christian Poetry, translated into Alliterative Verse*, London, 1952.

MAGOUN, F.P., and WALKER, J.A. *An Old English Anthology*, Dubuque, Iowa, 1950. (1–89)

NIST, J. 'Dream of the Cross', *Old English Newsletter*, x 2 (1977), 16–18. (1–89)

OLIVERO, F. *Traduzioni dalla poesia Anglo-sassone; con introduzione e note*, Bari, 1915.

RAFFEL, B. *Poems from the Old English*, Nebraska, 1961.

RISSANEN, P. 'Uni ristinpuusta', *Ikävöivä rakkaus*, Helsinki, 1987.

WAINEWRIGHT, R. *The Dream of the Holy Rood*, Ditchling, 1932.

WILLIAMS, M. *Word-Hoard*, London, 1946.

Complete or partial translations are also included in various of the editions and studies of the poem.

STUDIES: LITERARY, TEXTUAL AND EPIGRAPHIC

ALLEN, M.J.B. and CALDER, D.G. *Sources and Analogues of Old English Poetry: The Major Latin Texts in Translation*, Totowa, 1976.

ANDERSON, E.R. 'Liturgical influence in *The Dream of the Rood*', *Neophilologus*, lxxiii (1989), 293–304.

BAIRD, J.L. '*Natura plangens*, the Ruthwell Cross and *The Dream of the Rood*', *Studies in Iconography*, x (1984–86), 37–51.

BAMMESBERGER, A. 'Two archaic forms in the Ruthwell Cross inscription', *English Studies*, lxxv (1994), 97–103.

BAUER, A. *Ueber die Sprache und Mundart der altenglischen Dichtungen Andreas, Gûðlác, Phönix, hl. Kreuz und Höllenfahrt Cristi*, Marburg, 1890.

BENNETT, J.A.W. *Poetry of the Passion: Studies in Twelve Centuries of English Verse*, Oxford, 1982, pp. 1–31.

BERKHOUT, C.T. 'The problem of OE *holmwudu*', *Mediaeval Studies*, xxxvi (1974), 429–33.

BOENIG, R. 'The *engel dryhtnes* and mimesis in *The Dream of the Rood*', *NM*, lxxxvi (1985), 442–46.

BOLTON, W.F. 'Connectives in *The Seafarer* and *The Dream of the Rood*', *MP*, lvii (1959–60), 260–62.

——'Tatwine's *De Cruce Christi* and *The Dream of the Rood*', *Archiv*, cc (1964), 344–46.

——'*The Dream of the Rood* 9b: "Engel" = Nuntius?', *N&Q*, ccxiii (1968), 165–66.

——'The Book of Job in *The Dream of the Rood*, *Mediaevalia*, vi (1980), 87–103.

BRANDL, A. 'Zum ags. Gedichte *Traumgesicht vom Kreuz Christi*', *Sitzungsberichte der königlich preussischen Akademie der Wissenschaften*, 1905, 716–23. Reprinted in *Forschungen und Charakteristiken, von Alois Brandl zum 80 Geburtstag*, Berlin, 1936, pp. 28–35.

BRASWELL, B.K. '*The Dream of the Rood* and Aldhelm on sacred prosopopoeia', *Mediaeval Studies*, xl (1978), 461–67.

BREEZE, A. 'The Virgin Mary and *The Dream of the Rood*', *Florilegium*, xii (1993), 55–62.

——'*Deorc* "bloody" in *The Dream of the Rood*', *Éigse*, xxviii (1994–95), 165–68.

BRITTON, G.C. '*Bealuwara weorc* in *The Dream of the Rood*', *NM*, lxviii (1967), 273–76.

BRZEZINSKI, M. 'The Harrowing of Hell, the Last Judgment, and *The Dream of the Rood*', *NM*, lxxxix (1988), 252–65.

BUGGE, E.S. *Studien über die Entstehung der nordischen Götterund Heldensagen*, transl. O. Brenner, Munich, 1889.

BUNDI, A. 'Per la ricostruzione dei passi frammentari dell'iscrizione runica della Croce di Ruthwell', *Annali Istituto Universitario Orientale Napoli: Filologia Germanica*, xxii (1979), 21–58.

BURLIN, R.B. '*The Dream of the Rood* and the Vita Contemplativa', *SP*, lxv (1968), 23–43.

BURROW, J.A. 'An approach to *The Dream of the Rood*', *Neophilologus*, xliii (1959), 123–33. Reprinted in *Old English Literature*, ed. M. Stevens and J. Mandel, Lincoln, Nebraska, 1968, pp. 253–67.

CANUTESON, J. 'The Crucifixion and the Second Coming in *The Dream of the Rood*', *MP*, lxvi (1969), 293–97.

CAVILL, P. '"*Engel dryhtnes*" in *The Dream of the Rood* 9b again', *NM*, xciii (1992), 287–92.

CHAPPELL, V.A. '*Reordberendra gesyhthe* and Christian mystery: narrative frames in *The Dream of the Rood*', *Comitatus*, xviii (1987), 1–20.

CHASE, C.L. '*Christ III, The Dream of the Rood*, and early Christian passion piety', *Viator*, xi (1980), 11–33.

CHERNISS, M.D. 'The cross as Christ's weapon: the influence of heroic literary tradition on *The Dream of the Rood*', *Anglo-Saxon England*, ii (1973), 241–52.

CLELAND, J.H. 'The art of *The Dream of the Rood*', *Faith & Reason*, v 2 (1979), 3–25.

COOK, A.S. 'Cædmon and the Ruthwell Cross', *MLN*, v (1890), 77–78.

——'Notes on the Ruthwell Cross', *PMLA*, xvii (1902), 367–90.

——'Miscellaneous notes', *MLN*, xxii (1907), 207–09.

——'The date of the Old English inscription on the Brussels Cross', *MLR*, x (1915), 157–61.

D'ARDENNE, S.T.R.O. 'The Old English inscription on the Brussels Cross', *English Studies*, xxi (1939), 145–64, 271–72.

DAS, S.K. *Cynewulf and the Cynewulf Canon*, Calcutta, 1942.

DEERING, W. *The Anglo-Saxon Poets on the Judgment Day*, Halle, 1890.

DIAMOND, R.E. 'Heroic diction in *The Dream of the Rood*', *Studies in honor of John Wilcox*, ed. A.D. Wallace and W.O. Ross, Detroit, 1958, pp. 3–7.

DICKINS, B. 'A system of transliteration for Old English runic inscriptions', *Leeds Studies in English*, i (1932), 15–19. Reprinted separately, Norwich, 1950.

DUBS, K.E. '*Hæleð*: heroism in *The Dream of the Rood*', *Neophilologus*, lix (1975), 614–15.

EBERT, A. 'Über das angelsächsische Gedicht *Der Traum vom heiligen Kreuze*', *Berichte über die Verhandlungen der königlich sächsischen Gesellschaft der Wissenschaften zu Leipzig*, Phil.-Hist. Classe, xxxvi (1884), 81–93.

EDWARDS, R.R. 'Narrative technique and distance in *The Dream of the Rood*', *Papers on Language and Literature*, vi (1970), 291–301.

ELLIOTT, R.W.V. *Runes: an Introduction*, Second edition, Manchester, 1963.

FANGER, C. 'A suggestion for a solution to Exeter Book Riddle 55', *Scintilla*, ii–iii (1985–86), 19–28.

FARACI, D. 'Aspetti eroici nel Dream of the Rood', *Atti dell'Accademia Peloritana dei Pericolanti: Classe di Lettere, Filosofia e Belle Arti*, lviii (1982), 1–41.

FARINA, D.F. '*Wædum geweorðod* in *The Dream of the Rood*', *N&Q*, ccxii (1967), 4–6.

FINNEGAN, R.E. 'The *lifes weg rihtne* and the *Dream of the Rood*', *Revue de l'Université d'Ottawa*, li (1981), 236–46.

——'The Gospel of Nicodemus and *The Dream of the Rood* 148b–156', *NM*, lxxxiv (1983), 338–43.

FLEMING, J.V. '*The Dream of the Rood* and Anglo-Saxon monasticism', *Traditio*, xxii (1966), 43–72.

FLOREY, K. 'Community and self in *The Dream of the Rood*', *Connecticut Review*, i (1987), 23–29.

FORBES, M.D., and DICKINS, B. 'The inscriptions of the Ruthwell and Bewcastle Crosses and the Bridekirk font', *BM*, xxv (1914), 24–29.

——'The Ruthwell and Bewcastle Crosses', *MLR*, x (1915), 28–36.

FOUNTAIN, J.S. 'Ashes to ashes: Kristeva's *Jouissance*, Altizer's *Apocalypse*, Byatt's *Possession* and *The Dream of the Rood*', *Literature and Theology*, viii (1994), 193–208.

GRANT, R.J.S. '*The Dream of the Rood*, line 63b: a part-time idiom?', *NM*, xcii (1991), 289–95.

GRASSO, A.R. 'Theology and structure in *The Dream of the Rood*', *Religion and Literature*, xxiii (1991), 23–38.

GRAYBILL, R.V. '*The Dream of the Rood*: apotheosis of Anglo-Saxon paradox', *Proceedings of the Illinois Medieval Association*, ed. R.B. Bosse et al. Macomb, Illinois, 1984, pp. 1–12.

GRAU, G. *Quellen und Verwandtschaften der älteren germanischen Darstellungen des jüngsten Gerichtes*, Halle, 1908.

GREIN, C.W. 'Zur Textkritik der angelsächsischen Dichter', *Germania*, x (1895), 416–29.

HALL, J.R. ' "Angels ... and all the Holy Ones": *The Dream of the Rood* 153b–54a', *American N&Q*, xxiv (1986), 65–68.

HELDER, W. 'The *engel dryhtnes* in *The Dream of the Rood*', *MP*, lxxiii (1975), 148–50.

HERMANN, J.P. '*The Dream of the Rood*, 19A: *earmra ærgewin*', *English Language Notes*, xv (1978), 241–44.

HIEATT, C.B. 'A new theory of triple rhythm in the hypermetric lines of Old English verse', *MP*, lxvii (1969), 1–8.

——'Dream frame and verbal echo in *The Dream of the Rood*', *NM*, lxxii (1971), 251–63.

HILL, T.D. 'The cross as symbolic body: an Anglo-Latin liturgical analogue to *The Dream of the Rood*', *Neophilologus*, lxxvii (1993), 297–301.

HOLDSWORTH, C. 'Frames: time level and variation in *The Dream of the Rood*', *Neophilologus*, lxvi (1982), 622–28.

HOLLOWAY, J.B. '*The Dream of the Rood* and liturgical drama', *Comparative Drama*, xviii (1984), 19–37.

——'Crosses and boxes': Latin and vernacular', *Equally in God's Image: Women in the Middle Ages*, ed. J. Holloway et al., New York, 1990, pp. 58–87.

HOLTBUER, F. 'Der syntaktische Gebrauch des Genitives in *Andreas*, *Gûðlac, Phönix, dem heiligen Kreuz* und *Höllenfahrt*', *Anglia*, viii (1885), 1–40.

HOLTHAUSEN, F. 'Zur Textkritik altenglischer Dichtungen 7', *ES*, xxxvii (1907), 201.

HOPKINS, R.H. 'A Note on *Solomon and Saturn II*, 449 (Menner Edition)', *N&Q*, cciv (1959), 226–27.

HORGAN, A.D. '*The Dream of the Rood* and Christian tradition', *NM*, lxxix (1978), 11–20.

——'*The Dream of the Rood* and a homily for Palm Sunday', *N&Q*, xxix (1982), 388–91.

HOWLETT, D.R. 'Three forms in the Ruthwell text of *The Dream of the Rood*', *English Studies*, lv (1974), 1–5.

——'A reconstruction of the Ruthwell crucifixion poem', *Studia Neophilologica*, xlviii (1976), 54–58.

——'The structure of *The Dream of the Rood*', *Studia Neophilologica*, xlviii (1976), 301–06.

——'Two notes on *The Dream of the Rood*', *Studia Neophilologica*, l (1978), 167–73.

HUPPÉ, B.F. *The Web of Words: Structural Analyses of the Old English Poems 'Vainglory', 'The Wonder of Creation', 'The Dream of the Rood' and 'Judith'*, New York, 1970.

IRVINE, M. 'Anglo-Saxon literary theory exemplified in Old English Poems: interpreting the cross in *The Dream of the Rood* and *Elene*', *Style*, xx (1986), 157–81.

IRVING, E.B. 'Crucifixion witnessed, or dramatic interaction in *The Dream of the Rood*', *Modes of Interpretation in Old English Literature*, ed. P.R. Brown et al., Toronto, 1986, pp. 101–13.

ISAACS, N.D. 'Progressive identifications: the structural principles of *The Dream of the Rood*', *Structural Principles in Old English Poetry*, Knoxville, 1968, pp. 3–18.

JENNINGS, M. 'Rood and Ruthwell: the poetry of paradox', *English Language Notes*, xxxi (1994), 6–12.

JOHNSON, D.F. 'Old English religious poetry: *Christ and Satan* and *The Dream of the Rood*', *Companion to Old English Literature* ed. R.H. Bremmer, Amsterdam, 1994, pp. 159–87.

JONES, J.M. 'The metaphor that will not perish: *The Dream of the Rood* and the new hermeneutic', *Christianity and Literature*, xxxviii (1989), 63–72.

KASKE, R.E. 'A poem of the cross in the Exeter Book: *Riddle 60* and *The Husband's Message*', *Traditio*, xxiii (1967), 41–71.

KELLER, W. 'Zur Chronologie der ae. Runen', *Anglia*, lxii (1938), 24–32.

KEMBLE, J.M. 'On Anglo-Saxon runes', *Archaeologia*, xxviii (1840), 327–72.

——'Additional observations on the runic obelisk at Ruthwell; the poem of *The Dream of the Holy Rood*; ...', *Archaeologia*, xxx (1844), 31–46.

KILPIÖ, M. 'Hrabanus' *De laudibus Sanctae Crucis* and *The Dream of the Rood*, *Neophilologica Fennica*, xlv (1987), 177–91.

KING, A. 'The Ruthwell Cross—a linguistic monument: runes as evidence for Old English', *Folia Linguistica Historica*, vii (1987), 43–79.

KINTGEN, E.R. 'Echoic repetition in Old English poetry, especially *The Dream of the Rood*', *NM*, lxxv (1974), 202–23.

KIRBY, I.J. '*The Dream of the Rood*: a dilemma of supra-heroic dimensions', *Etudes de Lettres*, 4S, ii (1979), 3–7.

KLINCK, A.L. 'Christ as soldier and servant in *The Dream of the Rood*', *Florilegium*, iv (1982), 109–16.

LASS, R. 'Of data and "datives": Ruthwell Cross *rodi* again', *NM*, xcii (1991), 395–403.

LEE, A.A. 'Towards a critique of *The Dream of the Rood*', *Anglo-Saxon Poetry: Essays in Appreciation*, ed. L.E. Nicholson and D.W. Frese, Notre Dame, 1975, pp. 163–91.

LEE, N.A. 'The unity of *The Dream of the Rood*', *Neophilologus*, lvi (1972), 469–86.

LEHMANN, W.P. and DAILEY, V.F. *The Alliterations of the 'Christ', 'Guthlac', 'Elene', 'Juliana', 'Fates of the Apostles', 'Dream of the Rood'*, Austin, 1960.

LEITER, L.H. '*The Dream of the Rood*: patterns of transformation', *Old English Poetry*, ed. R.P. Creed, Providence, 1967, pp. 93–127.

LENTZNER, K. *Das Kreuz bei den Angelsachsen; gemeinverständliche aufzeichnungen*, Leipzig, 1890.

LE SAUX, F. 'Didacticism in *The Dream of the Rood*', *Etudes de Lettres*, ii–iii (1987), 167–77.

LOGEMAN, H. *L'Inscription Anglo-Saxonne du Reliquaire de la Vraie Croix au Trésor de l'Église des SS. Michel-et-Gudule à Bruxelles*, Ghent, 1891.

MACRAE-GIBSON, O.D. 'Christ the victor-vanquished in *The Dream of the Rood*', *NM*, lxx (1969), 667–72.

MAHLER, A.E. '*Lignum Domini* and the opening vision of *The Dream of the Rood*: a viable hypothesis?', *Speculum*, liii (1978), 441–59.

MARQUARDT, H. *Die Runeninschriften nach Fundorten*, 1, Göttingen, 1961.

MASTRO, M.L. DEL 'The *Dream of the Rood* and the *militia Christi*: perspective in paradox', *American Benedictine Review*, xxvii (1976), 171–86.

MCENTIRE, S. 'The devotional context of the Cross before A.D. 1000', *Sources of Anglo-Saxon Culture*, ed. P.E. Szarmach, Kalamazoo, 1986, pp. 345–56.

NAPIERKOWSKI, T.J. 'A dream of the cross', *Concerning Poetry*, xi (1978), 3–12.

Ó CARRAGÁIN, É. 'Crucifixion as Annunciation: the relation of *The Dream of the Rood* to the liturgy reconsidered', *English Studies*, lxiii (1982), 487–505.

——'*Vidi aquam*: the liturgical background to *The Dream of the Rood* 20a: *swætan on þa swiðran healfe*', *N&Q*, ccxxviii (1983), 8–15.

——'The Ruthwell crucifixion poem in its iconographic and liturgical contexts', *Peritia*, vi–vii (1987–88), 1–71.

OKASHA, E. *Hand-List of Anglo-Saxon Non-Runic Inscriptions*, Cambridge, 1971.

O'LOUGHLIN, J.L.N. '*The Dream of the Rood*', *Times Literary Supplement*, xxx (1931), 648.

ORTON, P. 'The technique of object-personification in *The Dream of the Rood* and a comparison with the Old English *Riddles*', *Leeds Studies in English*, NS, xi (1980), 1–18.

PAGE, R.I. 'Language and Dating in OE inscriptions', *Anglia*, lxxvii (1959), 385–406.

——'An early drawing of the Ruthwell Cross', *Medieval Archaeology*, iii (1959), 285–88.

——'The use of double runes in Old English inscriptions', *JEGP*, lxi (1962), 897–907.

——'A note on the transliteration of Old English runic inscriptions', *English Studies*, xliii (1962), 484–90.

——*An Introduction to English Runes*, London, 1973.

PASTERNACK, C.B. 'Stylistic disjunctions in *The Dream of the Rood*', *Anglo-Saxon England*, xiii (1984), 167–86.

PATCH, H.R. 'Liturgical influence in *The Dream of the Rood*', *PMLA*, xxxiv (1919), 233–57.

PATTEN, F. 'Structure and meaning in *The Dream of the Rood*', *English Studies*, xlix (1968), 385–401.

PAYNE, R.C. 'Convention and originality in the vision framework of *The Dream of the Rood*', *MP*, lxxiii (1976), 329–41.

PEZZINI, D. 'Teologia e poesia: la sintesi del poema anglosassone *Sogno della Croce*', *Rendiconti del' Istituto Lombardo*, cvi (1972), 268–86.

PICKFORD, T.E. '*Holmwudu* in *The Dream of the Rood*', *NM*, lxxvii (1976), 561–64.

——'Another look at the *engel dryhtnes* in *The Dream of the Rood*', *NM*, lxxvii (1976), 565–68.

PIGG, D.F. '*The Dream of the Rood* in its discursive context: apocalypticism as determinant of form and treatment', *English Language Notes*, xxix (1992), 13–22.

RAW, B.C. '*The Dream of the Rood* and its connections with early Christian art', *Medium Ævum*, xxxix (1970), 239–56.

RENOIR, A. 'Oral theme and written texts', *NM*, lxxvii (1976), 337–46.

RICCI, A. 'The chronology of Ango-Saxon poetry', *RES*, v (1929), 257–66.

RISSANEN, M. 'Two notes on Old English poetic texts', *NM*, lxviii (1967), 283–87.

RISSANEN, P. *The Message and the Structure of The Dream of the Rood*, Helsinki, 1987.

ROSS, A.S.C. 'The linguistic evidence for the date of the Ruthwell Cross', *MLR*, xxviii (1933), 145–55.

RYDBERG, V. 'Skalden Kadmon och Ruthwell-korset', *Göteborgs Handels- och Sjöfartstidning*, 24 September 1874, 3. Reprinted in *Skrifter af Viktor Rydberg*, xiv, Stockholm, 1899, pp. 516–23.

SARRAZIN, G. *Von Kädmon bis Kynewulf*, Berlin, 1913.

SAVAGE, A. 'Mystical and evangelical in *The Dream of the Rood*: the private and the public', *Mysticism: Medieval & Modern*, ed. V.M. Lagorio, Salzburg, 1986, pp. 4–11.

——'The place of Old English poetry in the English meditative tradition', *The Medieval Mystical Tradition in England: Exeter Symposium IV*, ed. M. Glasscoe, Cambridge, 1987, pp. 91–110.

SCHAAR, C. *Critical Studies in the Cynewulf Group*, Lund, 1949.

SCHLAUCH, M. '*The Dream of the Rood* as prosopopoeia', *Essays and Studies in Honor of Carleton Brown*, New York, 1940, pp. 23–34.

SCHMITZ, T. 'Die Sechstakter in der altenglischen Dichtung', *Anglia*, xxxiii (1910), 58–63.

SCHÜCKING, L.L. 'Das angelsächsische Totenklagelied', *ES*, xxxix (1908), 1–13.

SCHWAB, U. '*Das Traumgesicht vom Kreuzesbaum*: ein ikonologischer Interpretationsansatz zu dem ags. *Dream of the Rood*', *Philologische Studien: Gedenkschrift für Richard Kienast*, ed. U. Schwab and E. Stutz, Heidelberg, 1978, pp. 131–92.

——'Exegetische und homiletische Stilformen in *Dream of the Rood*', *Geistliche Denkformen in der Literatur des Mittelalters*, ed. K. Grubmüller et al., Munich, 1984, pp. 101–30.

SCRAGG, D.G. '*Hwæt/þæt* in *The Dream of the Rood*, line 2', *N&Q*, ccxiii (1968), 166–68.

SHEPHERD, G. 'Scriptural poetry', *Continuations and Beginnings*, ed. E.G. Stanley, London, 1966, pp. 1–36.

SISAM, K. 'Notes on Old English poetry', *RES*, xxii (1946), 257–68. Reprinted as 'The authority of Old English poetical manuscripts', *Studies*, pp. 29–44.

——'Dialect origins of the earlier Old English verse', *Studies*, pp. 119–39.

SKEMP, A.R. 'The transformation of scriptural story, motive, and conception in Anglo-Saxon poetry', *MP*, iv (1906–07), 423–70.

SMITH, J. 'The garments that honour the cross in *The Dream of the Rood*', *Anglo-Saxon England*, iv (1975), 29–35.

STEVENS, W.O. *The Cross in the Life and Literature of the Anglo-Saxons*, New York, 1904.

STEVICK, R.D. 'The meter of *The Dream of the Rood*', *NM*, lxviii (1967), 149–68.

SWANTON, M.J. 'Ambiguity and anticipation in *The Dream of the Rood*', *NM*, lxx (1969), 407–25.

TATE, G.S. 'Chiasmus as metaphor: the *figura crucis* tradition and *The Dream of the Rood*', *NM*, lxxix (1978), 114–25.

TAYLOR, P.B. 'Text and texture of *The Dream of the Rood*', *NM*, lxxv (1974), 193–201.

TRAUTMANN, M. *Kynewulf, der Bischof und Dichter*, Bonn, 1898.

TRIPP, R.P. '*The Dream of the Rood* 9b and its context', *MP*, lxix (1971) 136–37.

WEIGHTMAN, J. *The Language and Dialect of the later Old English Poetry*, Liverpool, 1907.

WHITMAN, F.H. '*The Dream of the Rood*, 101a', *The Explicator*, xxxiii (1975), 70.

WILCOX, J. 'New solutions to Old English riddles: Riddles 17 and 53', *Philological Quarterly*, lxix (1990), 393–408.

WOLF, C.J. 'Christ as hero in *The Dream of the Rood*', *NM*, lxxi (1970), 202–10.

WOOLF, R. 'Doctrinal influences on *The Dream of the Rood*', *Medium Ævum*, xxvii (1958), 137–53.

WRENN, C.L. 'The value of spelling as evidence', *Trans. Philological Society*, 1943, 14–39. Reprinted in *Word and Symbol: Studies in English Language*, London, 1967, pp. 129–49.

WÜLCKER, R.P. 'Ueber den Dichter Cynewulf', *Anglia*, i (1878), 483–507.

THE RUTHWELL CROSS

ALLEN, J.R., and ANDERSON, J. *The Early Christian Monuments of Scotland*, Edinburgh, 1903.

BAILEY, R.N. 'The Ruthwell Cross: a non-problem', *Antiquaries Journal*, lxxiii (1993), 141–48.

BROWN, G.B. *The Arts in Early England*, v, London, 1921.

BROWN, G.B., and LETHABY, W.R. 'The Bewcastle and Ruthwell Crosses', *BM*, xxiii (1913), 43–49.

BROWN, G.B., and WEBSTER, A.B. *Royal Commission on Ancient and Historical Monuments ... of Scotland*, vii, *County of Dumfries*, Edinburgh, 1920.

BROWNE, G.F. *The Ancient Cross Shafts at Bewcastle and Ruthwell*, Cambridge, 1916.

CASSIDY, B. ed. *The Ruthwell Cross*, Princeton, N.J., 1992.

COLLINGWOOD, W.G. 'The Ruthwell Cross in its relationship to other monuments', *Trans. Dumfries and Galloway Antiquarian Society*, S3, v (1918), 34–84.

——*Northumbrian Crosses of the Pre-Norman Age*, London, 1927.

CONWAY, M. 'The Bewcastle and Ruthwell Crosses', *BM*, xxi (1912), 193–94.

——'A dangerous archaeological method', *BM*, xxiv (1913), 85–89.

COOK, A.S. 'The date of the Ruthwell and Bewcastle Crosses', *Trans. Connecticut Academy*, xvii (1912), 213–361. Reprinted separately, New Haven, 1912.

CRAMP, R.J. 'The Anglian sculptured crosses of Dumfriesshire', *Trans. Dumfries and Galloway Antiquarian Society*, S3, xxxviii (1959–60), 9–20.

DINWIDDIE, J.L. *The Ruthwell Cross and its Story*, Dumfries, 1927.

FARRELL, R.T. 'Reflections on the iconography of the Ruthwell and Bewcastle Crosses', *Sources of Anglo-Saxon Culture*, ed. P.E. Szarmach, Kalamazoo, 1986, pp. 357–76.

HANEY, K.E. 'The Christ and the Beasts panel on the Ruthwell Cross', *Anglo-Saxon England*, xiv (1985), 215–31.

HEWISON, J.K. *The Runic Roods of Ruthwell and Bewcastle*, Glasgow, 1914.

HOWLETT, D.R. 'Two panels on the Ruthwell Cross', *Journal of the Warburg and Courtauld Institutes*, xxxvii (1974), 333–36.

HOWORTH, H.H. 'The great crosses of the seventh century in northern England', *Archaeological Journal*, lxxi (1914), 45–64.

KANTOROWICZ, E.H. 'The archer in the Ruthwell Cross', *Art Bulletin*, xlii (1960), 57–59. Reprinted in *Selected Studies*. New York, 1965, pp. 95–99.

KITZINGER, E. 'Anglo-Saxon vine-scroll ornament', *Antiquity*, x (1936), 61–71.

LETHABY, W.R. 'The Ruthwell Cross', *BM*, xxi (1912), 145–46.

——'The Ruthwell Cross', *Architectural Review*, xxxii (1912), 59–63.

——'Is Ruthwell Cross an Anglo-Celtic work?', *Archaeological Journal*, lxx (1913), 145–61.

MERCER, E. 'The Ruthwell and Bewcastle Crosses', *Antiquity*, xxxviii (1964), 268–76.

MEYVAERT, P. 'An Apocalypse panel on the Ruthwell Cross', *Mediaeval and Renaissance Studies*, ix (1982), 3–32.

MUIR, P.M. 'The Ruthwell Cross', *Trans. Scottish Ecclesiological Society*, i (1905), 135–40.

Ó CARRAGÁIN, É. 'Liturgical innovations associated with Pope Sergius and the iconography of the Ruthwell and Bewcastle crosses', *Bede and Anglo-Saxon England*, ed. R.T. Farrell, Oxford, 1978, pp. 131–47.

——'Christ over the Beasts and the Agnus Dei: two multivalent panels on the Ruthwell and Bewcastle Crosses', *Sources of Anglo-Saxon Culture*, ed. P.E. Szarmach, Kalamazoo, 1986, pp. 377–403.

SAXL, F. 'The Ruthwell Cross', *Journal of the Warburg and Courtauld Institutes*, vi (1943), 1–19. Reprinted in *England and the Mediterranean Tradition*, Oxford, 1945, pp. 1–19.

SCHAPIRO, M. 'The religious meaning of the Ruthwell Cross', *Art Bulletin*, xxvi (1944), 232–45.

——'The bowman and the bird on the Ruthwell Cross and other works', *Art Bulletin*, xlv (1963), 351–55.

WILLETT, F. 'The Ruthwell and Bewcastle Crosses', *Memoirs of the Manchester Literary and Philosophical Society*, xcviii (1957), 94–136.

f. 104ᵛ   Hwæt! Ic swefna cyst   secgan wylle
h[w]æt mē gemǣtte   tō midre nihte,
syðþan reordberend   reste wunedon.

Þūhte mē þæt ic gesāwe   syllicre trēow
on lyft lǣdan,   lēohte bewunden,   5
bēama beorhtost.   Eall þæt bēacen wæs
begoten mid golde;   gimmas stōdon
fægere æt foldan scēatum;   swylce þǣr fīfe
   wǣron
uppe on þām eaxlegespanne.   Behēoldon þǣr
   engel Dryhtnes ealle,
fægere þurh forðgesceaft.   Ne wæs ðǣr hūru   10
   fracodes gealga.
Ac hine þǣr behēoldon   hālige gāstas,
men ofer moldan   ond eall þēos mǣre gesceaft.

Syllic wæs se sigebēam,   ond ic synnum fāh,
forwunded mid wommum.   Geseah ic wuldres
   trēow,
wǣdum geweorðode,   wynnum scīnan,   15
gegyred mid golde;   gimmas hæfdon
bewrigene weorðlīce   wealdes trēow.
Hwæðre ic þurh þæt gold   ongytan meahte
earmra ǣrgewin,   þæt hit ǣrest ongan
swǣtan on þā swīðran healfe.   Eall ic wæs mid   20
   s[o]rgum gedrēfed.
Forht ic wæs for þǣre fægran gesyhðe.   Geseah
   ic þæt fūse bēacen

f. 105ʳ   wendan wǣdum ond blēom;   hwīlum hit wæs
   mid wǣtan bestēmed,

2 hwæt: *MS.* hæt
20 sorgum: *MS.* surgum

93

RUTHWELL TEXT

I

[+ Ond]geredæ hinæ Ḡod almehttig,   39
þā hē walde on ḡalḡu gistīḡa,   40
[m]odig f[ore allæ] men.   41
[B]ūḡ[a ic ni dorstæ . . . .]   42

II

[Āhōf] ic riicnæ K̄yniŋc,   44
heafunæs Hlafard, hælda ic ni dorstæ.   45
Bismærædu uŋket men bā ætḡad[re]; ic [wæs] miþ blōdæ
       [b]istēmi[d],   48
bi[goten of . . . .]   49

beswyled mid swātes gange,   Hwīlum mid since
     gegyrwed.
Hwæðre ic þǣr licgende   lange hwīle
behēold hrēowcearig   Hǣlendes trēow,   25
oððæt ic gehȳrde   þæt hit hlēoðrode.
Ongan þā word sprecan   wudu sēlesta:
   " Þæt wæs geāra iū,   (ic þæt gȳta geman),
þæt ic wæs āhēawen   holtes on ende,
āstyred of stefne mīnum.   Genāman mē ðǣr   30
     strange fēondas,
geworhton him þǣr tō wǣfersȳne,   hēton mē
     heora wergas hebban.
Bǣron mē ðǣr beornas on eaxlum,   oððæt hīe
     mē on beorg āsetton,
gefæstnodon mē þǣr fēondas genōge.   Geseah ic
     þā Frēan mancynnes
efstan elne mycle   þæt hē mē wolde on gestīgan.
Þǣr ic þā ne dorste   ofer Dryhtnes word   35
būgan oððe berstan,   þā ic bifian geseah
eorðan scēatas.   Ealle ic mihte
fēondas gefyllan,   hwæðre ic fæste stōd.
   Ongyrede hine þā geong hæleð,   (þæt wæs God
     ælmihtig),
strang ond stīðmōd;   gestāh hē on gealgan   40
     hēanne,
mōdig on manigra gesyhðe,   þā hē wolde mancyn
     lȳsan.
Bifode ic þā mē se beorn ymbclypte;   ne dorste
     ic hwæðre būgan tō eorðan,
feallan tō foldan scēatum.   Ac ic sceolde fæste
     standan.
Rōd wæs ic ārǣred.   Āhōf ic rīcne Cyning,
heofona Hlāford;   hyldan mē ne dorste.   45

RUTHWELL TEXT

III

[+]Krist wæs on rōdi.　　　　　　　　　　　　　56
Hweþræ þēr fūsæ fearran kwōmu　　　　　　　57
æþþilæ til ānum.　Ic þæt al bih[eald]　　　　58
Sār[æ] ic wæs mi[þ] sorḡum gidrœ[fi]d, h[n]aḡ[ic . . . .]59

IV

miþ strēlum giwundad.　　　　　　　　　　　62
Ālegdun hiæ hinæ limwœrignæ, gistōddun him [. . . . .]
　　　lícæs [hea]f[du]m;　　　　　　　　　　63
[bi]hea[l]du[n] hi[æ] þē[r . . . .]　64

Þurhdrifan hī mē mid deorcan næglum; on mē
    syndon þā dolg gesīene,
opene inwid-hlemmas. Ne dorste ic hira
    nǣnigum sceððan.
Bysmeredon hīe unc būtū ætgædere. Eall ic
    wæs mid blōde bestēmed,
begoten of þæs guman sīdan, siððan hē hæfde
    his gāst onsended.

Feala ic on þām beorge gebiden hæbbe   50
wrāðra wyrda. Geseah ic weruda God
þearle þenian. Þӯstro hæfdon
bewrigen mid wolcnum Wealdendes hrǣw,
scīrne scīman; sceadu forð ēode,
wann under wolcnum. Wēop eal gesceaft,   55
cwīðdon Cyninges fyll. Crist wæs on rōde.

Hwæðere þǣr fūse feorran cwōman
tō þām æðelinge. Ic þæt eall behēold.
Sāre ic wæs mid [sorgum] gedrēfed, hnāg ic
    hwæðre þām secgum tō handa,
ēaðmōd elne mycle. Genāmon hīe þǣr ælmih-   60
    tigne God,
f. 105ᵛ   āhōfon hine of ðām hefian wīte. Forlēton mē
    þā hilderincas
standan stēame bedrifenne; eall ic wæs mid
    strǣlum forwundod.
Ālēdon hīe ðǣr limwērigne, gestōdon him æt
    his līces hēafdum;
behēoldon hīe ðǣr heofenes Dryhten, ond hē
    hine ðǣr hwīle reste,
mēðe æfter ðām miclan gewinne. Ongunnon him 65
    þā moldærn wyrcan

59 sorgum *supplied from the Ruthwell text.*
65 moldærn: *MS.* moldӕrn

beornas on banan gesyhðe; curfon hīe ðæt of
   beorhtan stāne,
gesetton hīe ðǣron sigora Wealdend. Ongunnon
   him þā sorhlēoð galan,
earme on þā ǣfentīde; þā hīe woldon eft sīðian
mēðe fram þām mǣran þēodne; reste hē ðǣr
   mǣte weorode.

Hwæðere wē ðǣr [h]rēotende gōde hwīle   70
stōdon on staðole, syððan [stefn] ūp gewāt
hilderinca; hrǣw cōlode,
fǣger feorgbold. Þā ūs man fyllan ongan
ealle tō eorðan; þæt wæs egeslic wyrd!
Bedealf ūs man on dēopan sēaþe. Hwæðre mē   75
   þǣr Dryhtnes þegnas,
frēondas gefrūnon, ...
gyredon mē golde ond seolfre.

Nū ðū miht gehȳran, hæleð mīn se lēofa,
þæt ic bealu-wara weorc gebiden hæbbe, .
sārra sorga. Is nū sǣl cumen   80
þæt mē weorðiað wīde ond sīde
menn ofer moldan ond eall þēos mǣre gesceaft,
gebiddaþ him tō þyssum bēacne. On mē Bearn
   Godes
þrōwode hwīle. Forþan ic þrymfæst nū
hlifige under heofenum, ond ic hǣlan mæg   85
ǣghwylcne ānra þāra þe him bið egesa tō mē.
Iū ic wæs geworden wīta heardost,
lēodum lāðost, ǣrþan ic him līfes weg
rihtne gerȳmde, reordberendum.
Hwæt, mē þā geweorðode wuldres Ealdor   90
ofer holmwudu, heofonrīces Weard,

70 hrēotende: MS. reotende
71 stefn supplied by Kluge.

swylce swā hē his mōdor ēac,   Mārian sylfe,
ælmihtig God,   for ealle menn
geweorðode   ofer eall wīfa cynn.

  Nū ic þē hāte,   hæleð mīn se lēofa,   95
þæt ðū þās gesyhðe   secge mannum,
onwrēoh wordum   þæt hit is wuldres bēam,
sē ðe ælmihtig God   on þrōwode
for mancynnes   manegum synnum
ond Ādomes   ealdgewyrhtum.   100
Dēað hē þǣr byrigde;   hwæðere eft Dryhten
    ārās
mid his miclan mihte   mannum tō helpe.
Hē ðā on heofenas āstāg.   Hider eft fundaþ
on þysne middangeard   mancynn sēcan

f. 106ʳ   on dōmdæge   Dryhten sylfa,   105
ælmihtig God,   ond his englas mid,
þæt hē þonne wile dēman,   sē āh dōmes geweald,
ānra gehwylcum   swā hē him ǣrur hēr
on þyssum lǣnum   līfe geearnaþ.
Ne mæg þǣr ǣnig   unforht wesan   110
for þām worde   þe se Wealdend cwyð.
Frīneð hē for þǣre mænige   hwǣr se man sīe,
sē ðe for Dryhtnes naman   dēaðes wolde
biteres onbyrigan,   swā hē ǣr on ðām bēame
    dyde.
Ac hīe þonne forhtiað,   ond fēa þencaþ   115
hwæt hīe tō Criste   cweðan onginnen.
Ne þearf ðǣr þonne ǣnig   unforht wesan
þe him ǣr in brēostum bereð   bēacna sēlest.
Ac ðurh ðā rōde sceal   rīce gesēcan
of eorðwege   ǣghwylc sāwl,   120
sēo þe mid Wealdende   wunian þenceð."

113 wolde *corrected from* þrowode; þro *erased and* l *interlined.*

    Gebæd ic mē þā tō þān bēame   blīðe mōde,
elne mycle, þǣr ic āna wæs
mǣte werede. Wæs mōdsefa
āfȳsed on forðwege; feala ealra gebād   125
langung-hwīla. Is mē nū līfes hyht
þæt ic þone sigebēam sēcan mōte
āna oftor þonne ealle men,
well weorþian. Mē is willa tō ðām
mycel on mōde, ond mīn mundbyrd is   130
geriht tō þǣre rōde. Nāh ic rīcra feala
frēonda on foldan. Ac hīe forð heonon
gewiton of worulde drēamum, sōhton him
    wuldres Cyning;
lifiaþ nū on heofenum mid Hēahfædere,
wuniaþ on wuldre. Ond ic wēne mē   135
daga gehwylce hwænne mē Dryhtnes rōd,
þe ic hēr on eorðan ǣr scēawode,
on þysson lǣnan līfe gefetige
ond mē þonne gebringe þǣr is blis mycel,
drēam on heofonum, þǣr is Dryhtnes folc   140
geseted tō symle, þǣr is singal blis;
ond hē þonne āsette þǣr ic syþþan mōt
wunian on wuldre, well mid þām hālgum
drēames brūcan. Sī mē Dryhten frēond,
sē ðe hēr on eorþan ǣr þrōwode   145
on þām gealgtreowe for guman synnum.
Hē ūs onlȳsde ond ūs līf forgeaf,
heofonlicne hām. Hiht wæs genīwad
mid blēdum ond mid blisse þām þe þǣr bryne
    þolodan.
Se Sunu wæs sigorfæst on þām sīðfate,   150

127 ic *interlined.*
132 on *erased after* foldan.

mihtig ond spēdig,   þā hē mid manigeo cōm,
gāsta weorode,   on Godes rīce,
Anwealda ælmihtig,   englum tō blisse
ond eallum ðām hālgum   þām þe on heofonum
    ǣr
wunedon on wuldre,   þā heora Wealdend cwōm, 155
ælmihtig God,   þǣr his ēðel wæs.

152 o *erased before* on.

1. **Hwæt.** A conventional extra-metrical introductory interjection. Thus also begin *Andreas, Beowulf, Exodus*, etc.

2–3. Compare the style and substance of *Daniel* 122–3, *frægn þa ða mænigeo hwæt hine gemætte, þenden reordberend reste wunode*.

2. **hwæt.** MS. *hæt* was retained by some early editors but makes no sense in this context. An appropriate form is needed to introduce the subordinate clause, and most editors adopt Grein's emendation *hwæt*. The VB scribe commonly omits a letter (cf. *Andreas* 1478, *HÆT* for *HWÆT*). In any case the consonant group *hw* is not infrequently simplified to *h* in later OE MSS. (cf. Blake, *N & Q*, ccvi (1961), 166). Repetition of a form with different meanings in succeeding lines is characteristic of this poet's wordplay. Scragg (*N & Q*, ccxiii (1968), 166–8) has argued for the emendation *þæt*, originally favoured by Bouterwek and Kemble. This makes for more straightforward syntax, providing a simple adjectival clause to amplify *swefna cyst*, but would lack agreement of gender (fem. *cyst*, neut. *þæt*). Occasional scribal confusion between *h* and *þ* is found in some later OE MSS. but no certain instance can be cited from VB.

me gemætte 'I dreamed'. The verb *(ge)mætan* is often impersonal, taking a dative object to specify the person involved; cf. ME *me mette*, NE 'it occurred to me', ON *dreymði mik*. See N. Wahlén, *The Old English Impersonalia*, i, pp. 60–2.

3. **Reordberend**, 'voice-bearing ones', is a pres. pple. kenning for 'men', apparently made (abstract+*berend*) by analogy with e.g. *feorh- gast- sawl-berend*. The concept is similar to Latin *linguae*, which recurs frequently in Vulgate usage as the equivalent of *nationes, tribus* (cf. Rankin, *JEGP*, ix (1910), 66). With the exception of *sawlberend* in *Beowulf* 1004, no kenning of this group is found outside religious verse. *Reordberend* is used here with a fine negative effect, at once emphatic both of the silence that surrounds the visionary and of the carelessness of those that sleep, ignoring the messenger of Salvation. An ironic recall occurs at 89.

reste wunedon. Cf. *Beowulf* 2902, *wunað wælreste; Paris Psalter*, cxxxi, 15, *rest … wunian*. In this context the verb might be taken as intransitive with *reste* as dat. sg., 'were at rest' (cf. Wülfing, § 71), but Klaeber (*AB*, xvii (1906), 102), citing use of the verb in *Andreas* 131, 1310, 1697, prefers to take *reste* as acc. sg. ' resting-place ', i.e. ' were occupying their beds '.

4–7. þuhte me þæt ic gesawe. . . . Verbal parallels occur in similar dream situations in *Daniel* 497 ff. and *Elene* 72 ff., each beginning lines with *puhte him (þæt)* . . .; *Elene* also has a comparative adj. together with the verb *geseon* in the subjunctive: *ænlicre . . . gesege*. But any verbal parallel might be simply due to a general similarity in the situation (cf. Patch, *PMLA*, xxxiv (1919), 235–7).

4. syllicre. This use of the comparative is unusual. Cook suggested that a line might have been omitted, comparing *Elene* 74. Others (F. E. C. Dietrich, *Disputatio*, p. 12, n. 30; Herzfeld, *Archiv*, cxvii (1906), 189) would supply a negative (*ic ne*, or *ne syllicre*), comparing usage in *Andreas* 471, 499 and *Elene* 73–4. Most recent editors, however, follow Klaeber (*AB*, xvii (1906), 102; *MP*, iii (1905–6), 251–2.) in simply assuming an absolute use of the comparative: ' the most wonderful, very wonderful '.

5. on lyft lædan. Pope considers *lædan* possibly an error for the rare verb *leodan* ' to spring up ', but with the exception of Bouterwek (who read *liðan* ' schweben '), all editors accept the MS. reading; cf. *Guthlac* 467, *We þec in lyft gelæddun*. An infinitive following a finite verb (*gesawe* 4) occasionally has a passive sense in OE prose (M. Callaway, *The Infinitive in Anglo-Saxon*, p. 121) but not elsewhere in verse. L. L. Schücking (*Untersuchungen zur Bedeutungslehre der angelsächsischen Dichter-sprache*, pp. 56–7) attempted to reconcile the form as an active construction: 'in der Luft tragen ', assuming the subject to be *engel* (9). But there is no reason why, as in e.g. *Geseah . . . penian* 51–2, the construction should not be passive here—' It seemed to me as if I beheld a most wonderful tree borne up into the air '.

The Constantinian concept of the cross towering into the sky was familiar from Invention and Exaltation liturgies (e.g. York Breviary, *Hoc signum crucis erit in celo. . . . Et intuens in celum: vidit signum crucis Christi*, SS, lxxv, 270, 272, 554; and cf. the Blickling Easter Homily, *seo rod ures Drihtnes bið aræred on þæt gewrixle para tungla*, EETS, lviii-lxxiii, p. 91). For the significance of this towering link between heaven and earth see p. 51.

leohte bewunden. The same phrase is used of the Saviour himself in *Christ* 1642. In *Elene* 733 it is the noblest of angels who *geond lyft farað leohte bewundene*. The brilliance of the cross is a familiar feature of the Constantinian tradition (cf. *Elene* 88–94, *Riddle XXX* 2, *bewunden mid wuldre*, or Tatwine's cross riddle, cited p. 67, n. 4). Perhaps this phrase also derives from a form of contemporary liturgy.

6. In *Guthlac* 1309 the same line is used of the light which appears at the death of the saint.

Beacen is used of the cross also at 21, 83 and 118. Used commonly as the equivalent of *vexillum* (cf. Napier, 1.1861; *Beowulf* 2776–7), it must clearly be understood as the sign of the victorious Christ militant (cf. Bewcastle Cross *siğbecn*). Deriving from the Constantinian *labarum*, the early fathers' conception of a *crucis vexillum* (cf. pseudo-Augustine, *PL*, xxxix. 2051) survives into the seventh century through the most famous of Fortunatus' cross panegyrics or the writings of e.g. Julianus of Toledo (*PL*, xcvi. 500), and thus into church liturgy (cf. Durham Ritual, SS, cxl, p. 94).

7. **begoten mid golde.** The verb *begeotan* is used in an unusual way here to build up our oblique view of the cross; a poetic anticipation of its use in 49 is contrived: ' sprinkled with gold . . . with blood '. The verb occurs nowhere else in OE verse in this sense (and only in a single doubtful case, *Elene* 1247, in any other), and it might well have been chosen here for its startling effect.

gimmas stodon. For the contemporary jewelled cross see pp. 48, 52. The verb *standan* most commonly means ' to remain, be fixed '. But it is also used of light in the sense ' to gleam or shine in a beam ' (*cf. Beowulf* 726, 1570, etc.), and with the subject *gimmas* this may represent the most apposite meaning. Taken in conjunction with *æt* in the following line, it should perhaps be rendered ' shone forth from ' (cf. Swaen, *Neophilologus*, xxi (1936), 58). Very occasionally, however, the same verb is used to refer to the issue of moisture (cf. Ælfric, *Homs*, i, p. 86). The jewels of the cross (invariably red stones like the garnets of St. Cuthbert's pectoral cross or contemporary Kentish jewels) conventionally represent the various wounds of Christ (cf. Blickling Homily I, *He sealde his pone readan gim; pæt wæs his pæt halige blod*, EETS, lviii, pp. 9–11). Various connotations may therefore be present in the verb *standan* here.

8. **fægere.** Some earlier editors, following Bouterwek, read *feowere*, which they assume forms a reasonable contrast with *fife*

in the next half-line, the scribe's eye presumably having taken the MS. form from *fægere* (10). But emendation is unnecessary. The presence of a numeral in the second half-line by no means requires another in the first, and the device of repetition occurs commonly throughout the poem.

æt foldan sceatum. This collocation is not unusual in OE verse (cf. 43, or *Daniel* 501, *Exodus* 429, *Phoenix* 3, etc.), but in this context dat. pl. *sceatum* is ambiguous (cf. Klæber, *Anglia*, xxxv (1912), 115–16). Sometimes, as at 43, it means ' surface ', so that some thus translate ' at the surface of the earth ' i.e. ' at the foot of the cross ' (cf. Rankin, *JEGP*, ix (1910), 78). But this is difficult to visualise in iconographical terms. Ebert (*Leipzig Berichte*, xxxvi (1884), 83) tried to overcome the difficulty by seeing these gems at the foot-rest of the cross, but there is no reason to suppose that *folde* means ' suppedaneum ', and visually it seems equally improbable. Frequently, however, *sceat* has the meaning ' corner ', and its use in the plural here suggests a more convincing reading: ' at the corners of the earth ' (cf. *Christ* 878–9, *feowerum foldan sceatum, þam ytemestum eorþan rices*, or lines of an Exaltation cross panegyric in the York Missal, *terrarum comprehendit quattuor confinia*, SS, lx, p. 102). For this equation of the cross with the four corners of the earth see pp. 50–1.

þær fife wæron. Here, as at 30–5, etc., *þær* might have less a local than an existential sense (cf. Quirk, *London Medieval Studies*, ii (1951), 32).

Jewels are found in varying numbers decorating the contemporary ' crux gemmata ', but attention is commonly drawn to the quincunx of bosses (perhaps representing jewels) found at the junction of certain types of Anglo-Saxon sculptured stone cross; they are found superimposed on the breast of Christ on a late cross from Lancaster (W. G. Collingwood, *Northumbrian Crosses*, fig. 128). The clearest and most pertinent interpretation of the five jewels in this context is that they represent the five wounds received by Christ on the cross, although contemporary exegetes also sometimes associate number five and the cross with certain virtues (cf. Honorius or Stephanus, *PL*, clxxii. 559–60, 1298).

9. eaxlegespann. This combination is found nowhere else in OE, nor is there any recognisable cognate form. MS. spacing *eaxle ge spanne* suggests that the scribe took pains over an unfamiliar word, carefully inflecting the first element like the last. Some editors correct this inflection to *eaxlgespanne*, although the spelling *eaxle-* might merely represent a phonetic variant (cf. Klaeber, *AB*, xvii (1906), 102). It would be tempting to identify this with the ' axle-tree ' or centre-piece of the cross, although ' axle ' in this sense of wheel-centre is not otherwise recorded before the thirteenth century (H. Kurath and S. M. Kuhn, *Middle English Dictionary*, i, pp. 579–80). A quincunx of jewels at this point is a natural and common feature of contemporary crosses. However, there are clearly present in the compound fem. *eaxl* ' shoulder ' and *gespann* ' that which links or stretches '. It might therefore simply refer to the beam of the gallows along which Christ's arms were stretched, although the ' crux gemmata ' normally has jewels along all four arms.

Beheoldon þær engel Dryhtnes ealle. The MS. line gives awkward but not impossible syntax if we assume m. nom. pl. *ealle* to be the subject, and m. acc. sg. *engel* the object of the sentence: ' All beheld there the angel of the Lord '. *Engel* in this case, as in *Christ* 104, *Christ & Satan* 585 or *Soul & Body I* 27, might be used to mean 'Christ' (cf. Augustine, *PL*, xxxv. 1596). But unless this represents a case of poetic anticipation, we are not yet pre-pared for even so indirect a reference to the person of Christ himself at this stage in the poem.

Most editors assume that *engel* in some way forms the subject of the sentence, paralleling *halige gastas*, which occurs together with the same verb at 11. But *Beheoldon* demands a plural subject and neither nom. pl. nor collective sg. *engel* is elsewhere recorded. Some simply emend to the plural *englas*. Krapp, referring to examples of genitives with *eall*, suggests *engla*. More drastically Dickins–Ross, followed by Lehnert and Fowler, read *engeldryht* ' hosts, orders of angels ' (a compound otherwise not found, but cf. *engla gedryht*, *Christ* 1013). This makes good sense and metre but requires the omission of the remainder of the line, *-nes ealle*. The division is marked by a MS line-break, but how far this may have affected the scribe is debatable. More recently Pope's (pp. 101, 111, 223) restoration: *engeldryhta feala (fela)* ' many angelic hosts ' ingeniously accounts for the entire MS. line; insular *f* and *s* are easily confused.

Others, concerned to improve the metre, had simply omitted a word: e.g. Campbell–Rosier *ealle*, and Mossé *dryhtnes*. But as it stands the MS. line forms a quite satisfactory hypermetric verse, the middle of three, 8–10 (cf. Bolton, *N&Q*, ccxiii (1968), 165–6).

10. **fægere þurh forðgesceaft.** As it stands, pl. *fægere* would refer to the subject of the previous line, nom. pl. *ealle*, although if the common emendation *englas* be accepted, it might more sensibly refer to its object. However, it may be that this is either a simple error, the form *fægere* being taken from its appearance as the opening word of line 8, or that the final *-e* has been introduced into the m. acc. sg. by analogy.

The poetic compound *forðgesceaft* is ambiguous. It is used to mean both ' creation, the created world ' (e.g. *Riddle LXXXIV* 9) and ' future destiny or state ' (e.g. *Beowulf* 1750). This diversity might be reconciled by taking the second element *gesceaft* (elsewhere ' creation ', 12, 55, 82) in its primary sense of ' what is created, ordained ', with *forð* indicating either its continuing or future existence. The compound might then be rendered ' that which has been ordained or created to be ' (Pope). This would be in accordance with a temporal use of *þurh* (cf. Wullen, *Anglia*, xxxiv (1911), 467). Bosworth–Toller expand: ' the state of the angels whose tenure of heaven was to continue for ever '. Sweet, also assuming *englas* to be the subject of the sentence, would translate ' beautiful through the future, in eternity ', and Cook ' were created fair '. Similar phrases are found used of angels elsewhere (cf. Ælfric, *Homs*, i, p. 10, *fæger gesceapen*). But here it might equally appropriately apply to Christ.

fracodes. Sweet and Cook emended to the more usual *fracoðes*, and Magoun *fracuðes*. The MS. form seems a quite permissible variant, however (cf. *Beowulf* 1575; Napier, 1.4455; Wright, 89.5). It is possible that by this allusion the poet intended to distinguish Christ's cross from those of the two thieves, but these are invariably called *sceapan* in OE (cf. Patch, *PMLA*, xxxiv (1919), 247). The sentence is no doubt merely an instance of Anglo-Saxon litotes.

gealga ' gallows '. This designation of the cross recurs at 40 and 146 (*gealgtreow*) and in *Christ & Satan* 509, 548 and *Menologium* 86. The Anglo-Saxons were unacquainted with crucifixion at first hand. There is no vernacular equivalent for Latin *crucifigere* and Gospel glossators are obliged to resort to only very approximate synonyms like *cwylman*, or *prowigan scolde*. Most commonly, however, they simply use *hon* ' to hang '. The use of *gealga* in such contexts (e.g. Durham Hymnal, SS, xxiii, p. 78) is simply due to the accommodation of an alien concept. Care is often taken over the definition, as in the Durham Ritual gloss cited in note to *gealgtreow*, 146. The solution to this difficulty is identical in cognate languages (cf. R. v. Raumer, *Die Einwirkung des Christenthums auf die Althochdeutsche Sprache*, pp. 361–3; Kahle, *Arkiv för Nordisk Filologi*, N.S. xiii (1901), 145).

11. **Ac** is used in the *Dream*, as in the *Seafarer*, as an adversative conjunction following a negative, even when the negative precedes it by several lines, as at 110–15 (Bolton, *MP*, lvii (1959–60), 260–2). If the use of *ac* seems to imply that angels would hardly have paused to look at the cross of a malefactor, this is simply one of the paradoxical ironies involved in the situation. Angels gazing on the cross are a commonplace of contemporary crucifixion iconography.

12. This line recurs at 82. The collocation *men ofer moldan* is found frequently in OE verse (e.g. *Andreas* 594, 1484; *Christ* 421; *Guthlac* 1230, etc.), and survives commonly into ME.

13. **sigebeam.** This kenning is found in OE verse only here and in *Elene* (seven times), where similar epithets (*sigebeacen, sigores tacen*) are applied to the cross. The conception was apparently of wider currency, however; the Bewcastle Cross inscription begins + *þis sigbecn*. Contemporary hymns and liturgy commonly contain the formula *o crux, signum triumphale* (e.g. York Missal, SS, lx, p. 103) and the OE kenning may have derived from such sources (cf. Patch, *PMLA*, xxxiv (1919), 247–8). The victory alluded to is not simply that of conspicuous warrior converts like Constantine or Oswald who fought under its protection (see pp. 42, 45), but that resulting from Christ's own struggle with Satan at his crucifixion—*earmra ærgewin* 19, *ðam miclan gewinne* 65.

Fah is ambiguous in this context. Its primary and most frequent use seems to have been to mean ' stained ', glossing e.g. *varius vel discolor* (Wright, 163.13, etc.), but common figurative use in association with crime (cf. *mane fah, Andreas* 1599, *Beowulf* 978) seems to have led to a secondary meaning ' guilty ' (cf. *Gesetze*, i, p. 160). Its use here therefore provides a dual contrast between visionary and emblem, *syllic sigebeam*, both in its visual brightness and innocent virtue.

13b–14a. Cf. *Christ & Satan* 155–6, *Nu ic eom dædum fah*,

gewundod mid wommum, or *Elene* 1242–3.   The physical impact of sin is a common concept in OE verse, cf. *Alms-Giving* 9, *Andreas* 407, *Christ* 757 (*synwund*), 1313, 1321, etc.

14. **wuldres treow**.   Cf. *Elene* 89, 827, 866, 1251, and *Dream* 97, *wuldres beam*.

15. As at 22, the sense of **wædum** is obscure.   But, with the exception of Campbell–Rosier, who suppose it to allude to the jewels, there is general agreement that the reference must be to some kind of cloth trappings adorning the cross.   Ebert (*Leipzig Berichte*, xxxvi (1884), 85), drawing attention to the eleventh-century gloss *mataxa: wæde* (Wright, 450.33) and the fact that processional crosses are sometimes depicted hung with chains, visualised decorative silk cords or tassels.   But the most straight-forward reference would seem to be to the ritual shrouding of crosses with a veil or pall on Good Friday to be dramatically revealed with the Resurrection services of Easter Sunday.

The image is equally reminiscent, however, of the *labarum*, the Christian military standard first raised by Constantine and later adopted by the western church.   It was described by Eusebius thus:

> From the crosspiece of the spear was suspended a cloth, a regal piece (βασιλικὸν ὕφασμα) covered with a profuse embroidery of most brilliant stones, and which being also richly interlaced with gold, presented an indescribable degree of beauty to the beholder. This banner was square in form. . . .
>
> (*PG*, xx. 945)

In employing just this imagery in ' Vexilla regis ', Fortunatus uses the words *Arbor decora et fulgida ornata regis purpura*, rendered in one OE version: *eala þu treow þu eart wlitig ond scinende gefrætewod mid purpuran rægle ond blode þes cynges* (H. Gneuss, *Hymnar und Hymnen im englischen Mittelalter*, p. 352).   Similar words occur in a cross poem by Hrabanus Maurus (cited in note to *wenden wædum ond bleom*, 22).   *Purpura* is regularly glossed *godeweb* (cf. Napier, 1.461, 1059, etc.), denoting some rich kind of cloth. At the same time *wæd* is used to gloss *iacinthus*, *sandix* (Napier, 8.374, etc.)—in which there is almost certainly semantic con-fusion with OE *wād*,- purple being the colour both of kings and death.   It is used on one occasion to gloss *indumentum* ' pall ' (Napier, 8.372).   In this context it is revealing that purple was the colour of vestments and ornaments demanded by church ritual during the Lenten season of mourning that led up to Good Friday (cf. note to *wenden wædum ond bleom*, 22).

geweorðode. The MS. form is retained by most editors although some follow Sievers (*PBB*, x (1885), 518) in emending to the uninflected form *geweorðod* on metrical grounds. Both inflected and uninflected pp. forms occur in the MS. (cf. Brunner, § 414).

Wynnum presents an ambiguity between abstract and visual qualities attributed to the cross, similar to that in 13. It might be interpreted as the dat. pl. of *wynn*, ' joy, gladness ', which would be appropriate to the personality of the cross as it is later presented, a symbol of joy in heaven. Alternatively it might be taken as an adverbial use of the instrumental, ' pleasantly ' (cf. *Phoenix* 7, 27, 313). But litotes is unexpected here. Perhaps, as Dickins–Ross suppose, a more extreme sense akin to the OS adverb *wânum* ' brilliantly ' or the adjectives OE *wenlic*, OS *wânlik* ' beautiful ', is best understood in this context.

16. The variant pps. **gegyred** and **gegyrwed** (23) exist side by side; for a comparison of the two forms see Brunner, § 408.

17. **bewrigene**. Some editors, following Kemble, emend to the uninflected form *bewrigen* of 53; but such pp. variants are not uncommon in the MS. (cf. notes to 15 and 16).

The metre of 17b is technically defective, ideally requiring a further syllable to smooth out the line, and the emendation *Wealdendes* (the form of 53, and cf. *Hælendes treow*, 25) first suggested by Dietrich (*Disputatio*, p. 13, n. 30) has commonly found favour. As Dickins–Ross point out, this might be palaeographically credible if we assume an intermediate MS. form *wealdēdes*. However, the VB scribe allows three-syllable half-lines elsewhere (cf. *Andreas* 489b, 1443a, *Soul & Body 1* 82b, 125a, *Elene* 318b, etc.). And MS. *wealdes* is semantically and syntactically tenable as a gen. sg. of *weald*, which might mean either ' forest ' (cf. 29) or ' power ', either of which would be poetically meaningful. The half-line might be metrically completed by a restoration *gewealdes* (cf. *Beowulf* 950, 1610, etc.). The MS. form is retained here as in some other editions like those of Sweet or Grein–Wülcker.

18. **Hwæðre** occurs in nine different places in the poem and there is no general agreement that it carries a uniform sense throughout. Ebert (*Leipzig Berichte*, xxxvi (1884), 91) and Sievers (*PBB*, ix

(1884), 138) considered it merely a loose connective continuing the narrative. Bolton (*MP*, lvii (1959–60), 260–2) prefers to read an adversative or concessive use throughout; comparing its use with that of *forþon* in *The Seafarer*, he recognises it as an organising device important to the didactic structure of the poem—a modulation between sections contrasting either degradation and glory or earthly impulse and spiritual duty. Particular note might be made of its use here, however (cf. 24, 38 or 70), where a shift in the direction of thought is underlined by an extra-metrical use of this conjunction (cf. Stevick, *NM*, lxviii (1967), 167–8). In each case (except 38) this marks the opening of a new section.

gold. The first half-line might be considered metrically ' false ', with alliteration falling on the second stress only. Holthausen (*ES*, xxxviii (1907), 201), comparing *wædum geweorðode* 15, proposed *godweb*, and Kluge *goldbleo*, as improvements.

19. earmra ærgewin. The allusion here is unclear. It might be possible to take *earmra* as a comparative adjective qualifying *ærgewin*, ' more wretched former struggle ', which would be appropriate to the Crucifixion. But comparison of adjectives regularly follows the weak declension, so that here we would expect *earmre*. The MS. form must therefore be considered the gen. pl. of an adjectival noun: ' the former struggle of wretched ones '. Kemble translated ' sufferers ', i.e. Christ and the cross together; or this might simply refer to all those *wergas* who had previously suffered on the cross (31). Cook, comparing the general sense of 30–48 and similar meanings of the adjective in e.g. *Christ & Satan* 73, *Guthlac* 405, 437 or *Phoenix* 442, expanded to ' the adversaries of Christ '. It might certainly be argued that here *earm* has the connotation of moral wretchedness (cf. *Gesetze*, ii, p. 59).

Ærgewin is otherwise unrecorded but the elements of the compound are straightforward. It seems improbable that in this context *ær-* should be interpreted in an intensive sense (cf. *ærglæd -god*) rather than in the usual adjectival sense ' former, ancient '. For the use of *gewin* cf. *Genesis* 296, 323, *Gifts* 89, *Guthlac* 115, 134, 961. No doubt here *ærgewin* refers to the ancient hostility of God's primeval adversaries, which being transferred to the Son culminated in the Crucifixion, seen by the poet as ' the great conflict ', 65. (Cf. *fyrngeflit, Elene* 903 f., *Panther* 34, and see generally A. Szogs, *Die Ausdrücke für*

' *Arbeit* ' *und* ' *Beruf* ' *im Altenglischen*, pp. 137–41.) This view of the Crucifixion as a battle is reflected in the use of heroic images: *hilderincas, strælum forwundod, fyll*, etc.

Anglo-Saxon theology seems to have envisaged Satan himself actually engineering the Crucifixion, as he is made to confess in *Juliana* 289–93 (and cf. *Christ* 564–73, *Elene* 207–10). Contemporary carved stone crosses sometimes represent this satanic involvement; a shaft at Dewsbury shows a devil devouring a human body drawn on the reverse side to that containing the crucified Christ. Similar is the concept which shows the ' serpens antiquus ' or some other monster crouched below or at the foot of a crucifixion, as on sculptures at Lancaster, Sinnington or Kirklevington (cf. W. G. Collingwood, *Northumbrian Crosses*, pp. 100–4).

After **ongytan, þæt** might introduce an adverbial clause of reason, but evidence for a causal *þæt* in OE verse is slender (Mitchell, *Neophilologus*, lii (1968), 292–3). This is therefore probably best rendered as a clause of time, ' when that . . .' (cf. note to 34).

20. With the exception of its occurrence in an ' Orientalum Mirabilis ' (EETS, clxi, p. 58, glossing *sudare*), where it might be understood to be miraculous, the verb **swætan** is found only here in the sense ' to bleed '. The associated noun *swat*, however, is used of both sweat and blood. The blood shed by Christ on the cross is described as *swat* here at 23, and in *Andreas* 968, *Christ* 1111, 1448, 1458, *Christ & Satan* 543, etc. At the same time *swat* is used of Christ's sweat in all OE versions of *Luke* xxii. 44 (cf. Lindisfarne Gospels gloss: *ond aworden wæs suat his suæ droppo blodes iornendes on eorðu*). It seems likely therefore that in the careful choice of this particular verb the poet obliquely anticipates both the bloody sweat of Gethsemane and the blood and water of Golgotha.

It is noteworthy that the source of blood on the cross should be represented as **þa swiðran healfe** when neither side is specified in the biblical narrative. But the early church assumed it to have been the right side for exegetical reasons (cf. Bede, *PL*, xci. 753), and contemporary Crucifixion scenes conventionally depict either a flowing wound or the spear-bearer himself on this side of Christ. Clearly therefore the poet's conception already anticipates the view of Christ himself or the cross rather than merely that of the beholder.

mid sorgum gedrefed. MS. *surgum* is otherwise unknown.
Some early editors, following Thorpe, emended to *sargum*,
similarly unrecorded elsewhere but presumably understood to be a
nominal form associated with *sargian* ' to afflict, make sad '.
But *sorgum* has the authority of the same phrase at 59 and in
Judith 88, although this is palaeographically less credible and
would represent the only instance of stressed *u* for *o* in the entire
MS.

21. Generally, as at 57, **fus** carries the sense ' eager, ready,
hastening ', but applied to the as yet impersonal *beacen* the
semantic issue is complex.

The most obvious extension of meaning is to ' moving, shifting '
(Cook, ' mobile '; Sweet, ' changing ') presumably in the sense of
the cross changing its dress and colours and therefore anticipating
the following line.   Some, like Dickins–Ross, suggest that the
meaning here is ' brilliant, shining ', but in instances cited the
sense of movement is equally present: in *Genesis* 154 it is used
of the third day of creation, and in *Beowulf* 1966 of the sun.   The
word *fus* is commonly associated with death, however, and Stern
therefore (*ES*, lxviii (1933–4), 168–9) comparing e.g. *Beowulf* 1241
or *Guthlac* 1148, 1228, prefers to translate ' doomed '.   Clearly,
within the poet's vision we must recognise not simply the church
year hastening to its sacrificial end, but a concrete symbol of
approaching death and the doom to come.   This *beacen* is at once
an emblem of death (Christ's) and of doom (that of both dreamer
and world).   At Judgement Day it is this symbol that will be
seen again in the heavens (cf. 135–44 and pp. 65, 78).

22. **wendan wædum ond bleom.** The infinitive is used here in a
passive sense following the finite *Geseah*, 21 (cf. note to *lædan*, 5).
The following dat. pl. forms represent instrumentals, meaning
' with respect to clothing and colours ' (cf. Wülfing, §§ 91–2).

This half-line is metrically incomplete, but as Sievers first
pointed out (*PBB*, ix (1884), 235; xii (1887), 471) a disyllabic
pronunciation of *bleom* would fill out the line appropriately (cf.
bleoum, *Solomon & Saturn* 150; *bleowum*, Alfred's *Boethius*, ed.
W. J. Sedgefield, p. 33).   The MS. form therefore probably
derives from an earlier uncontracted form, although only Bouterwek emends his text—*bleo[u]m*.   The form *bleom*, apparently
pronounced as a single syllable, is that used by Cynewulf: *Christ*
1391, *Elene* 758.

Varying colour is conventional to cross imagery; cf. Hrabanus Maurus, *Arbor sola tenens varios virtute colores, purpureo regis sub tactu roscida fulgens* (*PL*, cvii. 199) or the opening of Tatwine's cross riddle, *Versicolor cernor nunc, nunc mihi forma nitescit* (see p. 67, n. 4). The allusion is presumably to the changing colours appropriate to different seasons of the church year. A plain wooden cross, blood-red, the colour of death (Ælfric, *Homs*, ii, p. 254) was carried during Lent until Good Friday, while on Easter Sunday a magnificent and richly jewelled cross appeared (cf. J. W. Legg, *Notes on the History of the Liturgical Colours*). For the significance of the different materials see p. 52.

mid wætan bestemed. This image recurs commonly in OE verse (cf. *Andreas* 1239, 1475, *Exodus* 449, or referring specifically to the cross, *Christ* 1085). Each instance refers to *blod*, *dreor* or *swat*, and the phrase in this line clearly anticipates *mid blode bestemed* (48). In every case save one (*Beowulf* 486, *bestymed*) it is the non-WS form of the verb that is used, which almost certainly therefore represents a ' poetic ' word.

23. Beswyled is the pp. form of an otherwise unrecorded verb **beswyllan*, which must be associated with OE *swilian*, *swillan* ' to soak, drench '. Early editors altered to *besyled*, *besylwed* 'soiled ', but no emendation is necessary (cf. Klaeber, *AB*, xvii (1906), 102).

gang. The sense ' flow ' is apparently not recorded elsewhere, although this word is found applied to the sea (e.g. *Paris Psalter* xcii. 6, cxviii. 136; *Phoenix* 118) and cf. *on ðære ea gong* (Alfred's *Orosius*, EETS, lxxix, p. 74).

27. Wudu selesta might be compared with the concept of Fortunatus' ' Pange lingua ', *Crux fidelis, inter omnes arbor una nobilis* (*PL*, lxxxviii. 89). The choice of *wudu* may have been determined by metrical exigency, but it is not found elsewhere in poetry in this sense, and the blunt prosaic form here usefully reinforces with the shock of conjunction the paradox which underlies and supports the entire poem.

30. Genaman. Some editors alter to the more usual form *genamon* of 60, but for pret. pl. endings in *-an*, cf. 46, 57, 149. Verb preceding subject in an inversion of usual syntax puts greater emphasis on the opening element and thus underlines the violence experienced by the tree. This order is not unknown in prose but occurs more frequently in verse, where greater licence is taken to achieve poetic ends. It adds considerably to the dramatic

immediacy of the poem that many clauses and sentences begin
with verbs (cf. 31-3, 39, 40, 42, 44, etc.).

31. **Him** must be taken as an ethic dat. pl. with acc. *me* understood.

31b is technically ambiguous; either *me* or *wergas* might be
understood as the object of either *heton* or *hebban*. This might
therefore be interpreted as either ' they ordered their criminals to
carry me ' or ' they ordered me to bear their criminals '. The
former merely duplicates the content of the next line; the latter,
however, representing normal OE word order, accords well with
the dramatic sense in *wæfersyn*.

wergas. The cross is still clearly recognised in Anglo-Saxon
times as the instrument of a shameful death. In *Riddle LV* 12 it
is described as *wulfheafedtreo*; and cf. OS *Heliand* 5563 *waragtrewe*,
the OE gloss *furca: wearhrod* (Wright, 245.39, etc.) or the place-
names *Weargrod, Weargtreow* (A. H. Smith, *English Place-Name
Elements*, ii, p. 248).

34. **efstan elne mycle.** Similar phrases occur in *Beowulf* 1493,
efste mid elne, or *Christ* 1317, *mid . . . micle elne*; and cf. the use
of *elne mycle* 60, 123. A simple intensive might fit the context in
each of these examples, but cf. the cognates OS, OHG *ellian*, ON
eljan, Gothic *aljan* ' zeal '. The area of meaning might include
' eagerly, quickly, effectually, valiantly '.

þæt here, as at 107, introduces an adverbial clause of time,
' when that . . .' (the presence of *willan* preventing interpretation
as a clause of purpose ' in order that . . .'). The sense ' because '
would usefully underline the doctrinal point here, but see note to
19.

gestigan (cf. *gestah*, 40). The Durham Hymnal gloss renders
crucem volens ascenderas as *rode willende þu astige* (SS, xxiii,
p. 80); and cf. the York Breviary antiphon, *Antequam te ascenderet
dominus noster o beata crux: timor terrenum habuisti* (SS, lxxv.
88). The concept seems to derive from commentaries on the
Song of Solomon vii. 8, *Dixi ascendam in palmam et apprehendam
fructus eius*, which conventionally identify the palm tree as a
type of the cross (cf. Gregory or Alcuin, *PL*, lxxix. 536; c. 660).
The idea was taken into the Anglo-Saxon homiletic tradition (see
note to 40), where it becomes a conventional equivalent for the
crucifixion. It is used in a passive sense thus of Peter (e.g.
Ælfric, *Homs*, i, p. 382, *rode-hengene astah*), where, hung upside-

down, he can hardly be said to have 'mounted' the cross. In the *Dream*, however, the image is presumably still fresh and unconventional.

35-6. Ic þa ne dorste ... bugan (and cf. 42) must surely be connected with ' Pange lingua ', *Flecte ramos arbor alta, tensa laxa viscera, et rigor lentescat ille, quem dedit nativitas* (*PL*, lxxxviii. 89). **þa ... þa** is syntactically correlative as 39–41.

36. bifian. Vulgate *Matt.* xxvii. 51, *terra mota est* is rendered in some OE versions, *seo eorðe bifode* (CCCC. MS. CXL, etc.) and the same verb is conventionally used of this phenomenon in both verse and prose (cf. *Christ* 827, 881, 1144; Ælfric, *Homs*, ii, p. 258). It was apparently considered appropriate to such natural phenomena in earth (cf. Vitellius Psalter, ed. J. L. Rosier, lxxv. 9; ciii. 32) or woods and trees (cf. 42 and Alfred's *Boethius*, ed. W. J. Sedgefield, p. 102).

37-8. Ealle ic mihte feondas gefyllan. For such disjunction (and cf. 50–1) see R. Quirk and C. L. Wrenn, *An Old English Grammar*, § 146. *Mihte* denotes a conditional perfect, 'could have felled '. Recurring in both verse and prose, (e.g. *Beowulf* 2706 or the Blickling Easter Homily, EETS, lviii–lxxiii, p. 87), *feondas gefyllan* must have been a common collocation, surviving into ME (cf. Layamon's *Brut* 5632, etc.).

39-42. Patten's (*English Studies*, xlix (1968), 396–7) recognition of sexual imagery in *ongyrede, bifode, ymbclypte* and fem. *rod* lacks external support; the equation of cross and bride of Christ is unwarranted.

39. Ongyrede hine þa geong hæleð. The verb should be interpreted as reflexive with an acc., ' stripped himself ' (cf. Wülfing, § 377). For the biblical fact see e.g. *Matt.* xxvii. 31, glossed in the Lindisfarne version: *Ond æfter ðon bismeredon him ongeredon hine ðyryfte ond gegeredon hine mið his gewedum ond gelæddon hine þæt hia on rode genæglede.* Christ was only very rarely depicted naked at the crucifixion; cf. Gregory of Tours, *PL*, lxxi. 724–5.

RC 39. [+Ond]geredæ. The opening part of the inscription is now totally obliterated. There is room for about three or four characters but most editors restore merely *on-* from VB *ongyrede*. *On-* is said to have been visible in Duncan's original drawing (G. Stephens, *Old-Northern Runic Monuments*, i, p. 416, n. 2), and Haigh's transcript purports to have read *un-*. Bainbrigg, however, had clearly read + *ændgeredæ*. The opening + would be supported by that which began the third section on the opposite side of the shaft. The first character seems to be an æ-rune, but as commonly among early antiquarians Bainbrigg confuses ᚠᚠᚾ so that it might equally be taken to represent *a* or *o*.

The verbal prefix *and-* appears in OE as a doublet for *on-*, the former representing the stressed form usual in nominal or adjectival compounds, with *on-* appearing as its unstressed equivalent proper to verbs; confusion does, however, occasionally take place in verbal compounds (Campbell, § 73, n. 1). *Ond-* rather than *and-* predominates in northern texts (Campbell, § 130, n. 2) and has therefore been preferred here, although this element does not recur in the Ruthwell inscription and so is without close parallel (see Page, *Medieval Archaeology*, iii (1959), 288).

40. **gestah he on gealgan heanne.** The concept of climbing the gallows as into a tree, taken from early biblical commentaries (cf. note to *gestigan*, 34), occurs in early Latin hymns (e.g. Prudentius, *PL*, lx. 495). It is found conventionally in OE religious verse (cf. *Christ* 727, 1171, 1491, *Creed* 28, etc.) and in the vernacular homiletic tradition (cf. Blickling Homily VIII, *þa he on rode galgan astag*, EETS, lviii–lxxiii, p. 97).

Heanne is ambiguous; glossing both *vulgus, plebs* and *cacumine, fastigium* (Wright, 110.41; 378.28; 400.8), it can mean either 'shameful, vile' or 'lofty'. 'High, towering' is a common conception of the cross in the Constantinian tradition (cf. *on lyft lædan*, 5, *hlifige under heofenum*, 85 or *Christ* 1446, *Elene* 424, *Juliana* 309, 482, etc.); in the Durham Hymnal the phrase *arduum scandit* of an Easter hymn is glossed *heahnyssa he astah* (SS, xxiii, p. 70). But cf. note to *wergas*, 31.

RC 40. **on ǥalǥu.** For the form *ǥalǥu* see p. 33f. Like VB *gealgan*, after *on* this form might be interpreted either as an acc. or, stressing the direction, as a locative dat. (cf. *on rodi*, RC 56).

RC 41. **Fore** is found in several early transcripts and most editors restore thus.

42-3. **Bifode ic. . . .** These lines were compared by E. S. Bugge (*Götter- und Heldensagen*, p. 523) with ON *Voluspá: Scelfr Yggdrasisls askr standandi, ymr ik aldna tre en jotunn losnar*, but cf. note to *Weop eal gesceaft*, 55. A more apposite parallel might be drawn with words of Ephraem Syrus, who describes the pillar against which Christ was scourged trembling at his touch (*Hymni et Sermones*, ed. T. J. Lamy, i, cols. 477–9). The apocryphal *Gesta*

Pilati depicts standards bowing in reverence at the approach of Christ to his trial (ed. C. Tischendorf, *Evangelia Apocrypha*, pp. 341–2).

42. Beorn ' warrior, hero ' is an unusual epithet for Christ, found otherwise only in *Christ* 449, 530. Elsewhere in the *Dream* it is used of both *feondas* (32) and disciples (66).

Ymbclyppan is not so inappropriate a verb as Sweet supposed; it underlines the eager willingness with which Christ is seen to embrace his sacrifice. Its use here might be compared with that of *amplector* in contemporary Latin hymns or liturgy like the York Breviary antiphon, *desideravi te amplecti o bona crux* (SS, lxxv. 88). Cf. Patch, *PMLA*, xxxiv (1919), 253.

RC 42. After **[B]uḡ**- there is room for another twelve or thirteen rows of runes (i.e. 30–40 letters), down the north-east margin of the shaft. Most editors restore thus, paraphrasing VB 42b. Probably a paraphrase of either 43a or 44a followed, filling out to where the inscription again becomes decipherable, corresponding with VB 44b. Line 44a would be appropriate to the context of the monument and would provide in *rod* a suitable motivation for the congruence of *ba* (see note to *butu*, 48).

44. Rod wæs ic aræred. This collocation recurs frequently in OE verse (cf. *Andreas* 967, *Christ* 1064–5, *Elene* 885–6, *Guthlac* 179–80, etc.) and survives into ME (cf. *þe rode was op a-reride*, C. Brown, ed. *English Lyrics of the Thirteenth Century*, p. 122).

RC 44. Ahof was read by only Haigh and Stephens, although there are strokes, which might correspond to such runes, shown in early drawings like that of de Cardonnell; it might reasonably be restored from VB. For the double vowel in *riicnæ* and the terminal group in *kyniⲛc*, see pp. 28–9, 37.

45. The phrase **heofona Hlaford** ' Lord of the heavens, skies ' is apparently unparalleled in OE, but cf. *heofenes Dryhten* (64). Gen. pl. *heofona* is probably to be understood with the sg. sense of RC *heafunæs*. The use of the pl. form for the sg. sense ' heaven ' seems to have been conventional, however (cf. 103, 134, etc., *Christ* 778, *Phoenix* 626 or the Lindisfarne Gospels gloss, *regnum caelorum: ric heofna, Matt.* xiii. 24). A similar equation of ' skies ' and ' heaven ' occurs in Latin *caelum*.

Hyldan is used transitively here; cf. RC *hælda ic ni dorstæ*.

RC 45. dorstæ. Some early transcripts read the usual Northumbrian form *darstæ* (Campbell, § 767). But as shown by Gordon and de Cardonnell, the return of the second *o*-rune lateral is clear although the lateral itself is not. Cf. VB *dorste*.

46-7. C. Schaar (*Critical Studies*, p. 178) notices here the only true case of adversative asyndeton in the poem. For the phraseology cf. *Andreas* 1397, or *Christ* 1107-9, *þa openan dolg . . . geseoð . . . mid næglum þurhdrifan niðhycgende.*

46. deorcan. A dat. pl. suffix *-an* is not unusual in WS, probably introduced by analogy from dat. sg. or nom. acc. pl. forms (Campbell, § 656).

Adjectives like *sweart* or *brun* are commonly applied to the iron of e.g. weapons (cf. *Riddles XVII* 7-8, *XCIII* 18, etc.), although this contrasts directly with the Constantinian tradition, in which the nails of the Crucifixion are visualised as bright, shining jewels (e.g. *Elene* 1114-15; and cf. Fortunatus' *dulces clavos*, *PL*, lxxxviii. 89). Either of two further possible interpretations would make suitable sense in this context, however. *Deorc* is twice used to gloss *teter* (Wright, 50.17; Napier, 1.1248), indicating a subsidiary meaning ' hideous, horrible ' (cf. *Juliana* 460, *Wanderer* 89). Alternatively Dickins-Ross draw attention to probable Celtic cognate forms like O Irish *derg*, Gaelic *dearg* ' red, bloody '.

47. opene. Pope (p. 141, n. 25), remarking that the adjective ought to take the primary rather than secondary accent, suggests reading *opne*. But unorthodox metre occurs as the result of similar forms in other opening half-lines of VB: *geopenie, geopenigean, Elene* 791a, 1101a.

The combination **inwid-hlemm** occurs only here, a line-break separating the two elements in the MS. *Inwid* usually denotes ' wicked, malicious '. In *Christ* 1109 similar phraseology describing the nails includes the word *niðhycgende* ' bearing malice '; and cf. *Andreas* 1394, and the Vercelli homily cited in note to *strælum*, 62.

The second element *hlemm* usually denotes a sound of some kind and is associated with *hlemman* ' to clash, crash '; it is used of shields in battle (*Judith* 205) or a whale's jaws closing (*Whale* 61). O Frisian *hlemm* ' blow ' and Gothic *hlamma* ' trap, snare ' suggest that the semantic field of OE *hlemm* might have included ' sound, as of a blow ' and hence the blow or wound itself. For the association of blow and wound in this context see William of Malmesbury cited in note to *strælum*, 62.

nænigum sceððan. Many editors, seeking to provide regular alliteration, follow Sievers (*PBB*, xii (1887), 462) in the simple emendation to *ængum* or *ænigum*. But as Grein–Wülcker first noticed, lack of alliteration in a second half-line is by no means uncommon in VB verse, while the double negation is common OE usage. The same collocation occurs in *Christ* 1466, *se ðe nængum scod*.

48. **Bysmeredon hie.** This presumably refers to the mockery by the Jews (*Matt.* xxvii. 41, *Mark* xv. 31) rather than the slightly earlier mockery by Roman soldiers (*Matt.* xxvii. 29, *Mark* xv. 20). OE Gospel glosses invariably use *bysmerian* for *inludere, inlusere, deridere* in both incidents.

butu ætgædere. RC reads fem. *ba*, presumably in congruence with *rod*, understood, anticipating 56 or recalling 44. As both masc. *Crist* and fem. *rod* are understood in *unc*, VB employs neut. acc. *butu*. This is not uncommonly found in congruence with both masc. and fem. forms in early texts, however (Campbell, § 683; H. Bauch, *Die Kongruenz in der angelsächsische Poesie*, § 14a).

RC 48. **Bismærædu.** Most editors follow Stephens in emending to *bismæradu(n)*. The second *æ*, although clearly carved on the cross, cannot be justified historically; pret. pls. of weak class II verbs (or *bysmerian* might possibly represent a weak class III verb, cf. Campbell, § 764) normally have the penultimate vowel *a, o* or *u*. An error of this kind might have occurred due to the similarity of *æ* and *a*-runes, the carver's eye perhaps carrying over the form of the previous syllable.

uŋket. The normal acc. of the dual *wit* is *unc*, as VB. Forms in *-et* occur most frequently in late prose texts (Campbell, § 703).

ætgad[re]. The third character is now unclear but Haigh's transcript gives the etymologically correct velar form ᛢ (and might be compared with Gibb's reading of the ŋ-rune ᛤ). Several early transcripts read final *-e*.

blodæ. Duncan, de Cardonnell and Haigh (and cf. Ross, 149–51), read the archaic form *blodi* (cf. *rodi*, 56) after the preposition *miþ*. But as shown by Gibb the lateral strokes of the *æ*-rune are quite visible on the cross.

49. **Guma** is found nowhere else in quite this sense. It might have been assumed to be the direct equivalent of Vulgate *homo*, although the OE Gospels regularly render that *mann* (cf. *Mark* xv. 39, *John* xix. 5). A cognate form does occur in this sense in OS *Heliand* 5743, etc.

gast onsended. The death of Christ is frequently expressed thus in both verse and prose (cf. *Andreas* 1327, *Elene* 480; Vercelli Homily I, *Prosa*, xii, p. 38). The concept derives from biblical tradition: Lindisfarne Gospels gloss, *Matt.* xxvii. 50, *emisit spiritum: asende gast* (cf. Rankin, *JEGP*, ix (1910), 70–2).

RC 49. After the last decipherable characters **bi-** there is room for about another forty runes down the south-eastern margin of the shaft. Gibb read *bi·ot·n of* and *bigoten of . . .* might be sensibly restored from VB. Kaiser expands to: *bi[goten of his sidan . . .]*, and Casieri: *bi[goten of þæs guman sidan . . .]*.

50–1. **Feala ... wraðra wyrda.** For the syntax, cf. 79–80a, 125–6a and note to 37–8; and cf. *Finnsburh* 25–6, *fæla ic weana gebad, heardra hilda.*

52. **þearle þenian.** Some, following Kemble, interpret the verb here as a form of *þegnian* ' to serve ', but more direct sense is given if interpreted as a variant of *þennan* ' to stretch out '. Cf. the passive sense of: *Crist wæs on rode aðened* (*Benedictine Office*, ed. J. M. Ure, p. 97), and *mid apenedum earmum* (Vercelli Homily XI, VB f. 72ᵛ).

Collocation with the adverb *þearle* compares with the phraseology of Latin hymns like Fortunatus' ' Pange lingua ', *ut superni membra regis miti tendas stipite* or ' Vexilla regis ', *tendens manus vestigia* (PL, lxxxviii, 89, 95).

Þystro is the word chosen in each OE version of the Gospels to render *tenebrae* in the Vulgate account of this phenomenon (*tenebrae factae sunt super universam terram, Matt.* xxvii 45; cf. *Luke* xxiii. 44) and is conventional to poet and homilist alike (cf. *Christ* 1132–3, *Kentish Hymn* 28; Vercelli Homily I, *Prosa*, xii, p. 35).

54. **scirne sciman ... forð eode.** There has been some confusion as to the nature of the verb here. The elements *forð* and *eode* are separated in the MS., but *forð* has generally been assumed to form the prefix of some kind of compound verb. Cook (*MLN*, xxii (1907), 207) considered that such a form might have arisen as a scribal error for *sweðrode*, noticing the common collocation of *sceadu* with *swiðrian* and the closely similar context of *Andreas* 836–7, *scire scinan. Sceadu sweðerodon, wonn under wolcnum.*

No emendation is necessary, however. There are two possible interpretations of a compound *forðēode*. Some, following Kemble, understand it to represent the pret. of the rare weak verb *forðēon*, *forðȳwan* ' to oppress, overcome ', presumably cognate with OHG *farduhian* (cf. Campbell, § 753 (8), n. 3).   Thus, reading without a break between the half-lines and taking *sciman* as the object, we might translate: '... Lord's corpse; shadow overcame the bright radiance '.

Others, following Thorpe, take *forð-ēode* as the pret. of *forð-gān* ' to go, come forth ', a compound verb found occasionally in later prose (cf. B. Weman, *Old English Semantic Analysis and Theory*, pp. 101–2).   There is no reason, however, why the MS. reading should not represent an earlier stage in which *forð* was not a prefix but a separate adverb as in *forð gewiton*, 132–3 (cf. Pope, p. 228, n. 17).   Either way this second half-line might then stand by itself, *scirne sciman* being taken as the object of *hæfdon bewrigen*, paralleling and amplifying *Wealdendes hræw* in the previous line. This might then be rendered: '... the Lord's corpse, bright radiance; shadow went forth '.

55. **wann under wolcnum.**   For this collocation, especially associated with *sceadu, pystro,* cf. *Andreas* 836–7 (cited in note to 54), *Beowulf* 1374, *Guthlac* 1280. Although *wann* is occasionally already used to gloss *pallidus* (e.g. Napier, 23.34), it is most commonly used to mean ' dusky ', apparently denoting a rather vague shade, neither dark nor bright (Wyld, *Essays and Studies*, xi (1925), 89).

Weop eal gesceaft.   The lament of all creation at the death of Christ—a commonplace of contemporary literature (cf. *Christ* 1127–30, 1174–5, 1182 or Ælfric, *Homs*, i, pp. 108, 228; ii, p. 258)— may have derived from Leo the Great's crucifixion homilies (*PL*, liv. 324–5, 330, 341, etc.) or the apocryphal Gospel of Nicodemus, *in tua morte omnis contremuit creatura et universa sidera commota sunt* (ed. C. Tischendorf, *Evangelia Apocrypha*, p. 399).   The concept was familiar from classical elegies, however, and Cook draws attention to the parallel with Orpheus, at whose death all created things were said to have wept and with whom some early eastern theologians compared Christ.   Others, like Stephens or Hammerich, find a striking similarity with the ON account of nature's lament for Baldr (*Snorra Edda*, ed. F. Jónsson, (1926), p. 64 f.).   But as E. S. Bugge pointed out (*Götter- und Heldensagen*, pp. 59–61), any connection with the *Dream* is likely to have taken the form of influence from western Christian sources on ON literature rather than vice-versa.

The principal panel of the Ruthwell Cross depicts a similar theme, the inscription reading *IHS Christus Judex: aequitatis, bestiae et dracones cognoverunt in deserto salvatorem mundi*. The only part of the OE inscription on the upper shaft which remains even possibly legible has been tentatively interpreted [*wœp*]*dœ gisgæf*[*t*] (see p. 31).

56. **cwiðdon**. The collective noun *gesceaft*, supplied with a singular verb in the previous line, is given a plural verb here (and in 82–3). Abrupt change of number is not infrequent with collective nouns, however (cf. R. Quirk and C. L. Wrenn, *An Old English Grammar*, § 126).

The verb *cwiðan* is unknown to the Cynewulf canon (cf. M. Trautmann, *Kynewulf*, p. 40), but it occurs relatively frequently in the third part of *Christ* (891, 961, 1130, etc.), with which Das and Schaar would group the *Dream*.

RC 56. **Rodi** is presumably, like VB *rode*, dative in form with a locative sense. See also p. 37.

57. **fuse feorran cwoman**. For the semantic field of *fus* ' eager, hastening, moving, shining, doomed ', see note to 21. While no specific allusion is necessary, the adjectival noun *fuse* ' eager ones ' has commonly been identified with the disciples Joseph and Nicodemus, the descent from the cross following immediately afterwards (*cf. John* xix. 38–9). Ælfric describes Joseph coming *hrædlice, hraðe* (*Homs*, ii, p. 260). Wyatt, disturbed by what seems to be a departure from biblical tradition, finds *feorran cwoman* difficult to reconcile with Joseph and Nicodemus and instead interprets *fuse* as ' eager angels ', comparing RC 57–8, ' eager noble ones came from afar '. The subsequent actions of *beornas* and *hilderincas* (66, 72) are not those of angels, however, while RC *æþþilæ* (58) as a designation for disciples, although otherwise unrecorded, accords well with early heroic religious literary convention (cf. *Dryhtnes þegnas*, 75).

58. **to þam æðelinge**. Sweet, without comment, replaced this phrase with *æðele to anum*, normalised from RC. For a possible connection between VB and RC versions see p. 40. Christ is occasionally described elsewhere as *æðeling* (e.g. *Christ* 158, 448).

RC 58. **æþþilæ til anum**. Most assume a pronominal use of *anum* here in the sense of ' a lone, solitary person ', as in e.g. *Beowulf* 2461, *an æfter anum*. Rissanen, however (*NM*, lxviii (1967), 283–7), argues that no other instance occurs of OE or early

ME *an* as a pronoun independent of any other noun or pronoun, and no independent adverbial use of *an* ' alone ' before early ME. But the phrase *to anum* does occasionally occur to denote a union or coming together (cf. *ASC*, i, pp. 62–3) so that Rissanen would translate ' together, to the same place '.

59. MS. mid gedrefed. RC reads *mi[þ] sorgum gidrœ[fi]d*, and with the same phrase reduplicated at VB 20, all editors since Grein have inserted *sorgum*.

þam secgum to handa, literally ' to the men to hand ', i.e. ' to the men's hands ', Bosworth–Toller ' within reach '; cf. *Beowulf* 1983, *hæleðum to handa*; *Genesis* 1463, *to handa halgum*.

RC 59. Sar[æ] . . . sorgum. Dietrich read *sæ[re] . . . sargu*, and Zupitza–Schipper also restored *sare*. The first vowels of either form are quite clearly cut, however. Adjectival adverbs like *sare* commonly end in -*æ* in early texts (Campbell, § 661; and cf. Sievers, *PBB*, viii (1882), 326).

After **h[n]ag** there is room for some six rows of runes (i.e. about eighteen characters) down the south-west margin, which would just accommodate the remainder of the corresponding VB line with the exception of *hwæðre*, which is in any case grammatically and metrically unnecessary.

61. ahofon hine of ðam hefian wite. The verb is used in this sense elsewhere only in *Elene* 481–2, *þa siððan wæs of rode ahæfen rodera wealdend*. For the figurative equivalence of *rod* and *wite* cf. *ic wæs geworden wita heardost* (87); and for the sense ' punishment, torment ' cf. *Gesetze*, ii, pp. 246–7, and Keiser, p. 130.

þa hilderincas. *þa* might be construed either as adverbial ' then ' or as a plural determiner with *hilderincas* ' the, those warriors ' (Stevick, *NM*, lxviii (1967), 166). This heroic epithet for ' disciples ' occurs elsewhere only at 72.

62. standan steame bedrifenne. Neither *steam* ' moisture ', here ' blood ', nor *bedrifan* ' to drench, bespatter ', are otherwise recorded with just these senses. Bouterwek emended to *stane bedrifene*. But cf. *Andreas* 1494, *standan storme bedrifene*; and Dickins–Ross compare ON *driffin bloði*, *doggu* ' sprinkled with blood, dew '. The pp. *bedrifenne* takes the masculine form, so that here the cross must be understood as masc. *gealga* rather than fem. *rod*.

mid strælum forwundod ' wounded with arrows, darts '. Here, as Cook suggested, there may possibly be an allusion to words recorded of Joseph, the type of Christ in *Genesis* xlix. 23, or prophetic *Psalms* like *LXIII*, 3–4; but these can only have been distant echoes. Alternatively *stræl* might refer to the soldier's spear which pierced the side of Christ (19–20, 48–9) were it not for the plural form of the noun supported by the sense of *eall*. Most probably, however, the word simply represents an heroic metaphor for ' nails '; *gar* is used in the same way in *Christ & Satan* 507–9, *Ic eow þingade þa me on beame beornas sticedon, garum on galgum.* Pertinent comparisons might be drawn with words of a Judgement Day homily in the Vercelli Book: *Þonne hæfð þæt dioful geworht bogan and stræla. Se boga bið geworht of ofermettum; and þa stræla bioð swa manigra cynna, swa swa mannes synna bioð. Sumu stræl byð geworht of· niðe* ... (*Prosa*, xii, p. 103) or William of Malmesbury's description of a jewelled cross formerly at Glastonbury *de qua olim ex percussione sagittae sanguis plurimus virtute divina profluxit* (*PL*, clxxix. 1698).

Some early editors following Stephens, recognised in the use of *strælum* here a link with the Baldr myth, who was slain with *kastvaben*, but cf. note to 55.

63. gestodon him æt his lices heafdum; *him* might represent either the dat. sg. possessive made redundant in NE by *his*, or an ethic dat. pl., ' they placed *themselves* at the head of his body '. The dat. pl. *heafdum*, (also apparently the RC form), occurs in similar contexts elsewhere; cf. *OE Martyrology*: *heoldon þone lichoman, oðer æt þæm heafdum, oðer æt þæm fotum*, EETS, cxvi, p. 80, or Alfred's *Cura Pastoralis*: *ðone stan ðe æt his heafdum læg*, EETS, xlv, p. 101. (Similar use of the plural with *breostum* as at 118, and cf. Wülfing, § 133, is physiologically explicable). The form here must probably be understood as a locative sg. (cf. Campbell, § 574.4) conventionally applied to the head of a corpse or one similarly recumbent. The recognition of such a verbal convention might support Schücking's supposition (*ES*, xxxix (1908), 4–5) of a possible allusion here to the Germanic ' corpse-watching ' funerary rite (cf. note to *sorhleoð*, 67).

RC 63–4. These lines might be partially restored from VB forms. After *þe-* there is room for some six rows of runes (i.e. about eighteen characters) down the north-west margin of the shaft. Dietrich read the last line as: [*h*]*it* [*o*]*nv*[*li*]*t*[*un v*]*e*[*pende* ...] ' cum dolore intuentibus? '; but this is supported by no other early reading and the letters are now totally obliterated. A restoration like Kaiser's, however, *þe[r heafunæs hlaford]*, might well fill the remaining space in suitable accordance with the VB text.

65. Ongunnon him þa moldærn wyrcan. Dickins–Ross consider *onginnan* probably auxiliary here, as at 67, 73, preferring to translate 'they made' rather than 'they began to make' (cf. Wülfing, §§ 480–1).

Moldærn, literally 'earth-house', parallels *eorðscræfu* in *Andreas* 802–3. But Christ's tomb is clearly not conceived in terms of an earthen grave, nor yet the cave of ecclesiastical tradition. The OE Gospels render both *monumentum* and *sepulchrum* as simply *byrgenn* (cf. *Matt.* xxvii. 60–1). But here (and cf. *curfon hie ðæt of beorhtan stane,* 66) the poet seems to have had in mind one of the fine free-standing sculptured stone tombs familiar in late classical and earlier medieval Europe (cf. Vercelli Homily I, *Prosa,* xii, p. 42, Ælfric, *Homs,* ii, p. 262 or OS *Heliand* 5736–7).

A dot has been added both below and above the first element of the *æ* graph in *moldærn*. It is uncertain whether or not it is intended that the *æ* should stand or be emended to *e*. The normal expunction of a graph or part of a graph consists merely of a single dot below (cf. *Andreas* 637, *Exhortation* 21, *Judgment Day II* 155), although a form of double expunction is not unknown (cf. *Elene* 926). If this does represent double expunction, the spelling would conform with the scribe's previous writing *moldern* in *Andreas* 802. In certain instances, however (e.g. *Christ & Satan* 403), the addition of a dot above is apparently intended to reverse a single expunction. In any case, both simple deletion and expunction exist side by side in the Vercelli MS., and the latter might well represent alterations by a later hand. In view of this uncertainty it has been felt best, with Sweet and Kluge, to allow the original form to remain.

66. banan. The idea that the cross itself might be regarded as the 'murderer' of Christ seemed so improbable to some editors as to require correction. Sweet (second edition, 1879) supposed that *banan* might have been mistaken for e.g. *beorg* as at 32, with an original reading something like *on beorges sidan.* Others, supposing the 'murderers' to be the Jews and Romans of biblical tradition, adopt one of two interpretations. Some, like Wyatt, Wrenn (*RES,* xii (1936), 106) and Bolton, assume that *banan,* like *guman* (146), represents a known late WS gen. pl. form (Brunner, § 276, *Anm.* 5). Others simply emend to the conventional gen. pl. form *banana, banena* (cf. Schmitz, *Anglia*, xxxiii (1910), 60–1). All these difficulties seem to arise from a misconception as to the actual connotation of *bana*, however. This is a neutral word meaning simply ' slayer ' and should not be translated in any way that implies criminality. *Bana* may be used of one who slays by way of righteously executing the law, and also of the innocent instrument employed, to which no motive could possibly be ascribed (cf. *ASC*, ii, p. 47). Used thus of swords (e.g. *Beowulf* 2506), there is no reason why it should not apply to the cross here; the poetic personification employed simply heightens the tragic individual involvement.

67–9. Dickins–Ross suggest that better sense might be obtained by placing a full stop after *æfentide*, rather than taking what comes after as either a causal or temporal clause connected by *þa . . . þa.*

67. **sorhleoð galan.** The same phrase is used of the old man's elegy in *Beowulf* 2460; and cf. the ritual lamentation at the grave of Beowulf himself, 3148 ff. It might be regarded as no more than a high-flown expression for mourning (cf. Sievers, *PBB*, xxix (1904), 315, Klaeber, *AB*, xvii (1906), 100) although Schücking (*ES*, xxxix (1908), 4–5, 8–9) considered this, together with *gestodon æt lices heafdum* (63), indicative of an archaic Anglo-Saxon funerary rite (cf. *carmen funebre: licleoþ; luctum: wopleoþ, licsang, birielssang*, Napier, 1.899, 3504). The OS *Heliand* 5741–4 contains a similar note of lamentation.

68. **on þa æfentide.** Short-syllable fem. i-stem nouns early adopted ō-declension endings (Campbell, § 606) so that *þa æfentide* might technically represent either acc. sg. or pl. The note of time is presumably taken from e.g. *Matt.* xxvii. 57, *cum sero.*

69. **þeoden** is a word virtually confined to OE verse, save that the poetic phrase *þegen and þeoden* is occasionally taken into legal contexts (cf. *Gesetze*, i, p. 456).

mæte weorode ' with a small company '. For this use of a comitative dat. cf. *lytle werode*, *ASC*, i, pp. 46, 72, 74–6. That this does not refer to the personalised crosses is plain from *Hwæðere we . . .* (70). Bütow and Mossé recognised in this ' small company ' an allusion to the two Marys (cf. *Matt.* xxvii. 61, *Mark* xv. 47), but it is probably best interpreted as a simple case of OE litotes. At 124 the same phrase is used explicitly thus, paralleling *ana* ' alone ' in the previous line. We might well recognise here an ironic recall of the common formula *weorod unmæte* (*Andreas* 1219, 1682, etc.).

70. **hreotende.** MS. *reotende* ' lamenting, weeping ' might well stand so far as meaning is concerned, and is retained thus by e.g. Grein, Bütow and Bolton. But orthodox alliteration requires the emendation of either *reotende* or *gode*. Craigie simply replaced *gode* by *rume* ' widely ', but this is syntactically awkward and palaeographically incredible. Grein, followed by Stephens and Ebert (*Leipzig Berichte*, xxxvi (1884), 87) altered *gode* to *rode*, which would be more understandable as a scribal error, but appositive to *we*, gives only poor sense.

The emendation of *reotende* has greater support. Kemble and Cook supposed the verb to have been *geotende* ' dripping ', pointing out that while there is no external evidence for the cross weeping, it is said to be drenched with moisture at 22–3 and 62. Most, however, follow Grein (*Germania*, x (1865), 425) in assuming that the scribe wrote *reotende* for its synonymous near homonym *greotende*. This would provide a parallel in syntax, substance and metre with line 24. But while the omission of a single letter is not unknown to the VB scribe, the loss of initial *h-* before the liquids *l* or *r* is an almost regular feature of later texts, including VB (Brunner, § 217, *Anm.* 2). This makes restoration of the synonym *hreotende* (as by Bouterwek) at least equally credible. This would incidentally place emphasis on *Hwæðere* (which bears alliteration also in e.g. *Beowulf* 2442).

71. **stefn.** MS. *syððan up gewat* clearly involves an omission although no lacuna exists in the MS.; *syððan* stands at the end of a line and no doubt a word was missed in passing over to the next. A form is required that both fits alliteratively and accounts grammatically for gen. pl. *hilderinca* (72). Grein and Sweet suggested *storm*, perhaps comparing e.g. *Exodus* 460, *storm up gewat*. But *stefn*, first supplied by Kluge, is eminently suited to this context. It alliterates with *staðol* elsewhere (cf. *Daniel* 560, 581); it parallels *sorhleoð* (67) convincingly, and suits the sense of *hilderinca*. Simply to insert *stefn*, however, produces an unusual hypermetric verse, and some editors choose to omit *syððan* (cf. Pope, p. 101).

73. **Feorgbold** occurs only here although parallel poetic compounds like *feorhhus*, *sawelhus* are found. The concept is confined

to religious OE literature and probably derives from e.g. Vulgate *terrestris domus* (2 *Corinthians* v. 1) rendered by Wærferth *þis eorðlice hus ures lichaman* (*Prosa*, v, p. 296). No doubt from such biblical sources derive parallel conceptions in Latin hymns of e.g. Prudentius (*PL*, lix. 884).

76. gefrūnon; cf. *frīneð* 112. Compensatory lengthening following the loss of *g* before *n* seems to be characteristically WS, occurring in both early and late texts (Campbell, § 243, n. 2).

76b. Although no lacuna exists in the MS., a half-line or more appears to have been omitted from the text. Stephens supplied *fram me hofon*, and Grein *hie me þa of foldan ahofon*, which might be compared with *Elene* 843–4, *ahof of foldgræfe*. Dickins–Ross suggest wording closer to that of *Elene: hofon of foldegræf*. But while such restorations might clarify the narrative, none has MS. authority and the sense is adequate without addition. Such ' missing ' second half-lines are not infrequent in the poetical MSS., and while commonly restored hypothetically, may have been deliberately left thus by the OE poet (cf. G. P. Krapp, *The Junius Manuscript*, p. 170).

77. Grein supplied *and* at the beginning of the line, assuming it to have been lost with what went before and justifying it as an extra-metrical syllable. This was adopted thereafter by only Krapp and Kaiser, although Sweet–Onions followed Kluge's suggestion of opening with an additional syllable in *gegyredon*. No addition is necessary, however.

Precious metals figure strongly in the Constantinian cross-reliquary tradition (see p. 44f), as in the OE prose account of the Invention in which Helena orders that the cross *bewyrcan mid golde and mid seolfre and mid diorwurþum gimmum* (EETS, xlvi, p. 15). And cf. *Elene* 88–90, 1022–6, *Riddle LV* 3–5, Ælfric's Exaltation sermon (EETS, xciv–cxiv, p. 144) or the York Breviary Invention readings (SS, lxxv, p. 273).

78. This line recurs in a Redemption context in *Elene* 511; and cf. *Andreas* 811, *Nu ðu miht gehyran, hyse leofesta*. The use of the vocative with *se* recurs in a similar formula at 95, and cf. *Beowulf* 1474. *Gehyran* probably implies here ' might hear generally, anywhere ', anticipating 80 ff.

79. MS. **bealu-wara weorc** has been questioned on the supposition that *bealu-wara* could not be equated with *sarra sorga* in 80. The form *bealuwa*, however, was noticed to parallel similar miseries in e.g. *Juliana* 311–13 or *Paris Psalter* lxv. 10. Grein therefore proposed reading *bealuwa* (*weorn*) ' a multitude of evils ', assuming the form to represent a gen. pl. noun. Later (*Germania*, x (1865), 425) he suggested a reading closer to the MS., *bealuwra* (*weorc*), taking it to be a gen. pl. adjective paralleling *sarra*. The most straightforward interpretation, however, is that of Stephens, taking *bealu-wara* as the gen. pl. of a compound noun, *bealu* ' misery, evil '+*ware* ' inhabitants '. This word is otherwise unrecorded but is quite explicable as analogy from e.g. *halig-ware*. Britton (*NM*, lxviii (1967), 275–6) draws attention to the description of devils as e.g. *bealowes gast* (*Christ & Satan* 681, 718, etc.), pointing out that *bealu-wara weorc* in apposition to *ic*, ' I, the work of devils (dwellers in misery), have suffered grievous sorrows ', accords well with statements in 30–3.

Weorc occasionally occurs as the object of verbs like *ðolian*, *ðrowian* in e.g. *Beowulf* 1418, 1721. It is a known, although rare, metaphor for ' pain, sorrow ' (A. Szogs, *Die Ausdrücke für ' Arbeit ' und ' Beruf ' im Altenglischen*, p. 126), arising perhaps as a result of confusion with *wærc* ' dolor ' (cf. Campbell, § 227, n. 2).

85. **hlifige under heofenum.** This is clearly within the Constantinian tradition and reminiscent of the poem's opening lines (see pp. 42–6, 51, 64). Cf. the phrase *hlifode to heofontunglum* (*Daniel* 500) used of the tree which appears in the dream of Nebuchadnezzar, or *Riddle LIII* 1, *Ic seah … beam hlifian*.

86. This line would be rendered literally: ' each one of those to whom (*þe him*) is (or ' will be ') awe of me '; the idiom *æghwylcne anra* (cf. *anra gehwylc*, 108) governs the genitive (cf. Wülfing, § 333 f). For apparent lack of congruence in the later part of the construction see H. Stoelke, *Die Inkongruenz zwischen Subjekt und Prädikat im Englischen und in den verwandten Sprachen*, pp. 55–7. For the use of *þara þe* with *ænig* cf. *Andreas* 377–9, *Beowulf* 842–3, 1461. On the possible future sense implicit in *bið* compared with this poet's otherwise regular use of *is*, cf. K. Jost, *Beon und Wesan; eine syntaktische Untersuchung*, p. 10 f.

87f. Cf. Chrysostom, ' Yet that cursed, abominable thing, symbol of the vilest punishment, is now made lovely and desirable … and the symbol that all formerly dreaded is now thus eagerly sought out by all, found everywhere among men … (*PG*, xlviii. 826).

88. **leodum laðost.** *Elene* 976–7 describes the cross as *Iudeum . . . wyrda laðost.*

88b–89a. Cf. *Riddle LXII* 3–4, *ond me weg sylfa ryhtne geryme.* **Lifes weg** is a straightforward rendering of a common biblical concept (cf. *Vitellius Psalter*, ed. J. L. Rosier, xv. 11, *vias vite: wegas lifes.* For the direct equation ' crux, vitae via ', see the pseudo-Chrysostom, *PG*, lii. 839.

91. The compound **holmwudu** occurs only here and its meaning is therefore obscure. OE *holm* most commonly means ' water, ocean ', with a later sense ' island ' presumably adopted from ON *holmr*. Kluge therefore glossed the MS. form ' schiff ', and Bolton ' sea-wood? ' (cf. H. Marquardt, *Die altenglischen Kenningar*, p. 229), but without resolving the difficulty. Kaske (*Traditio*, xxiii (1967), 64–7, n. 69) draws attention to the picture of the ' lignum vitae ' growing beside the waters of Paradise, to which contemporary readers might have recognised an allusion.

Since Kemble, however, most editors emend to read the known poetic compound *holtwudu* ' forest tree ' (cf. *Beowulf* 1369, *Phoenix* 171). This interpretation might be supported by the analogue the poet draws between the tree honoured above all others and Mary above all other women (92–3), and liturgical parallels in e.g. the hymn ' Pange lingua ', *Crux fidelis, inter omnes arbor una nobilis, nulla talem silva profert, flore, fronde, germine* (*PL*, lxxxviii, 89) or Exaltation antiphons in the York Breviary, *Super omnia ligna cedrorum tu sola excelsior* (SS, lxxv. 556–7). But unless the scribe unconsciously read Anglian *halm* ' trunk ', the alteration from *holt* to *holm* is not palaeographically credible.

One further possibility remains. In commenting on the Domesday Book place-name *Homestreu*, Ekwall (*AB*, xxxv (1924), 28) suggested that *holm* might have had the sense of OS *holm* ' hill '; (and cf. Stephens' gloss ' hill-tree ', and Grein ' lignum montis '). While this sense is unrecorded in OE, it certainly exists in early ME (cf. Layamon's *Brut* 20712, 20861). With this sense the compound *holmwudu* might provide a powerful oblique reference to the gallows of Golgotha (cf. *beorg*, 32), the wood on the hill now made into a towering symbol of victory. It is interesting that a ' Mons Calvariae ' at St. Albans was originally known as Holmhurste (*Gesta abbatum monasterii S. Albani*, ed. H. T. Riley, *RS*, xxviii (1867–76), i, p. 18). For *ofer* in the sense ' passing over, more than ', cf. Wülfing, § 772.

92. **swylce swa.** For the use of this combination as a conjunctive adverb see E. E. Ericson, *The Use of ' swa ' in Old English*, p. 37. A similar link between Mary and the cross is made by Irenaeus, *Patrologia Orientalis*, xii. 684–5.

93. It is unlikely that **for** simply duplicates the local sense in *ofer* (94), which is in any case normally expressed by *for*+dat. Here *for*+acc. should probably be rendered ' for the sake of . . .', or better ' on behalf of . . .', underlining Mary's representative role with the latent implication that this too might also apply to the cross.

98. **se ðe . . . on þrowode.** Compare the phraseology of 145 and *Christ* 1154, *Menologium* 85–6 or Benedictine Office, *þe he syððan on þrowode* (ed. J. M. Ure, p. 95). For this kind of relative construction cf. Curme, *JEGP*, xi (1912), 186–9.

100. **Ealdgewyrht** occurs elswhere only in *Beowulf* 2657, and then in a different sense; but this must clearly be equated with the more frequent *ærgewyrht* (cf. *Christ* 1240, *Elene* 1301, *Guthlac* 987, 1079, *Juliana* 702). The conception of Christ as a second Adam redeeming the fault of the first is commonplace in medieval theology; cf. Fortunatus (*PL*, lxxxviii. 264) or the seventh-century Bobbio Missal Invention liturgy (ed. E. A. Lowe, p. 87).

101. **Deað he þær byrigde.** This concept (recurring at 113–14 and cf. *bitran deaðe*, *Christ* 1474–5, *Daniel* 223) might derive directly from e.g. Vulgate *gustare mortem* (*Matt.* xvi. 28, *Mark* ix. 1, rendered in the CCCC. MS. CXL version as *dead onbyrigan*), or indirectly from liturgical use like that of the Leofric Missal (ed. F. E. Warren, p. 141). It is commonly used in connection with the fruit of the palm tree, itself taken as a type of the cross (see note to *gestigan*, 34; and cf. Alanus de Insulis, *PL*, ccx. 225).

102a is barely hypermetric as it stands and Kluge, followed by Pope (p. 101), suggests reading *miht* rather than *mihte* so as to make a normal line.

102b. **mannum to helpe.** The formula *hæleðum*, *guman*, *leoðum to helpe* recurs frequently in OE verse (cf. *Beowulf* 1709, 1961, *Christ* 427, 1173, *Elene* 679, 1011, etc.).

103–21. G. Grau (*Quellen und Verwandtschaften der älteren germanischen Darstellungen des jüngsten Gerichtes*, p. 175) supposed this part of the cross speech might derive from Ephraem Syrus, but the development of ideas is a natural and easy one.

103. **He ða on heofenas astag.** This phraseology (and cf. *Christ* 737) is reminiscent of the Creed, *ascendit ad caelus*, which in turn presumably derived from e.g. *Mark* xvi. 19, *adsumtus est in caelum*, rendered by the OE Hatton version, *he astah in to heofene*.

104. Cf. *Andreas* 1502, *on middangeard mancynn secan*, or *Christ* 523–4, 945–7.

106. **ond his englas mid.** For this type of construction with *mid* (and cf. *Andreas* 237, *Beowulf* 889, *Christ* 1521, *Daniel* 353), see E. Hittle, *Zur Geschichte der altenglischen Präpositionen ' mid ' und ' wið '*, pp. 101–2.

107–8. Cf. the phraseology of *Judgment Day II* 95–6, *heah-þrymme cyninge her wile deman anra gehwylcum be ærdædum*.

107. **þæt . . . wile deman.** For the construction following *þæt* see note to 34. For *deman* construed with a dat. object, see Wülfing, §§ 75, 78.

Se ah domes geweald is primarily a legal phrase (cf. *Gesetze*, i, p. 308, ii, p. 101) but occurs in verse elsewhere, e.g. *Christ* 228, *Elene* 725, *Gifts* 27, etc.

108. **ærur.** This form of double comparative is familiar Northumbrian usage (cf. H. C. A. Carpenter, *Die Deklination in der nordhumbrischen Evangelienübersetzung der Lindisfarner Hand-schrift*, p. 273). *Ærur* is unknown to the Cynewulfian canon (cf. M. Trautmann, *Kynewulf*, p. 40) but occurs (beside *ærra*) in *Beowulf* 809, 2654, 3168, and therefore probably arose early.

109. **on þyssum lænum life.** This common Christian formula recurs at 138, and cf. *Beowulf* 2845, *Seafarer* 65–6, etc.

geearnaþ. As at 118, a future perfect sense might be implied by *ærur*; cf. *Christ* 1233, *swa hi geworhtun ær*.

110. This line is rhetorically echoed at 117, working out the poem's conclusion in terms of a parallel antithesis: ' None need be unafraid . . . none need be very afraid '. The same form is employed by Hwætberht; see p. 67, n. 3.

112. **sie.** Regular metrical scansion would suggest disyllabic pronunciation here, as terminally elsewhere in *Bede's Death Song* (Northumbrian version) 2, *Beowulf* 682, 1831, 2649 or *Juliana* 280 (cf. C. Richter, *Chronologische Studien zur angelsächsischen Literatur*, pp. 79–80).

113. **deaðes wolde.** In writing first *deaðes prowode* the scribe seems to have been influenced by the form of 84 or 98.

115. **Fea** is ambiguous. It might be taken, as Grein and most
subsequent editors suppose, as a rare adverb (cf. *Libri Psalmorum*,
ed. B. Thorpe, cxxxiv. 18), to be rendered: '. . . and little think of
what they will try to say '. Alternatively, as e.g. Bolton prefers,
it might be taken as a nom. pl. adjectival noun, to be rendered
'. . . and few think of what they will try to say '.

117. **Ænig unforht** repeats and parallels 110. The prefix *un*-
almost always denotes a negative in OE but here the very opposite
sense is required. Bouterwek altered to *ænigum fyrht*, which
might be an understandable error only if the scribe wrote at
dictation. Grein read first *onforht* and later (*Germania*, x (1865),
425), followed by most editors, *anforht*—with the prefix understood as an intensive, ' very afraid, terrified '. But Wülcker's
revision, and more recently Bolton, Lehnert and Magoun, returned to the MS. form. The prefix *un-* is not unknown as an
intensive; cf. *unæt, unhirwan, unstenc* etc.; and from the Vercelli
MS. might be added at least *untrywan, untimbrum* (ff. 2^r, 73^v).
Word-play of this kind is characteristic of the *Dream* poet.

118. Tatwine's cross riddle concludes with a similar statement;
see p. 67, n. 4. It is unlikely that this refers to the wearing of
pectoral crosses here (where *in* might mean ' on '), the use of which
must always have been limited. But it might allude to the
contemporary baptismal practice of pectoral unction and thus
embrace the whole community of baptised Christians (cf. Alcuin,
PL, ci. 613). Physical and spiritual significances are meaningfully juxtaposed in the seventh-century Bobbio Missal rite:
*Accipe signum crucis tam in fronte quam et in corde semper esto
fidelis* (ed. E. A. Lowe, p. 71). It might simply thus imply the
common metaphorical sense of e.g. *Christ & Satan* 201–5, *Gemunan
we þone halgan drihten . . . beoran on breostum bliðe gepohtas* (or cf.
Christ 1072, *Genesis* 656, *Guthlac* 797 f.). Such abstract use of the
symbol was widely encouraged from earliest Christian times
(cf. p. 43, n. 1).

On the use of dat. pl. **breostum** where the sg. might have been
expected after *þearf*, 117 (and cf. *Wanderer* 113) see note to
heafdum, 63.

120. **of eorðwege.** For this use of *of* construed with a dat. (as
in the similar context of *Elene* 735, *of eorðwegum up geferan*) see
Wülfing, §§ 734, 739.

122a. **Gebæd ic me þa to þan beame** apparently echoes 83a, *gebiddaþ him to þyssum beacne.* Bouterwek and Kemble altered *þan* to *þam*, but the MS. form is found as a perfectly acceptable masc. dat. sg. in late WS and Northumbrian texts (Brunner, § 337).

125. afysed on forðwege. For similar collocations cf. *Exodus* 129, 248, *Guthlac* 801, 939, 945, *Menologium* 218. Motion is implicit in *afysan*, and acc. rather than dat. forms everywhere follow *on* (although cf. *Wanderer* 81, *in forðwege*). Pope therefore, like Klaeber (*AB*, xvii (1906), 102), prefers to read *forðweg* here, thus forming a straightforward A- rather than an expanded D-type verse.

126. langung-hwil. The two elements of this form are separated by MS. line-division, but the former is uninflected and most editors understand it to represent a compound noun. Occurring only here, however, its exact meaning is obscure. The element *hwil* clearly refers to a time of duration, occurring in parallel compounds like *gescæp-, sige-hwil*, but *langung* has been variously interpreted. Bütow, supposing that it referred to the injuries mentioned at 50–1 or 79–80, suggested the meaning ' times of iniquity or injustice ', but this interpretation lacks external support. Dickins–Ross drew attention to the Paris Psalter gloss, *taedio: langunga* (cxviii. 28), but their extension of this to ' accidia ' (cf. Fleming, *Traditio*, xxii (1966), 63) is misleading; at this time *taedium* normally means ' weariness, unease '. OE *langung* usually denotes simply ' longing, yearning ', often of a religious kind (cf. Blickling Homily XII, EETS, lviii–lxiii, pp. 131, 135). Use in this sense is in perfect accordance with the text at this point. The poet, inspired with a spiritual longing for the kingdom of heaven, in the anticipation of which lies his *lifes hyht* (126), often yearns to set out, *afysed on forðwege* (125). The same association of *langung* with hope and eagerness for a journey occurs in *Resignation* 98f, *Seafarer* 45–50, etc.

Lifes hyht recurs at 148. The semantic field of *hyht* includes the closely associated senses of ' hope, faith, joy ' (cf. *Christ* 864, *Elene* 797, *Guthlac* 659, *Resignation* 37, etc.). This Christian ' hope ' is commonly juxtaposed with the cross symbol in contemporary Latin hymns and liturgy; cf. *o crux ave spes unica* (SS, lxxv, p. 156; xxiii, 270, 552).

127. sigebeam secan. Fleming (*Traditio*, xxii. (1966), 65–6) draws attention to the common early penitential practice of ' going to the cross '. But penitence is less dominant than faith and joy at this point in the poem, and a more pertinent parallel might be drawn with words of a probably eighth-century insular cross panegyric from the Book of Cerne, *Securus ergo et gaudens venio ad te* (ed. A. B. Kuypers, p. 161). There clearly exist in **secan mote** here both present and future senses.

128. **Ana** is unlikely here to have either an exclusive Pharisaical sense, or that of ' friendlessness ' (cf. 131–2). Rather, the poet finds his *hyht* in that he alone, because of his vision, is in a more favourable position than others to adore the cross.

130. **Mundbyrd** normally glosses *patrocinium* (Wright, 36.36, 276.34, etc.) and seems to have been used primarily as a legal term denoting the protection granted by a superior in return for a bond of service (*Gesetze*, ii, p. 150). Here the cross stands in the position of spiritual patron to the visionary who now adores it, *well weorþian* (129). It is perhaps therefore best rendered ' my source (*or* hope) of protection '. Cf. *Guthlac* 542, or *Resignation* 109, where it is Christ who is the penitent's *meahtig mundbora*.

133a is technically hypermetric but might be made normal by reading *woruld-dreamum* (Pope, p. 101). Trautmann and Schmitz (*Anglia*, xxxiii (1910), 61) preferred to alter *Cyning* to *Dryhten* for the sake of alliteration, but this is unnecessary.

134. **lifiaþ.** S. K. Das (*Cynewulf*, p. 36, n. 85), apparently recalling the formula *hlifige under heofenum* 85, suggested reading *hlifiað* here, which might suit the context equally well. Initial *h*-before the liquids *l* or *r* is characteristically lost in later texts (cf. note to *hreotende*, 70). This word begins a new MS. line so that the loss would be palaeographically doubly credible.

Heahfæder is normally used to gloss *patriarcha* (cf. Wright, 155.3, 307.36) and but for the singular number might have been thought to do so here. Instead it must be understood in the relatively rare sense of ' Almighty Father '. It occurs thus only once elsewhere in verse (*Christ & Satan* 654). The Lindisfarne and Rushworth Gospels use this unusual word to gloss *abba, pater* (*Mark* xiv. 36).

135. The common collocation **wuniaþ on wuldre** recurs twice before the end of the poem, at 143 and 155.

136. The form **hwænne** is found in late WS and Anglian texts (Brunner, § 79, *Anm.* 3). For the metre of the second half-line see C. Richter, *Chronologische Studien zur angelsächsischen Literatur*, p. 47.

137. A syntactical and metrical echo of this line occurs at 145.

138. **on þysson lænan life gefetige.** Grein suggested reading *of* for *on*, perhaps comparing usage like *of þyssum lænan life feran* (*gehweorfe*), *Genesis* 1211 or *Prayer* 73. But the MS. phraseology accords perfectly well with e.g. *Crist, þe sitt on heofonum . . . mid eallum þam halgum þe he on ðisum life gefette* (Ælfric, *Homs,* i, p. 248). And for *on*+dat. with verbs meaning ' take, seize, reach after etc.' cf. Wülfing, § 814.

For the rare dat. form **þysson** see K. D. Bülbring, *Altenglisches Elementarbuch,* § 568; and cf. *þan* (122).

139–41. **þær is blis mycel . . . þær is singal blis.** A. Brandl (*Geschichte der altenglischen Literatur,* i, p. 1031) recognised in this anaphora the influence of Latin homiletic rhetoric. An ultimate source might be Augustine or Gregory (*PL,* xl. 1351–3; lxxix. 657–8) but this general concept of the heavenly life is found throughout OE religious literature (cf. Blickling Homily V, EETS, lviii–lxxiii, p. 65, or the pseudo-Wulfstan, *Homilien,* ed. A. S. Napier, pp. 139–40). This kind of *þær*-clause is found extensively in non-Cædmonian religious verse (C. Schaar, *Critical Studies,* pp. 304–8).

141. **Geseted to symle** as an image of the heavenly life derives from biblical sources like *Luke* xiv. 15 or *Revelation* xix. 9. For the phrase *to symle* cf. *Beowulf* 489, 2104, *Daniel* 700, *Judith* 15, etc.

142. **He** is probably to be read as the subject of **asette,** presumably referring to *Dryhten* (140), with the object *me* understood or carried over from 139. Some, however, following Bouterwek, prefer to emend MS. *he* to *me* in order to provide the object, the subject being taken to refer right back to *rod* (136).

146. **Gealgtreow** normally means simply ' gallows ' (cf. Napier, 1.391, *patibulo: on gealgan treowe,* and note to *gealga,* 10). In this sense it is apparently unique to the *Dream* (cf. Rankin, *JEGP,* ix (1910), 62). Normally such a description of the cross is more explicit, as in the Durham Ritual gloss, *crucis patibulum: rodes galgatre* (SS, cxl, pp. 23, 124).

guman. Cook, Craigie and Sweet–Whitelock altered to the conventional gen. pl. *gumena,* but this is unnecessary (see note to *banan,* 66). Dickins–Ross draw attention to the gloss *cogitationes hominum*: *guman geðancas* (*Libri Psalmorum,* ed. B. Thorpe, xciii. 11). Probably here, *guma,* like its cognate *homo,* represents the generic sg. 'mankind '.

148. **Hiht wæs geniwad.** The same phrase occurs in similar contexts at Christ's entrance into heaven in *Christ* 529–30, and at the death of the saint in *Guthlac* 953.

149. **mid bledum ond mid blisse.** This collocation recurs frequently in OE verse; cf. *Christ* 1256, 1346, 1657, *Guthlac* 1374, *Rune Poem* 24, etc. For the semantic field of *bled* ' glory, prosperity, blessedness ' see Wyld (*Essays and Studies*, xi (1925), 87–8).

þam þe þær. *Þær* might be used here in an existential sense, or as a specific adverb of place referring to hell (cf. *Beowulf* 1123). Grein suggested that either two half-lines had been omitted from between 149a and b, or alternatively that *þær* was written in error for *ær*. The reading *ær* was adopted by Cook and Craigie, apparently comparing 154b or *Christ* 799, 916, 1260, etc.

150. The word **Sunu** is used of Christ elsewhere in phrases denoting a simple relationship (cf. *Christ* 110, *sunu soþan fæder*; *Elene* 461, *sunu meotudes*), but occurs nowhere else so bluntly in this direct theological sense. *Sunu* seems to be a direct rendering of Vulgate *filius* as found in glosses to e.g. *John* v. 21, viii. 35–6. For the common variation *Bearn Godes* (83) see Keiser, p. 83.

sigorfæst on þam siðfate. This might refer either to the Harrowing of Hell as a whole or merely to Christ's return to heaven, depending upon whether or not a pause is placed between 151a and b. The terms are those of heroic verse but occur in religious contexts elsewhere (cf. *Andreas* 1662, *Exodus* 522, etc.). In the Durham Hymnal we are told that Christ, *victor redit de barathro: sigefæst he gehwerfde of helle* (SS, xxiii, p. 83).

151. **manigeo.** Cook preferred the regular WS form *mænigeo* as at 112, and Bütow the more frequent Northumbrian *menigeo* (Campbell, § 193d, n.4). The MS. form *man-* is well documented, however.

156. **eðel.** Except in phrases like *engla eðel* (*Andreas* 642) this word applies to the worldly homelands of men rather than the heavenly, but used figuratively it can be extended to the true home of the spiritual peregrinus in exile here on earth (cf. *nu eft sceolon operne epel secan . . . þone ecean eðel*, Blickling Homilies II and XVII, EETS, lviii–lxxiii, pp. 23, 209). It is in this sense that *eðel* is used in the conclusions to parts I and III of *Christ* (436, 1639) and in *Creed* 32, 37.

GLOSSARY

The glossary lists occurrences of all forms found in the texts. Those of the Ruthwell Cross inscription are intercalated with corresponding Vercelli Book forms and are preceded by the abbreviation RC. The order of words is alphabetical; æ follows ad-; words prefixed by ge-follow geāra; ð and þ are treated as one letter and follow t. The gender of nouns is indicated by the abbreviations m., f. and n. (noun being implied). The numbers after sv. and wv. refer to the classes of strong and weak verbs respectively. The remaining abbreviations used are self-explanatory. The glossary is intended to be used with the notes, which supplement it.

ac *conj.* but 11, 43, 115, 119, 132.

Ādom *prop. name gen. sg.* Ādomes 100.

æfentīd *f.* evening-time; *acc. sg.* æfentīde 68.

æfter *prep. w. dat.* after 65.

æghwylc *adj.* each, every; *f. nom. sg.* 120.

æghwylc *pron.* everyone; *m. acc. sg.* æghwylcne (ānra) 86.

ælmihtig *adj.* almighty; *m. nom. sg.* (RC almehttig) 39, 93, 98, 106, 153, 156; *m. acc. sg.* ælmihtigne 60.

ǣnig *pron.* any, anyone; *m. nom. sg.* 110, 117; *m. dat. sg.* (*neg.*) nǣnigum 47.

ǣr *adv.* before, formerly 114, 118, 137, 145, 154; *comp.* ǣrur earlier 108; *sup.* ǣrest first 19.

ǣrgewin *n.* former struggle, strife; *acc. sg.* 19.

ǣrþan *conj.* before 88.

æt *prep. w. dat.* at 8, 63.

ætgædere *adv.* together (RC ætgadre) 48.

æðeling *m.* lord, prince; *dat. sg.* æðelinge 58.

æþþilæ *adjvl. noun* noble ones; *nom. pl.* RC 58.

āfȳsan *wv.* 1 to impel, urge forward; *pp. m. nom. sg.* āfȳsed 125.

āgan *pret. pres. v.* to have, possess; *1 sg. pres.* (*neg.*) nāh 131; *3 sg. pres.* āh 107.

āhēawan *sv.* 7 to hew, cut down; *pp. m. nom. sg.* āhēawen 29.

āhebban *sv.* 6 to raise, lift up (lift down, remove 61); *1 sg. pret.* āhōf 44; *3 pl. pret.* āhōfon 61.

ālecgan *wv.* 1 to lay down; *3 pl. pret.* ālēdon (RC ālegdun) 63.

ān *adj.* one; *wk. m. nom. sg.* āna 'alone' 123, 128; *m. dat. sg.* RC ānum 58; *gen. pl.* ānra 86, 108; *see* æghwylcne (ānra) *and* (ānra) gehwylc.

Anwealda *m.* sovereign, lord; *nom. sg.* 153.

ārǣran *wv.* 1 to rear, raise up; *pp. m. nom. sg.* ārǣred 44.

ārīsan *sv.* 1 to rise, arise; *3 sg. pret.* ārās 101.

āsettan *wv.* 1 to set, place; *3 pl. pret.* asetton 32; *3 sg. pres. subj.* āsette 142.

āstīgan *sv.* 1 to mount, ascend; *3 sg. pret.* āstāg 103.

140

āstyrian *wv.* 1 to move, remove;
pp. m. nom. sg. **āstyred** 30.

bā *adj.* both; *f. acc.* RC 48.
bana *m.* slayer; *gen. sg.* **banan**
66.
bēacen *n.* symbol, sign, standard;
nom. sg. 6; *acc. sg.* 21; *dat. sg.*
bēacne 83; *gen. pl.* **bēacna**
118.
bealu-ware *m. collective nn.*dwellers
in evil, evil men; *gen. sg.*
bealu-wara 79.
bēam *m.* tree, part of a tree or ray of
light; *nom. sg.* 97; *dat. sg.* **bēame**
114, 122; *gen. pl.* **bēama** 6.
bearn *n.* son, child; *nom. sg.* 83.
bedelfan *sv.* 3 to bury; *3 sg. pret.*
bedealf 75.
bedrīfan *sv.* 1 to cover, drench,
soak; *pp. m. acc. sg.* **bedrifenne**
62.
begēotan *sv.* 2 to sprinkle, shed,
pour out; *pp. n. nom. sg.*
begoten 7, (RC **bigoten**) 49.
behealdan *sv.* 7 to behold, gaze on,
watch over; *1 sg. pret.* **behēold**
25, (RC **biheald**) 58; *3 pl. pret.*
behēoldon 9, 11, (RC **bihealdun**)
64.
bēon *see* wesan.
beorg *m.* mound, hill; *acc. sg.* 32;
dat. sg. **beorge** 50.
beorht *adj.* bright, shining; *wk. m.*
dat. sg. **beorhtan** 66; *sup. n. acc.*
sg. **beorhtost** 6.
beorn *m.* man, warrior; *nom. sg.*
42; *nom. pl.* **beornas** 32, 66.
beran *sv.* 4 to bear, carry; *3 sg.*
pres. **bereð** 118; *3 pl. pret.*
bǣron 32.
berstan *sv.* 3 to burst, break 36.

bestēman *wv.* 1 to make wet; *pp.*
m. n. nom. sg. **bestēmed** 22, (RC
bistēmid) 48.
beswyllan *wv.* 1 to soak, drench;
pp. n. nom. sg. **beswyled** 23.
bewindan *sv.* 3 to wrap, wind
round; *pp. n. acc. sg.* **bewunden**
5.
bewrēon *sv.* 1 to cover, clothe; *pp.*
bewrigen(e) 17, 53.
bifian *wv.* 2 to tremble, shake 36;
1 sg. pret. **bifode** 42.
biter *adj.* bitter, painful; *m. gen.*
sg. **biteres** 114.
blēd *m.* glory, blessedness; *dat. pl.*
blēdum 149.
blēo *n.* colour; *dat. pl.* **blēom** 22.
blis *f.* gladness, pleasure, bliss;
nom. sg. 139, 141; *dat. sg.*
blisse 149, 153.
blīðe *adj.* joyful, glad; *n. dat. sg.*
122.
blōd *n.* blood; *dat. sg.* **blōde** (RC
blōdæ) 48.
brēost *n.* breast, heart; *dat. pl.*
brēostum 118.
brūcan *sv.* 2 to enjoy, partake of
144.
bryne *m.* burning, (hell)fire; *acc.*
sg. 149.
būgan *sv.* 2 to bend, bow down 36
(RC **būga**) 42.
būtū *adj.* both; *n. acc.* 48.
byrigan *wv.* 1 to taste; *3 sg. pret.*
byrigde 101.
bysmerian *wv.* 2 *or* 3 to mock,
insult; *3 pl. pret.* **bysmeredon**
(RC **bismærædu**) 48.

ceorfan *sv.* 3 to carve, cut out;
3 pl. pret. **curfon** 66.
cōlian *wv.* 2 to cool, grow cold; *3*
sg. pret. **cōlode** 72.

Crist *prop. name nom. sg.* (RC **Krist**) 56; *dat. sg.* **Criste** 116.

cuman *sv.* 4 to come; *3 sg. pret.* **cōm** 151, **cwōm** 155; *3 pl. pret.* **cwōman** (RC **kwōmu**) 57; *pp. m. nom. sg.* **cumen** 80.

cweðan *sv.* 5 to say, declare 116; *3 sg. pres.* (*future sense*) **cwyð** 111.

cwīðan *wv.* 1 to lament, mourn; *3 pl. pret.* **cwīðdon** 56.

Cyning *m.* King; *acc. sg.* (RC **Kyniŋc**) 44, 133; *gen. sg.* **Cyninges** 56.

cynn *n.* kin, race; **wīfa cynn** ' woman-kind ' *acc. sg.* 94.

cyst *f.* choice, choicest, best; *acc. sg.* 1.

dæg *m.* day; *gen. pl.* **daga** 136.

dēað *m.* death; *acc. sg.* 101; *gen. sg.* **dēaðes** 113.

dēman *wv.* 1 (*w. dat.*) to judge 107.

dēop *adj.* deep; *wk. m. dat. sg.* **dēopan** 75.

deorc *adj.* dark; *wk. m. dat. pl.* **deorcan** 46.

dolg *n.* wound; *nom. pl.* 46.

dōm *m.* judgement; *gen. sg.* **dōmes** 107.

dōmdæg *m.* Doomsday, Judgement Day; *dat. sg.* **dōmdæge** 105.

dōn *anom. v.* to do; *3 sg. pret.* **dyde** 114.

drēam *m.* joy, delight; *nom. sg.* 140; *gen sg.* **drēames** 144; *dat. pl.* **drēamum** 133.

Dryhten *m.* Lord; *nom. sg.* 101, 105; *voc. sg.* 144; *acc. sg.* 64; *gen. sg.* **Dryhtnes** 9, 35, 75, 113, 136, 140.

durran *pret. pres. v.* to dare; *1 sg. pret.* **dorste** 35, 42, (RC **dorstæ**) 45, 47.

ēac *adv.* also 92.

ealdgewyrht *f. n.* old or former action; *dat. pl.* **ealdgewyrhtum** 100.

Ealdor *m.* prince, lord; *nom. sg.* 90.

eall *adj.* all; *n. nom. sg.* 6; *f. nom. sg.* 12, **eal** 55, 82; *n. acc. sg.* (RC **al**) 58, 94; *m. nom. pl.* **ealle** 9, 128; *m. acc. pl.* **ealle** 37, (RC **allæ** 41), 74, 93; *gen. pl.* **ealra** ' in all ' 125; *m. dat. pl.* **eallum** 154.

eall *adv.* all, completely 20, 48, 62.

earm *adj.* wretched; *m. nom. pl.* **earme** 68; *as noun, m. gen. pl.* **earmra** 19.

ēaðmōd *adj.* humble; *n. nom. sg.* 60.

eaxl *f.* shoulder; *dat. pl.* **eaxlum** 32.

eaxlegespann *n.* cross-beam, junction of the cross; *dat. sg.* **eaxlegespanne** 9.

efstan *wv.* 1 to hurry, make haste 34.

eft *adv.* afterwards, again 68, 101, 103.

egesa *m.* awe, fear; *nom. sg.* 86.

egeslic *adj.* fearful, dreadful; *f. nom. sg.* 74.

ellen *m.* strength, courage, zeal; *dat. sg.* **elne** 34, 60, 123.

ende *m.* end, edge; *dat. sg.* 29.

engel *m.* angel; *acc. sg.* 9; *nom. pl.* **englas** 106; *dat. pl.* **englum** 153.

eorðe *f.* earth, ground; *gen. sg.* **eorðan** 37; *dat. sg.* 42, 74, 137, 145.

eorðweg *m.* earth, earthly way; *dat. sg.* **eorðwege** 120.

ēðel *m.* country, homeland; *nom. sg.* 156.

fæger *adj.* fair, beautiful; *n. nom. sg.* 73; *m. nom. pl.* **fægere** 8, 10; *wk. f. dat. sg.* **fægran** 21.

fæste *adv.* firmly, securely 38, 43.

fāh *adj.* stained, guilty; *m. nom. sg.* 13.

fēa *adv.* little 115.

feala *indecl. n. pron.* much, many 50, 125, 131.

feallan *sv.* 7 to fall 43.

fēond *m.* fiend, foe, evil man; *nom. pl.* **fēondas** 30, 33; *acc. pl.* 38.

feorgbold *n.* body, the dwelling of the spirit; *nom. sg.* 73.

feorran *adv.* from afar (RC **fearran**) 57.

fīf *adj.* five; *m. nom. sg.* **fīfe** 8.

folc *n.* people; *nom. sg.* 140.

folde *f.* earth, ground; *gen. sg.* **foldan** 8, 43; *dat. sg.* 132.

for *prep.* for, because of, for the sake of, before, in front of; *w. dat.* 21, 99, 111, 112, 113, 146; *w. acc.* (RC **fore** 41), 93.

forgiefan *sv.* 5 to give, grant; *3 sg. pret.* **forgeaf** 147.

forht *adj.* afraid; *m. nom. sg.* 21.

forhtian *wv.* 2 to be afraid; *3 pl. pres.* (*future sense*) **forhtiað** 115.

forlǣtan *sv.* 7 to leave; *3 pl. pret.* **forlēton** 61.

forð *adv.* forth, away 54, 132.

forþan *conj.* therefore 84.

forðgesceaft *f.* creation, that which is pre-ordained; *acc. sg.* 10.

forðweg *m.* a going forth, departure; *dat. sg.* **forðwege** 125.

forwundian *wv.* 2 to wound badly; *pp. m. nom. sg.* **forwunded** 14, **forwundod** 62.

fracod *adjvl. noun* wicked, vile one; *gen. sg.* **fracodes** 10.

fram *prep. w. dat.* from, away from 69.

Frēa *m.* Lord; *acc. sg.* **Frēan** 33.

frēond *m.* friend; *nom. sg.* 144; *nom. pl.* **frēondas** 76; *gen. pl.* **frēonda** 132.

frīnan *sv.* 3 to ask; *3 sg. pres.* (*future sense*) **frīneð** 112.

fundian *wv.* 2 to come; *3 sg. pres.* **fundaþ** 103.

fūs *adj.* hastening, eager, doomed; *n. acc. sg.* **fūse** 21; *as noun, m. nom. pl.* **fūse** (RC **fūsæ**) 57.

fyll *m.* fall, death; *acc. sg.* 56.

fyllan *wv.* 1 to fell, cut down 73.

galan *sv.* 6 to sing 67.

gān *anom. v.* to go; *3 sg. pret.* **ēode** 54.

gang *m.* flow; *dat. sg.* **gange** 23.

gāst *m.* spirit, soul; *acc. sg.* 49; *nom. pl.* **gāstas** 11; *gen. pl.* **gāsta** 152.

gealga *m.* gallows; *nom. sg.* 10; *acc. sg.* **gealgan** (RC **galgu**) 40.

gealgtrēow *n.* gallows-tree; *dat. sg.* **gealgtreowe** 146.

geāra *adv.* long ago; **geāra iū** ' very long ago ', 28.

gebīdan *sv.* 1 to endure; *1 sg. pret.* **gebād** 125; *pp. m. nom. sg.* **gebiden** 50, 79.

gebiddan *sv.* 5 (*w. refl. dat.*) to pray, worship; *3 pl. pres.* **gebiddaþ** 83; *1 sg. pret.* **gebæd** 122.

gebringan *wv.* 1 to bring; *3 sg. pres. subj.* **gebringe** 139.

gedrēfan *wv.* 1 to trouble, distress; *pp. nom. sg. m.* **gedrēfed** 20 (RC **gidrœfid**) 59.

geearnian *wv.* 2 to earn, gain, deserve; *3 sg. pres.* **geearnaþ** 109.

gefæstnian *wv.* 2 to fasten, make fast; *3 pl. pret.* **gefæstnodon** 33.

gefetian *wv.* 2 *or* 3 to fetch; *3 sg. pres. subj.* **gefetige** 138.

gefrīnan *sv.* 3 to hear of; *3 pl. pret.* **gefrūnon** 76.

gefyllan *wv.* 1 to fell, strike down 38.

gegyrwan *wv.* 1 to adorn; *pp. n. acc. sg.* **gegyred** 16, **gegyrwed** 23.

gehwylc *pron.* each, every; *m. ins. sg.* **gehwylce** 136; *m. dat. pl.* **gehwylcum** 108; *see* **ānra** (**gehwylc**).

gehȳran *wv.* 1 to hear, understand 78; *1 sg. pret.* **gehȳrde** 26.

gemǣtan *wv.* 1 (*impers. w. dat.*) to dream; *3 sg. pret.* **gemǣtte** 2.

gemunan *pret. pres. v.* to remember; *1 sg. pres.* **geman** 28.

geniman *sv.* 4 to take away, seize; *3 pl. pret.* **genāman** 30, **genāmon** 60.

genīwian *wv.* 2 to renew, restore; *pp. m. nom. sg.* **genīwad** 148.

genōg *adj.* enough, many; *m. nom. pl.* **genōge** 33.

geong *adj.* young; *m. nom. sg.* 39.

gerihtan *wv.* 1 to direct; *pp. f. nom. sg.* **geriht** 131.

gerȳman *wv.* 1 to open, prepare, make way for; *1 sg. pret.* **gerȳmde** 89.

gesceaft *f.* creation; *nom. sg.* 12, 55, 82.

gesēcan *wv.* 1 to reach (by seeking) 119.

gesēon *sv.* 5 to see, behold; *1 sg. pret.* **geseah** 14, 21, 33, 36, 51; *1 sg. pret. subj.* **gesāwe** 4.

gesettan *wv.* 1 to set, place; *3 pl. pret.* **gesetton** 67; *pp. n. nom. sg.* **geseted** 141.

gesīene *adj.* visible; *m. nom. pl.* 46.

gestandan *sv.* 6 to stand; *3 pl. pret.* **gestōdon** (RC **gistōddun**) 63.

gestīgan *sv.* 1 to mount, ascend 34 (RC **gistīga** 40); *3 sg. pret.* **gestāh** 40.

gesyhð *f.* sight, vision; *acc. sg.* **gesyhðe** 96; *dat. sg.* 21, 41, 66.

geweald *n.* power, control; *acc. sg.* 107.

geweorðan *sv.* 3 to become; *pp. m. nom. sg.* **geworden** 87.

geweorðian *wv.* 2 to honour, adorn; *3 sg. pret.* **geweorðode** 90, 94; *pp. n. acc. sg.* **geweorðode** 15.

gewinn *n.* conflict, struggle; *dat. sg.* **gewinne** 65.

gewītan *sv.* 1 to go, depart; *3 sg. pret.* **gewāt** 71; *3 pl. pret.* **gewiton** 133.

gewyrcan *wv.* 1 to make; *3 pl. pret.* **geworhton** 31.

gimm *m.* gem, jewel; *nom. pl.* **gimmas** 7, 16.

giwundian *wv.* 2 to wound; *pp.* RC **giwundad** 62.

God *m.* God; *nom.* 39, 93, 98, 106, 156; *acc.* 51, 60; *gen.* **Godes** 83, 152.

gōd *adj.* good, great; *f. acc. sg.* **gōde** 70; *sup. m. nom. sg.* **sēlesta** 27; *sup. n. acc. sg.* **sēlest** 118.

gold *n.* gold; *acc. sg.* 18; *dat. sg.* **golde** 7, 16, 77.

guma *m.* man, *collectively* mankind; *gen. sg.* **guman** 49, 146.

gyrwan *wv.* 1 to dress, adorn; *3 pl. pret.* **gyredon** 77.

gȳta *adv.* yet, still 28.

habban *wv.* 3 to have; *1 sg. pres.* **hæbbe** 50, 79; *3 sg. pret.* **hæfde** 49; *3 pl. pret.* **hæfdon** 16, 52.

hǣlan *wv.* 1 to heal, save 85.

hælda *see* **hyldan**.

Hǣlend *m.* Saviour; *gen. sg.* **Hǣlendes** 25.

hæleð *m.* man, hero; *nom. sg.* 39; *voc. sg.* 78, 95.

hālga *m.* holy one, saint; *dat. pl.* **hālgum** 143, 154.

hālig *adj.* holy; *m. nom. pl.* **hālige** 11.

hām *m.* home, dwelling; *acc. sg.* 148.

hand *f.* hand; *dat. sg.* **handa** 59.

hātan *sv.* 7 to command; *1 sg. pres.* **hāte** 95; *3 pl. pret.* **hēton** 31.

hē, hit *pron.* he, it; *m. nom. sg.* 34, 40 *etc*; *n. nom. sg.* **hit** 19, 22, 26, 97; *m. acc. sg.* **hine** 11, 39, 61, 64, RC **hinæ** 39, 63; *m. gen. sg.* **his** 49, 63, 92, 102, 106, 156; *m. n. dat. sg.* **him** 63, 65, 67, 108, 118; *nom. pl.* **hī** 46, **hīe** 32, 48 *etc*, RC **hiæ** 63, 64; *gen. pl.* **heora** 31, 155, **hira** 47; *dat. pl.* **him** 31, 83, 86, 88, 133.

hēafod *n.* head; *dat. sg.* **hēafdum** 63.

hēah *adj.* high, lofty; *m. acc. sg.* **hēanne** 40.

Hēahfæder *m.* God the Father; *dat. sg.* **Hēahfædere** 134.

healf *f.* half, side; *acc. sg.* **healfe** 20.

heard *adj.* hard, severe; *sup. n. nom. sg.* **heardost** 87.

hebban *sv.* 6 to lift up, bear aloft 31.

hefig *adj.* oppressive, grim; *wk. n. dat. sg.* **hefian** 61.

help *f.* help, aid; *dat. sg.* **helpe** 102.

heofon *m.* heaven, sky; *gen. sg.* **heofenes** 64, RC **heafunæs** 45; *acc. pl.* **heofenas** 103; *gen. pl.*

heofona 45; *dat. pl.* **heofenum** 85, 134, **heofonum** 140, 154.

heofonlic *adj.* heavenly; *m. acc. sg.* **heofonlicne** 148.

heofonrīce *n.* kingdom of heaven; *gen. sg.* **heofonrīces** 91.

heonon *adv.* hence, from here 132.

hēr *adv.* here 108, 137, 145.

hider *adv.* (to) here 103.

hilderinc *m.* warrior; *nom. pl.* **hilderincas** 61, *gen. pl.* **hilderinca** 72.

Hlāford *m.* Lord; *acc. sg.* (RC **Hlāfard**) 45.

hlēoðrian *wv.* 2 to speak; *3 sg. pret.* **hlēoðrode** 26.

hlifian *wv.* 2 to rise, tower; *1 sg. pres.* **hlifige** 85.

hnīgan *sg.* 1 to bend, bow down; *1 sg. pret.* **hnāg** 59.

holmwudu *m.* wood on the hill; *acc. sg.* 91.

holt *m. n.* forest, wood; *gen. sg.* **holtes** 29.

hrǣw *m. n.* corpse; *nom. sg.* 72; *acc. sg.* 53.

hrēotan *sv.* 2 to weep; *pres. ppl. m. nom. pl.* **hrēotende** 70.

hrēowcearig *adj.* sorrowful, troubled; *m. nom. n. acc. sg.* 25.

hūru *adv.* certainly, indeed, however 10.

hwā *pron.* who; *n. acc. sg.* **hwæt** 2, 116.

hwænne *conj.* (the time) when 136.

hwǣr *conj.* where 112.

hwæt *interj.* what, well, lo, behold 1, 90.

hwæð(e)re *conj.* however, but, nevertheless, yet 18, 24, 38, 42, (RC **hweþræ**) 57, 59 *etc*.

hwīl *f.* while, time; *acc. sg.* **hwīle** 24, 64, 70, 84; *dat. pl. as adv.* **hwīlum** ' at times ' 22, 23.

hyht *m.* joy, hope; *nom. sg.* 126, **hiht** 148.

hyldan *wv.* 1 to bend, bow down (RC **hælda**) 45.

ic *pron.* I; *nom. sg.* 1, 4, 13 *etc*; *acc. sg.* **mē** 30, 31, 32 *etc*; *dat. sg.* 2, 4, 46 *etc*; *nom. pl.* **wē** 70; *acc. pl.* **ūs** 73, 75, 147a; *dat. pl.* 147b; *dual acc.* **unc** (RC **uŋket**) 48.

in *prep. w. dat.* in 118.

inwid-hlemm *m.* malicious wound; *nom. pl.* **inwid-hlemmas** 47.

iū *adv.* long ago 28, 87.

k *For RC forms with initial* **k**, **k̄** *see corresponding head-words with initial* **c**.

lǣdan *wv.* 1 to be raised, lifted up 5.

lǣne *adj.* transitory, fleeting; *n. dat. sg.* **lǣnum** 109; *wk. n. dat. sg.* **lǣnan** 138.

lang *adj.* long; *f. acc. sg.* **lange** 24.

langung-hwīl *f.* time of longing; *gen. pl.* **langung-hwīla** 126.

lāð *adj.* hostile, hateful; *sup. m. nom. sg.* **lāðost** 88.

lēode *f.* people, men; *dat. pl.* **lēodum** 88.

lēof *adj.* dear; *wk. m. voc. sg.* **lēofa** 78, 95.

lēoht *n.* light; *dat. sg.* **lēohte** 5.

libban *wv.* 3 to live; *3 pl. pres.* **lifiaþ** 134.

līc *n.* body; *gen. sg.* **līces** (RC **līcæs**) 63.

licgan *sv.* 5 to lie; *pres. ppl. m. nom. sg.* **licgende** 24.

līf *n.* life; *acc. sg.* 147; *gen. sg.* **līfes** 88, 126; *dat. sg.* **līfe** 109, 138.

limwērig *adj.* weary in limb; *m. acc. sg.* **limwērigne** (RC **limwǣrignæ**) 63.

lyft *m. f. n.* air; *acc. sg.* **(on) lyft** ' on high ' 5.

lȳsan *wv.* 1 to redeem 41.

mænigo *f.* multitude; *dat. sg.* **mænige** 112, **manigeo** 151.

mǣre *adj.* great, glorious; *wk. f. nom. sg.* 12, 82; *wk. m. dat. sg.* **mǣran** 69.

mǣte *adj.* small; *n. dat. sg.* 69, 124.

magan *pret. pres. v.* to be able; *1 sg. pres.* **mæg** 85; *2 sg. pres.* **miht** 78; *3 sg. pres.* **mæg** 110; *1 sg. pret.* **meahte** 18, **mihte** 37.

man *m.* man, one, they, people; *nom. sg.* 73, 75, 112; *nom. pl.* **menn** 12 (RC 48) 82, 128, *acc. pl.* **menn** (RC 41) 93; *dat. pl.* **mannum** 96, 102.

mancyn(n) *n.* mankind, men; *acc. sg.* 41, 104; *gen. sg.* **mancynnes** 33, 99.

manig *adj.* many; *m. gen. pl.* *as pron.* **manigra** 41; *f. dat. pl.* **manegum** 99.

Māria *prop. name* Mary; *acc. sg.* **Mārian** 92.

mēðe *adj.* tired, exhausted; *m. nom. sg.* 65; *m. nom. pl.* sorrowful 69.

micel *adj.* great; *m. nom. sg.* **mycel** 130; *f. nom. sg.* 139; *m. dat. sg.* **mycle** 34, 60, 123; *wk. f. dat. sg.* **miclan** 102; *wk. n. dat. sg.* 65.

mid *prep. w. dat.* with, by among 7, 14, 16, 20 *etc* (RC **miþ** 48, 59, 62); *as adv.* ' together with ' 106.

mid *adj.* middle; *f. dat. sg.* **midre** 2.

middangeard *m.* world; *acc. sg.* 104.

miht *f.* might, power; *dat. sg.* **mihte** 102.

mihtig *adj.* mighty, powerful; *m. nom. sg.* 151.

mīn *poss. adj.* my; *f. nom. sg.* 130; *m. voc. sg.* 78, 95; *m. dat. sg.* **mīnum** 30.

mōd *n.* heart, spirit; *dat. sg.* **mōde** 122, 130.

mōdig *adj.* brave, courageous; *m. nom. sg.* 41.

mōdor *f.* mother; *acc. sg.* 92.

mōdsefa *m.* mind, spirit; *nom. sg.* 124.

moldærn *n.* grave, tomb; *acc. sg.* 65.

molde *f.* earth; *acc. sg.* **moldan** 12, 82.

mōtan *pret. pres. v.* to be able, may; *1 sg. pres.* **mōt** 142; *1 sg. pres. subj.* **mōte** 127.

mundbyrd *f.* allegiance, protection; *nom. sg.* 130.

nægl *m.* nail; *dat. pl.* **næglum** 46.

nāh *see* **āgan**.

nama *m.* name; *dat. sg.* **naman** 113.

ne *neg. particle* not 10, 35, 42 *etc,* RC **ni** 45.

niht *f.* night; *dat. sg.* **nihte** 2.

nū *adv.* 78, 80, 84 *etc.*

of *prep. w. dat.* of, from, out of 30, 49, 61, 66 *etc.*

ofer *prep. w. acc.* over, upon, throughout, more than, contrary to, against 12, 35, 82, 91, 94.

oft *adv.* often; *comp.* **oftor** 128.

on *prep.* in, on, upon, onto, into, at; *w. acc.* 5, 20, 32b, 40 *etc*; *w. dat.* 9, 29, 32a, 41, 46, 50, 56 *etc*; *postpositionally* 34, 98.

onbyrigan *wv.* 1 (*w. gen.*) to taste 114.

ond *conj.* and 12, 13, 22 *etc.*

onginnan *sv.* 3 to begin; *3 sg. pret.* **ongan** 19, 27, 73; *3 pl. pret.* **ongunnon** 65, 67; *3 pl. pres. subj.* **onginnen** 116.

ongyrwan *wv.* 1 to strip, disrobe; *3 sg. pret.* **ongyrede** (RC **ondgerede**) 39.

ongytan *sv.* 5 to perceive 18.

onlȳsan *wv.* 1 to redeem; *3 sg. pret.* **onlȳsde** 147.

onsendan *wv.* 1 to send forth, give up; *pp.* **onsended** 49.

onwrēon *sv.* 1 to reveal, disclose; *2 sg. imper.* **onwrēoh** 97.

open *adj.* open; *m. nom. pl.* **opene** 47.

oððæt *conj.* until 26, 32.

oððe *conj.* or, and 36.

reordberend *m.* speech-, voice-bearer, man; *nom. pl.* 3; *dat. pl.* **reordberendum** 89.

rest *f.* rest, resting-place; *dat. sg.* **reste** 3.

restan *wv.* 1 to rest; *3 sg. pret.* **reste** 64, 69.

rīce *n.* kingdom; *acc. sg.* 119, 152.

rīce *adj.* rich, powerful; *m. acc. sg.* **rīcne** (RC **riicnæ**) 44; *gen. pl.* **rīcra** 131.

riht *adj.* right, proper, true; *m. acc. sg.* **rihtne** 89.

rōd *f.* cross; *nom. sg.* 44, 136; *acc. sg.* **rōde** 119; *dat. sg.* **rōde** (RC **rōdi**) 56, 131.

sǣl *m. f.* time; *nom. sg.* 80.

sār *adj.* sore, painful; *f. gen. pl.* **sārra** 80.

sāre *adv.* sorely, deeply (RC **sāræ**) 59.

sāwl *f.* soul; *nom. sg.* 120.

sceadu *f.* shadow, darkness; *nom. sg.* 54.

scēat *m.* corner, surface; *acc. pl.* scēatas 37; *dat. pl.* scēatum 8, 43.

scēawian *wv.* 2 to see, behold; *1 sg. pret.* scēawode 137.

sceðöan *sv.* 6 to harm, injure 47.

scīma *m.* radiance, light; *acc. sg.* scīman 54.

scīnan *sv.* 1 to shine 15.

scīr *adj.* clear, bright; *m. acc. sg.* scīrne 54.

sculan *pret. pres. v.* to have to, be obliged to; *3 sg. pres.* sceal 119; *1 sg. pret.* sceolde 43.

se, sēo, þæt *def. art., demonst. adj. and pron.* the, that, those, who; *m. nom. sg.* 13, 42, 95 *etc, with long vowel in pronominal functions* 98, 107, 113, 145; *f. nom. sg.* sēo 121; *n. nom. sg.* þæt 6, 28a, 39, 74; *m. acc. sg.* þone 127; *f. acc. sg.* þā 20, 68, 119; *n. acc. sg.* þæt 18, 21, 28b, 58, 66; *m. gen. sg.* þæs 49; *m. n. dat. sg.* þām 9, 50, 58 *etc,* þān 122; *f. dat. sg.* þǣre 21, 112, 131; *m. n. nom. pl.* þā 46, 61; *m. gen. pl.* þāra 86; *m. dat. pl.* þām 59, 143, 149, 154.

sēaþ *m.* pit; *dat. sg.* sēaþe 75.

sēcan *wv.* 1 to seek out, visit 104, 127; *3 pl. pret.* sōhton 133.

secg *m.* man; *dat. pl.* secgum 59.

secgan *wv.* 3 to say, tell 1; *2 sg. pres. subj.* secge 96.

sēlest *see* gōd.

seolfor *n.* silver; *dat. sg.* seolfre 77.

sīde *f.* side; *dat. sg.* sīdan 49.

sīde *adv.* widely; wīde ond sīde ' far and wide ' 81.

sigebēam *m.* wood of victory; *nom. sg.* 13; *acc. sg.* 127.

sigor *m.* victory; *gen. pl.* sigora 67.

sigorfæst *adj.* triumphant, victorious; *m. nom. sg.* 150.

sinc *n.* treasure; *dat. sg.* since 23.

singal *adj.* continual, everlasting; *f. nom. sg.* 141.

sīðfæt *m.* expedition, journey; *dat. sg.* sīðfate 150.

sīðian *wv.* 2 to go, journey, depart 68.

sorg *f.* sorrow, distress; *gen. pl.* sorga 80; *dat. pl.* sorgum 20, 59.

sorhlēoð *n.* lament, dirge; *acc. sg.* 67.

spēdig *adj.* successful; *m. nom. sg.* 151.

sprecan *sv.* 5 to speak 27.

stān *m.* stone; *dat. sg.* stāne 66.

standan *sv.* 6 to stand 43, 62; *1 sg. pret.* stōd 38; *1 pl. pret.* stōdon 71; *3 pl. pret.* 7.

staðol *m.* position, foundation; *dat. sg.* staðole 71.

stēam *m.* moisture; *dat. sg.* stēame 62.

stefn *m.* trunk, root; *dat. sg.* stefne 30.

stefn *f.* voice, cry; *nom. sg.* 71.

stīðmōd *adj.* resolute, courageous; *m. nom. sg.* 40.

strǣl *m. f.* arrow, dart; *dat. pl.* strǣlum (RC strēlum) 62.

strang *adj.* strong, firm, powerful; *m. nom. sg.* 40; *m. nom. pl.* strange 30.

Sunu *m.* Son; *nom. sg.* 150.

swā *conj.* as, even as, just as 92, 108, 114; *see* swylce (swā).

swǣtan *wv.* 1 to bleed 20.

swāt *m. n.* blood; *gen. sg.* swātes 23.

swefn *n.* dream, vision; *gen. pl.* swefna 1.

swiðra *comp. adj.* right (hand); *wk. f. acc. sg.* swiðran 20.

swylce *conj.* and also 8, swylce (swā) ' just as ' 92.

sylf *pron.* (him-, her-)self; *f. acc. sg.* sylfe 92; *wk. m. nom. sg.* sylfa 105.

syllic *adj.* unusual, wonderful, marvellous; *m. nom. sg.* 13; *comp. n. acc. sg.* syllicre 4.

sym(b)el *n.* banquet, feast; *dat. sg.* symle 141.

synn *f.* sin; *dat. pl.* synnum 13, 99, 146.

syppan *adv.* afterwards 142.

syðþan *conj.* when, after 3, siððan 49, 71.

til *prep. w. dat.* to RC 58.

tō *prep. w. dat.* to, into, at, for, of 2, 31, 42, 43, 58 *etc.*

trēow *n.* tree, wood; *acc. sg.* 4, 14, 17, 25.

þā *adv.* then 27, 33, 35, 39 *etc.*

þā *conj.* when 36, 41, 42, 68, 151, 155, RC 40.

þǣr *adv.* there, then 8, 9, 11, 24, 31 *etc*, RC þēr 57, 64.

þǣr *conj.* where 139, 140, 141, 142, 156, when 123.

ðǣron *adv.* therein 67.

þæt *conj.* that, so that, in that, when 4, 19, 26, 29 *etc*, when that 34, 107.

þe *indecl. particle and rel. pron.* who, which, that 111, 118, 137; sē þe who, he who; *m. nom. sg.* 98, 113, 145; *f. nom. sg.* sēo þe 121; *m. gen. pl.* þāra þe 86; *m. dat. pl.* þām þe 149, 154.

þearle *adv.* severely, violently 52.

þegn *m.* thane, servant, follower; *nom. pl.* þegnas 75.

þencan *wv.* 1 to think, consider, intend; *3 sg. pres.* þenceð 121; *3 pl. pres.* þencaþ 115.

þenian *wv.* 1 to stretch out 52.

þēoden *m.* prince, lord; *dat. sg.* þēodne 69.

þes, þēos, þys *demonst. adj. and pron.* this; *f. nom. sg.* þēos 12, 82; *m. acc. sg.* þysne 104; *f. acc. sg.* þās 96; *n. dat. sg.* þyssum 83, 109, þysson 138.

þolian *wv.* 2 to endure, suffer; *3 pl. pret.* þolodan 149.

þonne *adv.* then 107, 115, 117, 139, 142.

þonne *conj.* than 128.

þrōwian *wv.* 2 to suffer; *3 sg. pret.* þrōwode 84, 98, 145.

þrymfæst *adj.* glorious; *m. nom. sg.* 84.

ðū *pron.* thou; *nom. sg.* 78, 96; *acc. sg.* þē 95.

þurfan *pret. pres. v.* to need; *3 sg. pres.* þearf 117.

þurh *prep. w. acc.* through, by virtue of, by reason of 10, 18, 119.

þurhdrīfan *sv.* 1 to drive through, pierce; *3 pl. pret.* þurhdrifan 46.

þyncan *wv.* 1 (*impers. w. dat.*) to seem, appear; *3 sg. pret.* þūhte 4.

þȳstro *f.* darkness, gloom; *nom. pl.* 52.

unc, uŋket *see* ic.

under *prep. w. dat.* under, beneath 55, 85.

unforht *adj. m. nom. sg.* unafraid 110; very afraid, terrified 117.

ūp *adv.* up 71.

uppe *adv.* up, above 9.

wǣd *f.* dress, clothing; *dat. pl.* **wǣdum** 15, 22.

wǣfersȳn *f.* show, spectacle; *dat. sg.* **wǣfersȳne** 31.

wǣta *m.* wetness, moisture; *dat. sg.* **wǣtan** 22.

wann *adj.* dark, black; *f. nom. sg.* 55.

wē *see* **ic.**

weald *m.* forest; *gen. sg.* **wealdes** 17.

Wealdend *m.* Ruler, Lord; *nom. sg.* 111, 155; *acc. sg.* 67; *gen. sg.* **Wealdendes** 53; *dat. sg.* **Wealdende** 121.

Weard *m.* Guardian, Lord; *nom. sg.* 91.

weg *m.* way, path; *acc. sg.* 88.

well *adv.* well, fully 129, 143.

wēnan *wv.* 1 to hope, look for; *1 sg. pres.* **wēne** 135.

wendan *wv.* 1 to alter, change 22.

weorc *n.* work, pain; *nom. acc. sg.* 79.

weorod *n.* host, multitude; *dat. sg.* **weorode** 69, 152, **werede** 124; *gen. pl.* **weruda** 51.

weorþian *wv.* 2 to honour, adore 129; *3 pl. pres.* **weorðiað** 81.

weorðlīce *adv.* worthily, magnificently 17.

wēpan *sv.* 7 to weep; *3 sg. pret.* **wēop** 55.

werg *m.* outlaw, criminal; *acc. pl.* **wergas** 31.

wesan *anom. v.* to be 110,117; *3 sg. pres.* **is** 80, 97, 126 *etc*, **bið** 86; *3 pl. pres.* **syndon** 46; *1 sg. pret.* **wæs** 20, 21, 29 *etc*; *3 sg. pret.* **wæs** 6, 10, 13 *etc*; *3 pl. pret.* **wǣron** 8; *3 sg. pres. subj.* **sī(e)** 112, 144.

wīde *adv.* widely, **wīde ond sīde** ' far and wide ' 81.

wīf *n.* woman; *gen. pl.* **wīfa** 94.

willa *m.* desire, purpose; *nom. sg.* 129.

willan *anom. v.* to will, wish, intend; *1 sg. pres.* **wylle** 1; *3 sg. pres.* **wile** 107; *3 sg. pret.* **wolde** 34, 41; *3 pl. pret.* **woldon** 68; *3 sg. pret. subj.* **wolde** 113.

wīte *n.* punishment, torture; *dat. sg.* 61; *gen. pl.* **wīta** 87.

wolcen *m. n.* cloud, sky; *dat. pl.* **wolcnum** 53, 55.

wom *m. n.* sin, stain; *dat. pl.* **wommum** 14.

word *n.* word, command; *acc. sg.* 35; *dat. sg.* **worde** 111; *acc. pl.* **word** 27; *dat. pl.* **wordum** 97.

woruld *f.* world; *gen. sg.* **worulde** 133.

wrāð *adj.* cruel; *f. gen. pl.* **wrāðra** 51.

wudu *m.* (piece of) wood; *nom. sg.* 27.

wuldor *n.* glory, splendour; *gen. sg.* **wuldres** 14, 90, 97, 133; *dat. sg.* **wuldre** 135, 143, 155.

wunian *wv.* 2 to live, dwell, be 121, 143; *3 pl. pres.* **wuniaþ** 135; *3 pl. pret.* **wunedon** 3, 155.

wynn *f.* joy; *dat. pl. as adv.* ' pleasantly, beautifully ' **wynnum** 15.

wyrcan *wv.* 1 to make 65.

wyrd *f.* fate, event; *nom. sg.* 74; *gen. pl.* **wyrda** 51.

ymbclyppan *wv.* 1 to clasp, embrace; *3 sg. pret.* **ymbclypte** 42.